JACKIE O.
SPECIAL MEMORIAL EDITION

Thursday, May 19, 1994—New York City

A cold rain swept the street in front of Jacqueline Kennedy Onassis's Fifth Avenue residence, mute testimony of the tragedy that was about to occur.

They began arriving, in twos and threes at first, then by the tens and scores: mourners, reporters, the curious—all drawn, inexorably, to be near her.

At Jackie's home, her family gathered. Caroline and John Jr.—the children of wealth and privilege who Jackie had raised to be upstanding, independent adults—were among the first. Both looked stunned by the sudden and unexpected severity of their mother's illness.

As the day grew darker, a candlelight vigil began outside. While more family members and friends braved the crowds to pay their last respects, people who had never seen Jackie anywhere but on television stopped to wish her well. Visitors from as far away as Japan and neighbors from as close as the building next door joined in remembering and mourning the former First Lady. Even the doorman of Jackie's building couldn't hide his grief.

The rumor that a priest had administered last rites sent shock waves around the globe, and tributes poured in from kings and queens, celebrities and dignitaries, the well-known and the unknown.

Then, at 10:15 p.m., the news came: Jackie had passed away peacefully with her beloved family at her bedside.

Never before has the United States produced a woman of such inimitable class and impeccable taste. Never again will the White House be graced by the glamour and elegance that distinguished Jackie all her life.

But who was this remarkable woman who created an international sensation with the "Jackie Look," yet remained an elusive enigma to all but those closest to her?

The public has eagerly followed every detail of Jacqueline Bouvier Kennedy Onassis's life from her wealthy childhood to her marriage to the world's richest man, from her days as the First Lady to her career as New York's most talented editor. *Jackie O.* is an often surprising, always fascinating look at the private tragedies and triumphs of the world's most famous woman.

JACKIE O.

HEDDA LYONS WATNEY

LEISURE BOOKS　　NEW YORK CITY

ACKNOWLEDGMENT:

The author is indebted to *The Bouviers* by John H. Davis as a research source for material on Jacqueline Onassis's childhood.

A LEISURE BOOK®

June 1994

Published by

Dorchester Publishing Co., Inc.
276 Fifth Avenue
New York, NY 10001

JACKIE O. revised and expanded edition

Printed in the United States of America.

JACKIE O.

PART ONE

CHAPTER ONE
Jackie—Goddess
With Clay Feet

Perhaps Ted Sorensen, High Poo Bah of the Irish Mafia, was stretching it when he quipped at John F. Kennedy's inauguration that, "This administration would do more for sex than Eisenhower's did for golf." But there is no doubt that the Kennedy days stimulated America's appetite for gossip about the peccadillos of the mighty to the extent that Washington bedrooms began to be as susceptible to scrutiny as those of Hollywood.

There had already been a preview of the "Kennedy style" years before that blustery January day in 1960 when John Kennedy became the thirty-fifth president of the United States. There was barely a newspaper editor in America or in Europe whose files did not include a photograph of Jack Kennedy, hiding his face with his hand, which was taken in the small hours of the morning outside the Georgetown home of Pamela Turnere. Miss Turnere, later to become his wife's personal secretary, was then attached to Jack Kennedy's Senate office.

The photograph had been taken by an irate neighbor of Miss Turnere whose religious and personal sensibilities were offended by the repeated visits of the married Senator to the apartment of the attractive young woman at a time when he was making his presidential bid. The woman had also accumulated a number of taped conversations between the two which made it clear that Kennedy wasn't visiting Miss Turnere to dictate letters.

The photographer-neighbor, dismayed that the incriminating photograph did not immediately make the front pages, took to haunting the Senator's public appearances during the primaries and later, the presidential campaign. She carried a sign displaying the photograph and a message explaining the circumstances under which it was taken.

Biographies of Jackie Kennedy have incorrectly reported that the photograph's sole appearance in print occurred in the *Washington Star* when the paper printed a photograph of the woman shoving her poster toward Kennedy, who only grinned. It was withdrawn after one edition following a telephone call from Bobby Kennedy who warned the managing editor that the Kennedys would own the paper "the next day" if he didn't withdraw it. Deciding that the story was of a "personal nature," the *Washington Star* pulled back, as even its reporters amassed evidence substantiating the nocturnal visits of the Democratic nominee to Miss Turnere's Georgetown digs.

However, one of the weekly scandal tabloids which began to proliferate in the late fifties *did* print the incriminating photograph with the banner, WHO IS THIS MAN? There was no mistaking Kennedy's trim figure and mop of thick hair. But incriminating? Hardly. Kennedy had made a mistake in starting to crouch down, and with one hand shielding his face, he just looked silly. There was no detail in the picture beyond the suggestion of a building behind a clump of trees where Kennedy had been accosted by the busybody neighbor. For all the photograph revealed, Kennedy might have been sneaking out of a late poker game or from a secret meeting with a group of politicians.

In today's climate of searching out the intimate details in the lives of the country's public figures, even *Camelot* alumni concede that the sexual capers of the handsome, young president would have turned him out of the White House long before he began emulating the precedent of Warren G. Harding, who favored the spacious White House closets as trysting places. Evidently aware of the historical significance of the event, Kennedy is supposed to have mentioned it to one of the White House chicks who was lured into a cupboard dalliance with the president.

There were plenty of rumors, of course, about JFK and brother Bobby, blind items in the gossip columns, accounts of presidential skinnydipping in the pools of Bel Air and along the beaches of Florida and Southern California, and the suicide of Marilyn Monroe. Marilyn's hero-worship of JFK, however, was at least something American women could identify with.

Enough was known of Marilyn's mercurial disposition and unhappy love affairs to eliminate the probability that the president or his brother, Bobby, was responsible for the overdose leading to her death. Yet there were insinuations that Marilyn's last telephone calls had been made to the White House. Much was made of the fact that the telephone company destroyed all the records of Marilyn's telephone calls during the critical last month of her life—an action that produced fodder for the many magazine articles and books about Marilyn asking questions about her suicide. Some questions remain unanswered to this day.

The records have stayed lost and this, among many curious facts connected with Jack Kennedy's relationship with Marilyn, leads to another incident involving the hyper-active sex life of President Kennedy.

It was told around Hollywood by one of the starlets of the era—a party girl really, who may have been talking about herself.

"I don't know. Maybe it's just gossip. I only know what I know. She didn't keep a diary, but she made notes about the times she spent with him. She kept them with her jewelry in a safe deposit box. For a kooky gal she was pretty careful about things like that.

"Anyway when this president died, his family swooped down on her and every other gal he'd screwed in Hollywood—maybe, even in the country. They were backed up by government agents—the F.B.I. maybe. I don't know. But she told me how they sweated it out of her—made her give up everything she had connected with him, autographed photos, the diary, a few little gifts that didn't mean a damn but could be identified. Those guys knew everything—more than she did."

While Jack Kennedy was president, Jackie was able to create her own life outside the rough and tumble world of her husband and the Irish Mafia. Although she had made a vivid impression on America as the model of an elegant First Lady and devoted mother, she was not spared criticism. The barbs hurled at her centered mainly around her bouffant hairdo, her extravagance (what little was known of it) and her folly in requesting White House servants to sign agreements protecting the Kennedy privacy. The document bound them to a promise not to publish accounts of their lives in the White House after their service had been completed.

There were complaints that Jackie's frequent trips abroad were unnecessary but they quieted down after Jackie conquered Paris and taciturn President De Gaulle on a State visit with President Kennedy, at a time when the relations of the United States and France had been frayed by the inability of American diplomats to understand the autocratic De Gaulle. His distrust of America was born of bitter experience during

World War II. He had not forgiven the Allies for recognizing the French Government of Vichy over De Gaulle's Free French movement which was given reluctant encouragement in England. De Gaulle had fled there after the destruction of the French fleet off the African coast.

The trip to France and England could be called "the greening of Jackie Kennedy" and the press lined up begging for interviews and photographs. Jackie had become an international celebrity, the epitome of a beautiful and famous woman who had everything—including the President of the United States. She had become more than a pretty, wealthy socialite who had married an ambitious millionaire Irishman and landed in the White House. Jackie began to emerge as a personality in her own right, well on the way toward becoming what she is today— the most well-known woman of our century.

Jackie's composure, her courage and strength in the face of the assassination of JFK in Dallas and the difficult period that came afterward, enlarged Jackie to a heroine of the dimensions of Joan of Arc.

The Kennedy era coincided with a striking evolution in the American press. The puff movie magazines had gotten stiff competition from scandal sheets like *Confidential, Uncensored* and *Whisper,* which unearthed and printed celebrity stories which, if somewhat inaccurate, were close enough to the truth to cause their subjects to squirm. When *Confidential* began selling an unprecedented four million copies every month and *Uncensored* achieved a circulation of one million steady readers, daily newspapers and monthly periodicals could no longer ignore the phenomenon—gossip and scandal-mongering were back in style. Not in the form of Walter Winchell-like blind items, but in cold fact, supported by evidence. Moreover, the Kennedys had made the public more aware of a new kind of celebrity—the men of power in Washington —household names whose extra-curricular activities had long enjoyed immunity from close scrutiny by the press.

Even the late Drew Pearson drew a bead on alcoholic senators and playboy congressmen in the form of blind items in his controversial column. Pearson identified himself, however tenuously, with Old Guard Washington correspondents who seldom hinted that anything untoward might be taking place in the capital's boudoirs.

That was all to change as a new breed of newspeople stood in the wings, waiting to take up the space vacated by Pearson, Walter Lippmann, Arthur Krock, the Alsop Brothers and other resourceful newspapermen who covered the smoke-filled rooms of politics—not the bedrooms. Jack Anderson, Maxine Cheshire and Barbara Howar were not bred in the fine tradition of conservative politics. They didn't exactly see Washington as *Sin City on the Potomac,* but they began to question the uniqueness of Washington's position, a national capital riddled with sex and booze scandals, where highly placed government officers consorted with call girls paid for by lobbyists and played footsies

with beauties imported by foreign governments
—all cloaked in the immunity granted them by a
friendly press.

Although Jackie Kennedy had not been involved in anything remotely resembling a sex
scandal and had nothing to do with Washington
lobbyists, her name was magic in the world of
publishing, both at the top of the magazine and
newspaper field as well as in the high circulation
items, the scandal sheets. She became the most
photographed and most written about woman in
history. Unwittingly, she opened the keys to
Washington's bedrooms and unleashed a Pandora's Box of newspaper reporters who would
slither in and out of Washington's secret world
of sex, payoffs, fixes, bribery and corruption.

"Americans get so bloody uptight about their
politicians," an English newspaperman once
remarked. "I remember an American correspondent who was in England doing a series on
our Parliamentary system and he was surprised
to hear all over London that the Prime Minister
was a transvestite. What's more, he owned a
fabulous woman's wardrobe and showed it to
friends who knew his fetish on the slightest
provocation.

"'Gawd!' gasped the American. 'How *Confidential* or the tabloids would explode over this!
How come they don't do something about it over
here? Hint at it, maybe.' I explained why not.
The libel laws, for one thing, are fantastically
strict in England. For another, did anyone really
care? In a little country like England lots of
people knew about the fellow. What interested

them was that he turned out to be a damned capable Prime Minister—in skirts or out of them."

There was some moderate sniping at Jackie in the first year of her widowhood when she rented the Washington home of Averill Harriman, the former Governor of New York and a prominent political figure nationally, on N Street. It was slight, almost apologetic and quickly answered in sectors of the press which complained that the public was thoughtless in not respecting Jackie's wish for privacy. Jackie's honeymoon with the press continued throughout that difficult year and well into her move to New York. Her years in Washington were over, and her reign as America's Pop Princess was about to begin.

Pop Princess In New York

During her first years in New York, Jackie could be seen in the flesh, now and again, in her fabulous leopard coat which had been given to her by Haile Selassie in 1963, or in the midnight-colored natural mink which made every other fur coat in town look shabby beside it. She'd be walking on Fifth Avenue with the children, lunching at the Russian Tea Room with director Mike Nichols, or getting into a taxi on Sutton Place. She was probably closer to being a "private person" during this time than at any other period since her marriage to Jack.

Then, in 1966, with Bobby's agreement or

perhaps not, Jackie took an action which resulted in the first crack in her image. In February 1964, both she and Bobby realized that a lot of books were going to be written about Jack's death in Dallas, and they knew that many would be sensational and ugly. They both felt there should be one book, at least, which was accurate, comprehensive, and written with the dignity that Jack deserved. They suggested to William Manchester—who had written *Portrait of a President* about Jack some years before—that he do one about the assassination. Manchester's earlier book, which had been described as "gushy" and "adoring," was probably the single most important qualification he had—but there were others. He was a conscientious journalist, a skilled interviewer, and above all, he was a gentleman. Manchester's publisher, Harper & Row, paid him an advance to sustain him through the writing of the new book; neither the Kennedy family nor the government gave him any financial assistance. Their contributions took the form of cooperation and availability. Word got around New Frontier circles that Manchester's book would be the unofficial official work, and scores of aides, friends, and relatives put themselves at his disposal, feeling more or less that it was their duty to Jackie and Bobby, and something which Jack would have wanted.

"Are you just going to put down all the facts, who ate what for breakfast and all that, or are you going to put yourself in the book, too?" asked Jackie. Manchester answered that he couldn't see how he would be able to keep himself out of it, weighing evidence and coming to conclusions. "Good," said Jackie emphatically.

Manchester moved his family from Connecticut to Washington, so that he would be close to most of the sources. (This was before Jackie's move to New York.) He spent extensive time in Dallas, long after the Warren Commission investigators had left. He interviewed scores of people, went through acres of newspaper clippings—and even submitted written questions and received written answers from President Lyndon Johnson. Mary Gallagher wanted him to hire her as his secretary, but he had no funds for this. After three years of work, *Death of a President* was complete. It was one of the most eagerly awaited publishing events of our time. The Warren Report had been published previously, and received with much criticism. It was hoped that Manchester's exhaustive, single-handed effort might shed further light on the tragedy of Dallas.

Just before publication, Harper & Row arranged for portions of the book to be printed in *Look* magazine—a perfectly legitimate promotional tactic followed by many publishers. At that point, Jackie stepped in, insisting that there were certain passages of the book which should be "censored." The ensuing flap, which involved lawyers, injunctions, and a great deal of publicity, did nothing to affect the book except to boost its sales. It did a great deal of harm to Jackie's image with the American people. There was nothing especially alarming about Manchester's account, which presented Jack Kennedy in a most favorable light, and which dwelled almost lovingly on Jackie. Passages which were supposedly unflattering to President Lyndon Johnson were not all that bad, simply showing that he was a sensitive and vulnerable human being in a terribly difficult position. In the end, the only people who were hurt by the book were those it presented most sympathetically—Jackie, and to a lesser extent, the Kennedy family. They'd have done much better to leave well enough alone.

There was also Jackie's celebrated problem with her cook, a young German girl named Anna Marie Hubst, who tried to add to her $125 a week by writing a cookbook. In it she revealed that Jackie often dieted, a not too surprising revelation since there are few women in this country who are not concerned with their weight. But either because of that, or because she felt the girl was "capitalizing" on her association with Jackie, she was summarily fired. The cookbook, which, like Manchester's book, was not all that exciting, enjoyed a modest surge in sales, and Anna Marie was besieged with job offers. Again, Jackie's image was tarnished, and again, in striking out to preserve her prized anonymity, she served only to create more unfavorable publicity about herself.

Through this period, she was guided in most things by her brother-in-law, Bobby. Their mutual loss brought them closer together, and it became apparent to others in the Kennedy family that Bobby was the only man who was able to "handle" the willful Jackie. On the other hand, Jackie found that in Bobby she often had an unexpected ally.

And during this time, editors of cheap magazines continued to exploit Jackie's face and fame as a gimmick to sell their wares. It is a truism in the trade that Jackie on the cover means money in the bank. Some of the headlines were lurid and tasteless, some of them sickly sentimental, and almost all of them were totally offensive. Perhaps celebrities eventually become inured to seeing their names and photos used in this way, though it's unlikely that the fastidious Jackie could be numbered among them. At any rate, all of them are concerned about the effect such things may have on their children and families. There is simply no telling what effect it has had on John and Caroline to see their mother's name bandied about this way. Endless stories appeared, and continue to appear, about her supposed feud with the Kennedy family, about the various men in her life, about her freewheeling spending patterns. And almost immediately after the assassination and with increasing frequency until 1968, there was equally intense speculation about Jackie's plans. She would never remarry, said some articles. She planned to devote her life to perpetuating Jack's memory and to raising his children. She would remarry when the children were grown, said others. She already was married, secretly, some said. Wistful liberals tried to link her name with that of

Adlai E. Stevenson, then Ambassador to the U.N. and an occasional escort of Jackie's. Nonsense, said other Jackie-watchers. Stevenson was a divorced man. Devout Jackie would never think of it!

Matchmakers linked her with an Argentine millionaire, and with writer and editor George Plimpton.

In 1965, Jackie and the children went to England, where Queen Elizabeth dedicated a portion of the meadow at Runneymede, where the Magna Carta was signed, in perpetual memory of John F. Kennedy. It was a moving ceremony, and an occasion for Jackie to renew her friendship with David Ormsby-Gore, now Lord Harlech, who had been the British ambassador to Washington during the Kennedy years, and a good friend of Jack's. Naturally, international gossips assumed that engagement plans would be announced soon—but they weren't.

Insults Mrs. Roosevelt

The Manchester incident proved that Jackie had Clay Feet—and the Princess, who could do no wrong, now found herself exposed to the kind of press attention that she had been spared as First Lady out of respect for her husband's office and, as his widow, out of sympathy.

A new picture of Jackie began to emerge—a portrait of a tempermental, strong-willed woman, given to brooding and rudeness unless she got her own way. Some personal characteristics and habits which once were overlooked, notably Jackie's chain-smoking, were commented upon.

The day had long passed when smoking among women was viewed as shocking. What made it ridiculous was that so much effort was made to preserve Jackie's image as a non-smoker. No photo of her with a cigarette in hand ever crept into public print.

But other items about her smoking have; most recently in a book titled *I Love a Roosevelt*, written by Mrs. Elliot Roosevelt, the former Patricia Peabody of Seattle, the fifth wife of Elliot who served as Mayor of Miami for several years.

In recalling the details of Mrs. Eleanor Roosevelt's death, her daughter-in-law wrote that Jackie and President Kennedy arrived at the Roosevelt house in New York. Kennedy asked if General Eisenhower had arrived. "I'll bet," he said, "that in five minutes he'll have me backed against the wall giving me advice on how to run the country."

Kennedy was talking to Elliott at the time. Barely were the words out of his mouth when Eisenhower arrived. He shook hands all around and headed for JFK and, sure enough, backed him against the wall.

The book adds, "Jackie Kennedy sat regally on a couch nearby listening with cool unconcern to the scraps of talk floating about her. With an elegant gesture, Jackie took a cigarette from her purse and held it for a light . . . Elliott's sons were too mesmerized to react. They stared. Jackie balanced her unlit cigarette, waiting. At last, with a resigned sigh, she drew a match from her purse and lit it herself."

Ghouls' Gravy Train

Pique was at the root of her disenchantment with Eleanor Roosevelt. The former First Lady had withheld her endorsement of John Kennedy's vice-presidential bid in 1956 because of his reluctance to go on the record as opposing Senator Joseph McCarthy and his Witch Hunt. Kennedy had his reasons and they were politically sound. McCarthy had already stuck his head in the noose. There was no need for the Massachusetts senator to tie the knot. McCarthy, like himself, was an Irish Catholic, a minority in the world's most exclusive club, the United States Senate. Kennedy had nothing to gain by publicly deploring his tactics simply to satisfy Eleanor Roosevelt.

Mrs. Roosevelt understood his evasion—Jackie didn't. She nurtured her dislike of Mrs. Roosevelt to the end. Her disaffection with William Manchester grew out of the *Look* serialization. The fee paid Manchester for the installments was reported to be $665,000—a record high. Almost overnight Jackie turned on Manchester, equating him in her mind with the ghouls who were mopping up in what gossip columns called the *I Knew Kennedy* business. She had lived through the trauma of watching the principals in the assassination pick up considerable sums of money and in her mind's eye,

Manchester had simply jumped on the bandwagon.

It was a big mistake—even if there seemed ample reason for Jackie to leap out of her skin at the figure. It was also a grave injustice to Manchester.

Sympathetic Americans sent cash donations to Lee Harvey Oswald's wife and mother, to Jack Ruby and to others involved in the sensational events.

The family of Dallas Patrolman J.D. Tippit, shot dead when he tried to grab Oswald after the assassination, received more than $600,000 from 40,000 different persons. Abraham Zapruder, a Dallas clothing manufacturer who took movies of the assassination, contributed the $25,000 *Life* magazine paid him for films. The second largest donation was $12,000 from a Philadelphia publisher.

Oswald's mother, Marguerite, sold interviews to newspapers and magazines, appeared on several TV shows and began writing her memoirs. *The National Guardian*, a left wing weekly, sponsored a nationwide lecture tour during which Mrs. Oswald claimed her son was innocent but offered no evidence to support her theory.

Jack Ruby got $75,000 from a newspaper syndicate for his story. He also sold interviews to American and European magazines and to a TV network. Never before in all history had the prison cell of a murderer been crowded with so many reporters, photographers, columnists and writers.

Though he was supposed to be under maximum security guard in the Dallas jail, Ruby was allowed as many visitors as he wanted. He poured out his life's story to anyone who wished to listen—and could afford his price. At times, his narrow cell looked like a combination press room and TV studio.

Not least of those who were in on the JFK murder and its dramatic aftermath were the shapely strippers who performed in Ruby's two Dallas nightclubs. Solely on the strength of their association with Jack Ruby, these dolls commanded and received double their former peeling pay.

One of them stripped her way through Europe, where she was billed in various languages as "The Stripper Who Worked For Jack Ruby, Killer of President Kennedy's Assassin."

It takes years to create a Jackie, just as it takes years to grow a topiary tree. The soil and the climate must be just right, and the skilled hands of the gardener must bend the branches out of their natural shape to create, patiently, a shrub that looks like an animal or a geometric shape, and not the plant nature designed it to be. Such a creation takes time, knowledge, money, taste, and confidence that this is the way this natural creature should be molded.

Jackie is a product—of her time, of her class, and of her society. She is a purebred creature, superbly trained and nurtured to become just the person she is. She may be the last ultimate example of a vanishing species.

CHAPTER TWO
Jackie As A Little Girl

Knowing a bit about the Bouvier history, fortunes, and lifestyle, it is deceptively easy to start out a discussion of Jackie with allusions to the wealth and privilege into which she was born. Such allusions would be accurate only on the surface. Beneath that surface, the history of the Bouviers, and the life of Jacqueline Bouvier, is as full of financial uncertainty, family tragedy, social gaffes, and plain bad judgment as that of most families and most individuals.

It's true that she was born into comparative wealth—on July 28, 1929—but this was a bare three months before the stock market crashed in October. After that, Jackie's family (like many much richer and better connected) was to go through an extended period of financial uncertainty, of cutting corners, and of dipping into capital. Jackie and her sister, Lee, never exactly went hungry, but until her mother's remarriage to Hugh D. Auchincloss in 1942, there was much more preoccupation with money among her relatives than was really "good form."

The Bouviers were, in a sense, society, but never quite the utter bluebloods that adoring biographers used to imply in the days when Jackie was First Lady. They were Catholics—not so devastating a handicap as it used to be, but still too important to be overlooked. They were, for the most part, dark-haired and swarthy, with a Mediterranean look that set them apart from the fine-blonde ideal of WASP beauty. They were rather flamboyant in their tastes—Jackie's Aunt Maude dressed her bridesmaids in tangerine-colored dresses—and their actions sometimes went beyond the traditional limits of what was "done" and "not done."

Jackie's mother, the former Janet Lee, came of a wealthy enough family, but its wealth had been built up in a single generation, and for some reason this kind of energy and industry was looked down upon. It was supposed to be better to accumulate one's wealth slowly, avoiding the appearance of unseemly impatience.

Jackie's Phony Family Tree

That the Bouviers were an old and distinguished family long before the first Bouvier left France for America was a myth that originated with Jackie's paternal grandfather, John Vernour Bouvier II. Because he'd concocted such an intriguing story no one dared to dispute it—or even wanted to. The last to have called it a phony would have been Jackie's mother who liked to claim that she was a "Lee from the Maryland branch of the Lees."

So far as society arbiters could decide there have been no "Lees of Maryland" listed in the Blue Book. But family genealogy is an imperfect science, composed largely of what families decide they want to say about themselves. If they keep at it long enough, someone is bound to believe them.

What happens, though, when one becomes a First Lady and diligent researchers discover that granddaddy's carefully compiled volume on the Bouviers, lovingly put together with great detail and published under his own auspices, turns out to be totally false, the creation of a most imaginative mind? It was fascinating, but not composed of the stuff that makes for an acceptable family tree.

Once Jackie became the First Lady, however, the deception became moot. A lot of people suspected that the Bouvier blood wasn't quite as purple as the family wanted it believed. But now the experts went to work and uncovered the truth—that grandpa Bouvier had made up his background from whole cloth. They quietly filed their findings away.

From time to time the tabloids hauled out the findings of the experts and decked them with shrill headlines like JACKIE'S PHONY FAMILY TREE, but it didn't really matter. All the ancestry in the world didn't add up to one First Lady—a title Jackie may wear until the end of

her life, entitling her to a position at the head of
the line wherever she happens to stand.

It's difficult to imagine that a woman of Jackie's sophistication accepted the fairytale concocted by her grandfather, tracing their ancestry
back to the France of the eleventh century and
claiming kinship with Charles V—unless she
sincerely wanted to believe the fantasy. Perhaps
she needed to believe it. It had all been written
down in grandpa's book, *Our Forebears*, a copy of
which was duly presented to the Library of
Congress and circulated among the family's
friends and business acquaintances.

Actually, the first Bouvier, like many French
who immigrated to the United States in the early
part of the nineteenth century, had fled to avoid
vexations at home—not to discover America's
pot of gold. They were in trouble because of
taxation, their political views or, in the case of
Michel Bouvier, because he had been one of
Napoleon's soldiers in the Battle of Waterloo.
There was a price on his head, put there by
French royalists.

On arriving in Philadelphia at the age of
twenty-three he promptly took up the only trade
he knew, carpentry, and became successful at it.
There were enough French customers in Philadelphia to keep him busy. The most prominent
was Joseph Bonaparte, Napoleon's brother, who
arrived with caskets of jewels and established a
palatial residence. Young Michel Bouvier
helped build it.

The family's entrance into society came
through successful marriages of Bouvier's off-

spring, six daughters who were able to land wealthy and socially prominent husbands thanks to their carpenter father whose thrifty ways enabled him to build up a sizeable fortune by the time they were married off. Moreover, his craftsmanship was superb and in America, he discovered, skills won more respect than titles. The true origins of the Bouviers made a much more interesting saga of rags to riches than the souped-up concoction of grandpa Bouvier, who described his ancestor as a manufacturer of veneers and intimate of Joseph Bonaparte.

Of the five children of Jackie's paternal grandfather, John V. Bouvier, Jr., only one, her Aunt Maude, has never been divorced. Both her father, Jack, and his brother, Bud, died victims of the alcoholism which had wrecked their marriages and shattered their careers. Her Aunt Edith gradually withdrew from the world and became a virtual recluse in her Long Island house. The family was not exactly a model of psychological stability, any more than it embodied the refined virtues that old Social Register families pride themselves on.

Born when she was, Jackie never knew the really good times of the Bouvier family, when every male adult in the family was involved in Wall Street, riding high and confident at the crest of the greatest prosperity the family, or the nation, had ever known. Her great-uncle, Michel Charles Bouvier, was one of the oldest and most respected members of the stock exchange. Her grandfather, a lawyer by training, was a special partner in M. C. Bouvier & Co., and was put in charge of the branch office the firm had opened in East Hampton. Her father, John V. Bouvier III, was a successful specialist in trading on the floor of the exchange. He was making $75,000 a year on the exchange by the time he was thirty-five, and, until his marriage to Janet Lee, delighted in spending most of it on elegant clothes, pretty women, and good living.

To be sure, there were few shrewd, experienced investors who could perceive impending disaster through the golden haze of prosperity.

One, not too surprisingly, was the venerable M. C. Bouvier, who had seen, and survived, the panics of 1873, 1907, and 1917. At the height of his fortunes, he had assets amounting to around $7,500,000 on paper. During the speculative euphoria, he had maintained a prudent cash reserve of $1,600,000 and, before September, he had converted most of his holdings into gold, cash, or assorted, very reliable bonds. His attitude during the dismal days of the autumn of 1929 had been described as "maddeningly cool."

Unlike M. C., or financier Bernard Baruch, and that disturbingly brilliant Joe Kennedy, John V. Bouvier, Jr., had less of a feel for the market. He had made his first substantial investment only a few months before the crash: a $250,000 legacy from his mother whose value was cut at least in half by the time he withdrew it from the market on October 29. He had given up his law practice because of ill health, and his financial future depended almost entirely on the stock market. As a special partner in the M. C.

Bouvier firm, he was originally guaranteed an annual minimum of $15,000 a year on his ten percent of the profits from the firm. After the crash, his percentage remained the same, but his guaranteed minimum was cut to $10,000 a year. This did not present a bright financial future for a man of sixty-four with expensive tastes and a big family, particularly since his children seemed continually to be asking for money.

At first, John V. Bouvier, III actually made money by sensing trouble and selling short the stocks he specialized in a few weeks before the market collapsed. This practice, incidentally, was outlawed by the tough Securities and Exchange Commission rules put into effect by Joseph Kennedy after Franklin Roosevelt became president. After the dust cleared, it appeared that Jack had made a $100,000 profit in short sales from the crash. But prices plunged still lower, and by the sixth of November all of Jack's short-lived profits had been washed away.

The financial damage Jack suffered in the crash was humiliating, but the blow to his pride and manly self-confidence was infinitely worse. Not only had he lost his capital in the market, but he discovered after the crash that trading was so much reduced in volume that his income from commissions had dwindled terribly. He was forced to subdue his pride and ask his family for help, but all he could obtain was a $25,000 loan from his uncle, M. C. Bouvier. Everyone else in the family was in as bad shape as he.

In desperation, he made what must have seemed the ultimate sacrifice and went to his father-in-law, James T. Lee. A strict, moralistic man, who had never really approved of the wild young man his daughter had married, Mr. Lee agreed to help his son-in-law out, under some very galling conditions. First, Jack had to give up several club memberships. Then he had to promise to tone down his scale of living in general. And finally, he had to agree to let his father-in-law call the shots. In what must have been an agony of wounded vanity, Jack agreed, and he, his wife, and little Jacqueline moved into a luxury apartment building owned and managed by Mr. Lee, where they were allowed to live, rent free.

John V. Bouvier, Jr. still maintained his estate at East Hampton, with its gardener, chauffeur, two maids, and cook, its sunken Italian garden, and all the memberships in local beach and tennis clubs that made life there so enjoyable. Times were hard and getting harder, and yet no one in the family ever considered cutting down the standard of living. The money had to come from somewhere, though, and if incomes couldn't provide it, then it was necessary to dip into capital. This was a practice nobody liked to talk about, of course, and when necessity finally drove one member of the family to ask another for financial help, it always came as a shock.

In the summer of 1931, Jack and Janet rented a cottage on Egypt Lane, in East Hampton, where they spent the summer. Little Jacqueline was with them, of course, and they also brought Michel, the son of Jack's dead brother. And on July 28, 1931, Jackie made her first appearance in the society columns, as she attended a dog show on her second birthday. The photo is unmistakably of Jackie—with the wide-apart eyes, the snub nose, and the olive complexion that have become so familiar to celebrity watchers over the years.

Jackie's life, during those early years, was much happier than that of many American children. Living in her parents' comfortable Park Avenue apartment, playing in the park with her nanny, shopping for polo coats and leggings at Best's, or for her first riding habit at Millers, she had no way of knowing that there were 15 million unemployed in the nation, and that a lot of little girls went to bed hungry every night. Nor, when her parents brought her to East Hampton for the summer and she fell in love with her father's stable of hunters, could she have known that her own comfortable life was based on a very shaky foundation.

On the day before Roosevelt's inauguration in 1932, Jackie's sister, Caroline, was born. Like Jackie, she was given her mother's maiden name as a middle name and, almost immediately, people began to refer to her as Lee rather than Caroline.

Things appeared to be looking up for the family, although no one would have credited it to Mr. Roosevelt's drastic reforms. Anticipating the repeal of prohibition, Jack bought liquor stocks and they began to climb.

The Bouvier penchant for parties began to reassert itself. Jack threw a lavish fifth-anniversary party for himself and Janet. His father threw a huge luncheon party at East Hampton for Jackie's fourth birthday, and read some verses he had composed himself. And on Sunday, July 30, little Caroline Lee Bouvier was christened at St. Philomena's Church in East Hampton, and two hundred guests attended a garden party in celebration. The best part of the summer, from Jack's point of view and probably in the eyes of the adoring Jackie as well, was the first prize Jack won in a horse show with his chestnut hunter, Danseuse.

All this time, Jack's liquor stocks had climbed steadily, and by the middle of 1933 he had amassed $2 million in profits. He vowed that he'd keep it until he died—after all, he wasn't a playboy any longer, and he had two little daughters to look after—and put it in the bank. But that much money was a disastrous temptation for Jack. He withdrew it, sank it into the now-forgotten firm of Auburn Motors, and by September had nothing left. His net worth, by January, 1935, had sunk to $106,444.94. A healthy sum even by today's standards, but not very much, in reality, for a specialist on the stock exchange.

To make matters worse, the new head of the SEC was, in the words of one writer, "a man who knew all the angles because he had played them all," that canny Irishman, Joe Kennedy, so that before very long it was harder than ever for a man in Jack Bouvier's position to make up for his losses. Up until this time, the stock specialist had been in a position untrammeled by many rules, able to take advantage of his inside knowledge and ability to move fast in the market. With the new SEC rules, however, those days were past. Wall Streeters, who had never much liked Joe Kennedy in the first place and who had envied him his acumen, regarded his going to work for Roosevelt as nothing short of a defection, probably the worst since Benedict Arnold's.

At this point, some unheard-of stroke of luck was the only thing which could have revived Jack Bouvier's fortunes.

It came, with uncanny good timing, on July 29, 1935, when old M. C. Bouvier died. The dean of Wall Street had never married, and so his considerable estate with nearly $2-1/2 million in personal bequests, after taxes, went for the most part to his family. His nephew, John V. Bouvier, Jr., received in the neighborhood of $1 million —enough to finance a graceful old age. Jack Bouvier received only a token $5,000 in cash— but he was bequeathed all of M. C.'s brokerage business.

As a result, the new firm of Bouvier, Bishop & Co. was formed in September 1935, describing itself as "successors to M. C. Bouvier & Co.," whose partners were John V. Bouvier III, John V. Bouvier, Jr., and John G. Bishop, M. C.'s old partner.

In that year, Jack Bouvier managed to rake in $31,444 from commissions, and $3,442 in trading. It was a nice step upward from the previous year when he had earned only a little more than two thousand in commissions and when trading had led him to take a $43,000 bath. Of course, running true to Bouvier form, Jack also elevated his standard of living, so that his expenses ran to $39,692. His net worth at year's end was not perceptibly greater than the year before. But there is no doubt that Jack was convinced that life was getting better for him at long last.

In some respects, at least. For it was ironic that just as his luck began to run better financially, it was running out as far as his marriage was concerned. It had taken seven years for Jack and Janet to begin to realize that they were simply not made for each other. Janet was a serious-minded girl, conservative in her tastes, and careful about her friends. She was deeply concerned with doing the correct thing. As the daughter of a man who had earned himself a fortune, but who had never really made it into the best circles in New York society, Janet was somewhat unsure of herself and worried about what other people would think of her, her children, and her husband.

In late 1935 and early 1936, things deteriorated so severely between Jack and Janet, that, beginning on October 1, 1936, a trial separation went into effect. During this time, Jack was entitled to visit the girls "at all reasonable times and places" and "on Saturday afternoons and Sunday mornings as he may wish." But the girls were to remain in their mother's custody, and this was a deeply distressing thing for their father—more, perhaps, than the breakup of the marriage itself. And in the patterns of guilt, competition, and compensation that emerged in the ensuing years, this circumstance was to have a profound effect in shaping the character of the girls, particularly Jackie.

And so Jack moved into a single room at the Westbury Hotel, while his family remained in the luxurious duplex on Park Avenue, which Mr. Lee had assigned to them years before when Jack was down on his luck. Jack began paying the $1,050 a month for support and maintenance of Mrs. Bouvier and the children, and also took care of educational, medical and dental expenses.

Finances, too, took a turn for the worse, as if to add to Jack's troubles. The estate of M. C. Bouvier began to press him about that $25,000 loan from his uncle back in 1930, and Uncle Sam was giving him trouble about nearly $40,000 in back taxes. Though 1936 was not a bad year for him on the exchange, Jack's accountant calculated that if all real and contingent liabilities were settled by the end of the year, his net worth would sink to an all-time low of $56,000.

Perhaps the increasing financial pressure was what prompted Jack to return to his wife and children in March 1937, and make a final but unsuccessful attempt to live together. The family remained together until the end of August. After that, the separation became permanent and Janet Lee Bouvier quietly went off to Reno. At the time, Jacqueline was eight years old—old enough to be aware of the collapse of her world, but too young to absorb or understand the blow.

According to Berthe Kimmerle, the girls' governess from August 1937 to December 1938,

"They were very sorry, weeping little girls when Mr. Bouvier's custody would come to an end and they were compelled to return to their mother, who was staying with her father, Mr. Lee, in East Hampton."

This sums up the problem that was to dominate the rest of Jackie's girlhood and, to a lesser extent, Lee's as well. Their mother was undeniably a good mother and a woman of unimpeachable character; it was their father who possessed the kind of glamour, generosity, and sheer showmanship that appeals to little girls. Living at home with their mother was drab and colorless and ordinary. Being with their father was like a constant Christmas. Their mother conscientiously taught them manners, religion, how to dress—things which are infinitely more valuable to adults than they are to children. Their father taught them to have fun. He spoiled them relentlessly. He taught them how to get their own way. Their mother loved the girls—Jack worshipped them.

He regarded his time with his daughters as the supreme pleasure of his life, and gradually came to believe that the Lee family was trying to win them away from him. This spurred him on to compete more strenuously for the girls' affections, indulging them, giving in. Naturally, he sent them to the best private day school, Miss Chapin's. He planned elaborate treats for them, taking them to the stock exchange, the zoo, or riding in Central Park. When they grew older, his generosity took on greater dimensions—he maintained three hunters for them, opened charge accounts at Bloomingdale's, and squired them to posh French restaurants where he could be sure the other patrons would stare admiringly at the handsome trio.

Jack Bouvier had what might be called "star quality," and he made it part of his legacy to his daughters. Perhaps he knew that he would have little else to leave to them.

For the moment, at least, he also enjoyed two other advantages in dealing with his daughters. First, there was the financial power he had over them. With her $1,050 income from him, plus whatever her own family might occasionally contribute, Janet Lee Bouvier had a strictly budgeted existence with little leeway for extras. Jack himself was in a bad financial position, chronically spending more than he had, but he was able to give the girls a modest allowance of their own, and, depending on how much attention they paid him and whether or not he was pleased with them, he would make extra little presents to Lee and Jackie.

Another, less insidious form of love which Jack was able to share with his daughters was his remarkable, exuberant family. "Grampy" Bouvier—John V. Bouvier, Jr.—had a strong dynastic sense. He loved to have his children and grandchildren around him, and went to great lengths to devise games and contests to keep them amused. While the children were inclined to consider their visits to his Park Avenue apartment as tedious wintertime obligations, they regarded their summer visits to his East Hampton house, Lasata, as the high-water mark of the year. There were long, lazy rambles around the grounds of the estate, happy hours of playing golf or tennis, or swimming at the Maidstone Club. For young Jackie, what was best of all was the riding ring where she could practice with Danseuse. Aunt Edith, in her younger days, would entertain with an impromptu concert. There were a number of summer birthdays in the family, all celebrated with feasts of Long Island duckling and corn on the cob. And there were always plenty of children of all ages to play with.

Grandpa Bouvier—Aristocrat?

Grampy Bouvier was an aristocrat, or so he liked to think, and he reveled in the role of patriarch. He had never quite gotten over his impulse to run his children's lives—with the most benevolent will in the world, but with the firm certainty that he was correct and they weren't. He was determined, too, to instill a strong feeling of family loyalty among his grandchildren. They were Bouviers, and while their parents may have had their problems, they were all of good stock. He was a fascinating, contradictory old man who insisted that his family play golf with him on the nine-hole course at the Maidstone Club instead of the eighteen-hole course which they preferred, and who let it be known implicitly that he liked to win. Because he was, after all, the head of the family, a notorious tinkerer with his will, and the possessor of a modest fortune and a lovely estate, the younger Bouviers saw to it that he won most of the time. And yet he was the same man who would sit in a room where the children were having a wild time, having turned down his hearing aid so he could read his Macaulay in peace.

At lunch, the conversation would be dominated by Jack paying the most extravagant compliments to Jackie and Lee, then challenging the others to disagree with him. This practice, severely frowned upon by the English-descended aristocracy who believed children should be seen and not heard and should never overhear anything nice about themselves, has been described as "typically Latin."

And so it went for years, Jack conducting his all-out campaign to keep his daughters' love and loyalty, their mother trying quietly to bring them up as well-bred young ladies. It was a difficult time for Janet, trying to lead a genteel life on her $1,050 a month, living on the fashionable East Side of Manhattan during the winter, spending summers at her father's in East Hampton where her former husband was continually spiriting the girls away to Lasata. Unhappily, Jack's family and friends had sided with him after the divorce—not because they loved Janet the less, but because they loved Jack the more. Thus she found herself without many of the very friendships that had helped to make her years with Jack more bearable.

Liberated from the limitations and frustrations of being a husband, but keeping the privi-

leges and joys of fatherhood, Jack Bouvier glee-
fully returned to the playboy existence he had
led before his marriage. He moved from the
Westbury into a four-room apartment at 125
East Seventy-Fourth Street, and embarked once
again on the activity that had given him the most
pleasure all his life—courting women.

For six years, he enjoyed what he considered
the best of both worlds—the love and companionship of his daughters, on the one hand, and
his freedom to pursue the most beautiful and
desirable women in the city on the other.
Though he was never as rich as he would have
liked to be, he was able to support his daughters
and treat his ladies lavishly, and during this time
he was probably as happy as he had ever been, or
ever would be.

But it all hinged on one fact—Janet Bouvier
was a divorcee of very modest means. This
allowed Jack almost unlimited access to his
daughters, permitted him to appear lavish and
openhanded in contrast to Janet's necessarily
thrifty ways, and gave him the opportunity to be
the only continuing male presence in the girls'
lives.

This was all right for Black Jack Bouvier, but
it amounted to a lonely purgatory for Janet Lee
Bouvier. A normal, attractive, vital woman, she
was simply not the type to while away the rest of
her life as a penny-pinching divorcee. She
wanted to remarry, but she wisely took her time
about it. She was reluctant to make another
mistake, and the thought of possibly subjecting
Jackie and Lee to another divorce was utterly

repugnant to her. She was also concerned about the matter of social position—not just *any* rich man would do.

The right man came along in the person of Hugh D. Auchincloss, descended on his father's side from the first American Auchincloss, a Scottish merchant who became president of the American Dry Goods Association; and on his mother's side from Oliver B. Jennings, one of the founders of Standard Oil. Hugh Auchincloss had inherited social prestige which made the Bouviers look like Lions Clubbers, and a vast fortune which assured Janet and her daughters of unassailable security for the rest of their lives.

Most important, Auchincloss embodied all the virtues which Jack lacked, and which meant so much to Janet. He was steady, hard working, thrifty, and prudent, (though his wealth made it unnecessary), and respectful of traditional religion. His first two marriages had ended in divorce, but it was evident that he had found his ideal at last in Janet, as she had found hers in him.

They were married in McLean, Virginia, at one of Hugh's magnificent estates, in June 1942. For Janet Lee Bouvier Auchincloss, it was the beginning of the kind of life she had hoped to have with Jack. For Jack, it marked the beginning of the end. And for their daughters, Jackie and Lee, it marked the beginning of their development into individual, remarkable young women.

On Wall Street, observers of the scene noted that this was the time when Hugh Auchincloss's firm of Auchincloss, Parker, and Redpath became the butt of a classic saying—"Take a loss with Auchincloss." Black Jack Bouvier was credited with thinking it up.

Belle Of The Ball

During the painful years while her parents' marriage was breaking up, her relatives began to notice that Jackie tended more and more to withdraw into herself. As a little girl she had been outgoing, confident, and cheerful. But when her parents parted, Jackie, in her little-girl heart, took it as a personal humiliation and began erecting defenses to protect herself from the blame and ridicule that she anticipated.

And yet, her naturally extroverted personality would not be denied. The way it worked out, in the analysis of one relative, was that she developed an "apparent urge to be seen by an audience and admired, which was just as pronounced, in a way, as her shyness and reserve." Talking with just one person, on a one-to-one basis, she appeared to be painfully restrained and ill at ease. But given the limelight and an audience, at a horse show, perhaps, or at a big debutante party, Jackie became the incandescent belle of the ball.

Although her mother's marriage did, indeed, solve many of the problems which had beset her and her daughters, and opened the way to a more relaxed and confident view of life for all of them, the influence—or the damage—to Jackie's personality had already taken place. They moved from the dreary wartime city to the Auchincloss estate, Hammersmith Farm, at Newport, Rhode Island. One of the huge ocean-side "cottages" built by the very rich before there were such things as income taxes or servant problems, the beautiful old house must have seemed like a castle to Jackie and Lee. It seemed that not only Lasata, but its surrounding grounds and the sunken Italian garden could fit inside, with room to spare.

It was enormous, but by no means lonely. There were Auchincloss cousins to play with now, and visits from the children of "Uncle Hughdie's" previous marriages. And there was their mother, serene and smiling now, and big, ruddy-faced Uncle Hughdie himself. All of a sudden, it was a lot more fun to live with their mother than it had been to visit their father.

Realizing this, and knowing there was nothing he could do about it, Jack Bouvier sank slowly into depression. For the first time, he attended his father's Thanksgiving luncheon in 1942 without Jackie and Lee. His sisters noticed his morose state.

He was able to have his beloved daughters with him for the summer of 1943, when the Bouviers enjoyed another enthusiastic reunion —all but the men who were serving in uniform.

In the years that followed, Jack Bouvier felt his daughters slipping away from him, moving more and more into the orbit of the Auchincloss family. This was perfectly natural, as they were living with their mother and stepfather, but Jack could not accept it. It must have rankled him particularly to know that even though Hugh Auchincloss had all those millions, Jack's divorce agreement bound him to support his daughters at their private schools, stable their horses, and pay their charge accounts and allowances. Understandably, he became increasingly insistent that the girls spend time with him—but unfortunately, this was at a time in their own lives when life with their mother and stepfather was more exciting.

Jack's great dissatisfaction with the situation weighed heavily upon him. His temper grew short, and he drank too much. He indulged in angry outbursts at his father with the accumulated resentments of his lifetime. Afterward, Jack was always overcome with remorse; it was evident that his father was seriously ill, and after all, he was in his eighties. Beset by cancer, prostate trouble, and nervous disorders, he became more and more affectionate toward his docile twin daughters, Maude and Michelle, and more hostile toward the unconventional Edith and the rebellious Jack, who goaded his father into cutting him off. Jack and Edith sided with each other against the twins, and when his sister Michelle remarried, Jack swiftly moved into the void left in his father's affections and began to campaign for a reconciliation. He brought Jackie and Lee to his father's birthday party in the summer of 1947 to demonstrate that they still held him in affection, that they still considered themselves Bouviers first.

Jack's campaign succeeded, he was reinstated

in his father's will, and it was he who led the mourners at the old man's funeral in January 1948. But it was an ironic victory. When the will was probated, it was discovered that instead of the million-plus fortune which everyone expected to divide, there was only $824,000 in John V. Bouvier's estate. Dividing that among four children, ten grandchildren, innumerable charities, old servants, and other legatees was not going to leave anybody with much.

Out of the proceeds, Jack Bouvier came away with $100,000, and had a $50,000 loan excused. His last-ditch reconciliation with his father had paid off, but at the expense of his fellow heirs. A failure of personality prevented Jack from assuming the role of head of the family, and there were understandable resentments that kept the family from rallying around him.

Even with the generous legacy, Jack was far from rich, and it was out of the question for Lasata to remain in the family. Two years later, it was sold.

One interesting—and prophetic—anecdote about Jackie arises from the first year she spent at Miss Porter's. She wanted badly to bring Danseuse with her, but her mother and stepfather felt that an additional fee of $25 a month to board the horse, when there were others available at the school, was a needless extravagance. Jack Bouvier, virtually on his uppers at the time, could not pay it. So Jackie wrote a sweet note to John V. Bouvier, Jr., persuading him to foot the bill.

She was a good student, with a gift for languages, a great interest and some talent in art, and, obviously, a flair for writing. Her roommate at Miss Porter's was Nancy Tuckerman, who became a lifelong friend and whom Jackie later brought to Washington as a member of her White House staff.

Jackie spent the summers in Newport and East Hampton, playing tennis, dating socially prominent young men, and, always, riding. Her well-known passion for horses has continued undiminished through her adult years.

On the surface, anyway, Jackie seemed to be accepting the kind of role laid out for her. She was expected to learn to dress, to run a great house, to keep herself fit and beautiful, to marry well.

When she became America's heroine on a tragic November weekend almost twenty years in the future, she was compared to a thorough-bred. The comparison is a good one, for Jackie in many ways is similar to the noble animals she loves so much. Heredity has given her good looks and the kind of mind that is most congenial to the aristocratic way of life. Training has refined her innate qualities, and made her even more suited to the role of a rich man's wife, a leader in what is known as society, and a woman who will be a credit to her husband and family.

Debutante Of The Year

A thoroughbred is, by the standards of most people in the world, an outmoded and unrealistic creation, a beautiful ornament that only the rich can afford. A woman like this is not especially useful—but then, neither is a thoroughbred horse. Still, there is something sad and heroic about them both, something that speaks to the best potential in all of us.

During her teens, Jackie's evident superiority to other girls her age captivated society reporters and photographers. Her picture appeared repeatedly in the rotogravure sections of the newspapers. Cholly Knickerbocker nominated her "Debutante of the Year" in 1947.

In the fall of 1947, Jackie went off to Vassar—as usual, at the expense of her father. Jack was pleased that she was there, for Poughkeepsie was closer to New York than either Newport or McLean, Virginia, and he had hopes of seeing her often on weekends.

When, during the first couple of months, Jack visited his daughter, it was as if she were entertaining a movie star. In his early fifties, Jack still looked forty. He was one of those lucky men whose indulgences didn't show—on the outside, anyway. And Jackie stayed at his apartment when she came to New York for dances.

But Jack was so intent on keeping his daughter's love, and in particular, keeping it away from the Lees and the Auchinclosses, that he became unreasonable. Like most college freshmen, Jackie was self-centered and intent on enjoying herself; like most normal girls of her age, she was inclined to accept whatever was offered and ask for more without worrying about what she was giving in return.

He was unsure of himself in his relationship with Jackie. Too long had he enticed her with material things, with visits to Lasata, with little unexpected checks. He was probably uncertain of his ability to give his daughters real love by this point, and in his reduced circumstances, with Lasata sold, and with nothing really to offer that could compete with the Auchincloss riches, he was desperate. He insisted that Jackie go to a dentist in New York, rather than in Virginia, because he was sure that dental work in Virginia was only a ploy to take her away from him. He kept her horses at East Hampton. All he could afford in the way of a summer place was a modest rented cottage a good walk from the ocean, which couldn't compete with Hammersmith Farm or even Lasata, but he played knowingly on Jackie's affection for her horses.

He was boundlessly disappointed when Jackie announced that she intended to spend the summer of 1948 traveling through Europe with three friends: Judy Bissell, and Judy and Helen Bowdin. Under protest, feeling certain that the whole thing was Janet's idea, Jack paid his daughter's way. It was on this trip that Jackie first came in contact with the country of her Bouvier ancestors, and developed her passionate interest in the arts and culture of Europe.

Jackie spent two weeks with her father in East Hampton that summer before sailing for a year of studying in France. Once abroad, her cousin John Davis has pointed out, her relationships with her father improved considerably, since she was not in a position to choose Merrywood or Hammersmith Farm over his sunless East Seventy-Fourth Street apartment.

Jackie began her year with a two-month intensive course in French at the University of Grenoble, then moved to Paris for study of French history and literature at the Sorbonne. She lived at the home of the Countess of Renty, an impecunious aristocrat whose husband had died in a German concentration camp. In Paris, Jackie's friends included the exciting student life of the university, and the older, more elegant world of expatriate Americans. She bloomed, she blossomed, she came into her own in Paris, and Vassar had lost her forever.

Not even when Jack was hospitalized for a cataract operation did Jackie consider coming home; a decision which hurt Jack particularly since Lee, at the time, was at a horse ranch in Wyoming and told him she couldn't get away either.

When she finally did return from France, Jackie had made up her mind that the all-girl atmosphere of Vassar was just not her cup of tea. She enrolled, instead, at George Washington University. This was a severe blow to Jack, since George Washington, in Washington D.C., was even closer to the hated Auchincloss stronghold at McLean than Poughkeepsie had been to New York. Jack took it as a complete surrender by Jackie to her stepfather's family, and, ironically, one which he would have to pay for.

CHAPTER THREE
Jackie Finds Love

In line with her wish to lead an independent emotional life, Jackie had begun to date seriously. In the early part of 1951, she became engaged to John G. W. Husted, son of a prominent banker in New York. A Yale graduate, like Jack, who worked on Wall Street, again like Jack, he was precisely the sort of lad that Jack approved of. In Jack's eyes, his greatest virtue was, of course, that he lived in New York.

The couple saw each other on alternate weekends, first in New York, then at Merrywood. Jack was highly pleased with the arrangement.

But the engagement lasted only three months. What went wrong? It's hard to say—both Jackie and John might not know themselves, even today. They were both terribly young, and perhaps neither was really ready for marriage. Perhaps Jackie had some inner misgivings about marrying and living in New York, where her father would expect to see her often and where he might well feel he was competing with her husband in the same way he had felt he was competing with the Auchinclosses for Jackie's time and attention.

One day John took his fiancee to visit his mother who, with typical maternal pride, sweetly offered Jackie a snapshot of her son as a baby. "No, thank you," said Jackie. "If I want any photos I can take my own." It is not reported what Mrs. Husted replied to her prospective daughter-in-law. Presumably she was speechless.

At any rate, before long the engagement was at an end. Jack's hopes of having Jackie in New York permanently were shattered, and he was feeling very low about it. Then Jackie came through with an accomplishment that any parent would be proud of, and a momentary renewal of the hope that she would come to live in New York.

She won the 1951 Prix de Paris contest, sponsored by *Vogue* magazine, and enormously respected by people in the fashion, publishing, and social worlds. Competing with 1,280 other college girls, Jackie submitted a complete plan for an issue of *Vogue*, four technical papers on haute couture, and wrote an essay on "People I Wish I Had Known." The three that Jackie chose were the poet Charles Baudelaire, the playwright and wit Oscar Wilde, and the ballet director Sergei Diaghilev. The first prize was a job with the Paris edition of *Vogue* for six months, followed by six months at the magazine's New York office.

Predictably, since it would take Jackie out of the Auchincloss orbit for an entire year, and bring Jackie to New York for half that time, Jack Bouvier was enthusiastic about it. The Auchinclosses were less so. Whatever argument prevailed, Jackie declined the Prix de Paris, unknowingly casting the die for the shape of her life to come.

Inquiring Photographer

But after she left George Washington U., there was still the question of what to do with herself. Perhaps Jack's unrelenting opposition to the Auchinclosses, and his continuing suspicion that they were trying to win Jackie away from him had, in fact, aroused exactly those feelings in them. At any rate, it was Uncle Hughdie who organized matters so that Jackie would remain in Washington, until long after her father's death —if anyone could have seen into the future. Through his friend, Arthur Krock of *The New York Times,* he arranged for Jackie to have a fling at journalism, which had been thwarted when she gave up the opportunity with *Vogue.* Krock set up an interview with the publisher of the now-defunct *Washington Times-Herald,* and as a result she became the paper's inquiring photographer, at $42.50 a week. It was less than the $50 a week Jack Bouvier was willing to pay her as a secretary in his firm, but no doubt the job was much more appealing to her.

She began work for the *Times-Herald* in late 1951, asking a different question of several people every day, taking their photographs, and preparing a column with their answers beside their pictures. By March 1952, she had a by-line. The questions she asked were intriguing and harmless. At a dental clinic, she asked the staff members, "Are men braver than women in the dental chair?" Along Washington's "Antique Row" she asked dealers, "If you could keep one thing in your shop, what would it be?" She asked children why Santa's reindeer don't come down the chimney.

The chronology of Jackie's social life becomes a bit muddled during this period, possibly because she was so busy buzzing back and forth to New York and dating innumerable eligible young men in Washington. In *The New York Times Magazine*, writer Susan Sheehan stated that it was in January 1952 that the episode between Jackie and John Husted's mother took place, going on to say that the engagement was broken after three months. In *The Bouviers*, John Davis, a cousin of Jackie's, states that she became engaged to Husted in the first half of 1951.

Similarly, Mary Barelli Gallagher, Jackie's personal secretary who told all in *My Life with Jacqueline Kennedy*, says that friends of Jackie's, the Charles Bartletts, brought her together with a young Congressman from Massachusetts in June 1951. But John Davis, who is, after all, a relative, says that it was on May 8, 1952, at a dinner at the Bartlett's home that Jackie met Congressman John F. Kennedy.

The 1952 date seems more likely for the meeting which changed Jackie's life. Although Jack and Jackie got along well enough at the dinner, both Mrs. Gallagher and Mr. Davis agree that they did not begin to date regularly until several months later. Mrs. Gallagher says that the romance did not begin to become serious until after Jackie had interviewed him as a senator.

She asked him his opinion of the Senate Pages, and in her column she quoted him as saying: "I've often thought that the country might be better off if we senators and pages traded jobs. If such legislation is ever enacted, I'll be glad to hand over the reins to Jerry Hoobler, whom I've often mistaken for a senator."

Then she dashed across the hall to ask the same question of Vice-President Richard Nixon.

In the same column, Jackie quoted Page Jerry Hoobler as saying that the youthful Senator Kennedy was always being mistaken for a page, or even a tourist. "The other day, he wanted to use the special phones, but the cops told him, 'Sorry, Mister, those are reserved for senators.'"

In the middle of what turned out to be Jack Kennedy's courtship of the lovely Jackie Bouvier, her cousin, John Davis, lunched with her in Washington and asked her if there was anything to the rumors. Jackie, he reports, seemed not to take the young senator seriously because he had told her that he "intended to become president." To Jackie, that seemed quixotic, unrealistic. It was also said that the young senator was quite a man with the ladies, even while he was dating Jackie, and later.

During this time, Jackie definitely did have marriage on her mind—but it was the wedding of her younger sister, Lee, to Michael Canfield, son of publisher Cass Canfield, that she was thinking about. They were married April 18, at Merrywood, in a formal ceremony at which Jack Bouvier gave his daughter away. It was his first trip into Auchincloss territory. Reluctantly, he admitted that Merrywood was every bit as lovely as Lasata, and it must have been painful for him to compare the sumptuous Auchincloss way of life with the comparative little he had been able to give his daughters during the past ten years. Though he was proud of Lee and gratified that she looked so happy, though he was able to keep up a brave front and behaved pleasantly to Janet, her new husband, and her father, Jack very nearly broke down during the reception. It was quite possibly the worst ordeal of his life.

Lee's new husband, Michael, was a long-time friend who had moved in the same circles as the Bouvier girls. But Jackie's beau was another matter entirely. A third-generation Irishman from Boston, he had much less social cachet than the Auchinclosses or the Bouviers. The immense Kennedy wealth, moreover, was won in the stock market by his father, Joseph P. Kennedy, the head of Roosevelt's SEC, and, next to Roosevelt, the most hated man on Wall Street during the thirties and early forties.

John F. Kennedy, senator or not, was hardly the man that Jack Bouvier would have chosen for his beloved Jackie. But this was only the case on the surface. It turned out that the two men had more in common than a first name and nickname. Both loved the good life and were immensely successful with women. Both Black Jack Bouvier and Jack Kennedy suffered from slipped spinal discs. Both married beautiful women who were considerably younger—Janet being fourteen years younger than Jack Bouvier, Jackie twelve years younger than Jack Kennedy. And both men loved Jackie intensely—that was the most important quality they shared.

"Gay Young Bachelor"

Jack squired Jackie to the Eisenhower Inaugural Ball in January 1953. Naturally, Jackie was at her most resplendent in such a setting, and perhaps it was at this moment that Jack's heart capitulated. Or perhaps it was their separation in May, when Jackie's paper sent her to London to cover the coronation of Queen Elizabeth II. Or, quite possibly, Jack had fallen in love with Jackie months before and, as luck would have it, was forced to keep the romance a secret until the *Saturday Evening Post* came out with its big story about him. The problem was that the *Post* story was titled "The Senate's Gay Young Bachelor." In fact, in telephoning the news of her engagement to her Aunt Maude, Jackie begged her not to tell anyone, "because it wouldn't be fair to the *Saturday Evening Post.*"

Actually, Mary Gallagher reports, when the Senator saw the title of the article, he was livid with rage. His personal life might seem glamorous to the readers of the *Post*, but he wanted it known that he was a hard-working, serious Senator with an important political contribution to make.

When the official announcement did come, the Auchinclosses were delighted and not particularly surprised. Jack had been a frequent visitor at Merrywood, sometimes when Jackie wasn't there. He had even felt free to bring along his office staff to use the swimming pool!

It was decided that Jack and Jackie would be married on September twelfth at Hammersmith Farm in Newport. Archbishop Cushing would officiate. Lee would be her sister's matron of honor, and Jack Bouvier would again give one of his daughters away at a wedding where the Auchinclosses were hosts. The press began touting it as "the wedding of the year."

Jack Bouvier was determined to carry off his role at Jackie's wedding as well as he had handled his part at Lee's. He spent hours in the sun at East Hampton acquiring a magnificent tan. He went all out in putting together his wardrobe for the occasion—a made-to-order cutaway, striped trousers and vest, a new pair of expensive gray suede gloves and the pearl stickpin his late father used to wear. Jack Bouvier was a man who loved to look good, and knew how to.

On the evening of September eleventh, Jack Bouvier checked into the venerable Viking Hotel in Newport where, as father of the bride, he was accorded royal treatment. But as the hour of the wedding approached, he felt a mounting anxiety. If he took a couple of steadying drinks, who could blame him?

But as the night wore on into morning, and he kept making incoherent phone calls to Hammersmith Farm and to his sisters, who were staying at another hotel in Newport, it became painfully evident that Jack Bouvier was not going to make it to Jackie's wedding.

And so it was that the man who escorted Jackie Bouvier down the aisle at St. Mary's Church that day was not her adoring father, but the man he considered his rival for Jackie's love—Hugh D. Auchincloss.

Jackie As Mrs. JFK

For Jackie, the vibrant Leo who loves the spotlight and who tenses up in intimate conversation, there was something wonderfully fitting that her marriage to Jack should begin and end, with elaborate formal ceremonies, in bright autumn sunshine, with thousands of fascinated spectators. The high noon of her womanhood was spent as the wife of one of the most magnetic political personalities since Franklin Roosevelt. It was altogether appropriate that this period of her life should open with a ceremony as lighthearted and beautiful to look at as the closing ceremony was somber, grief stricken—and also poignantly beautiful to look at.

Jackie has always had a remarkable flair for the theater of real life; on such occasions, she shines forth like a first-magnitude star. And, on both occasions, the thought uppermost in Jackie's mind could easily have been the hallowed theatrical motto: "The show must go on."

In the tight-waisted, full-skirted wedding dress which fashion in the early fifties decreed, Jackie looked pretty enough, but she lacked the great feeling of style which she was later to exhibit. Her gown was eggshell taffeta, with a scooped neckline and little cap sleeves. The huge, bouffant skirt was ruffled, row on row, to the floor. She wore her grandmother's rose-point lace wedding veil. Her sister and the bridesmaids wore white, with claret-colored sashes. The flowers were orange blossoms.

The bridal luncheon, held at Hammersmith Farm, saw a heterogeneous crowd of 1,200 Social Registerites, financial figures, and artists from Jackie's side, mingling with the congressmen, senators, and ward-heelers from Jack's. Jack's brother, Bobby, who as best man had nearly lost the wedding ring, was there with his wife, Ethel. Jack Kennedy danced with his mother, who looked almost as young as the bride herself.

Back at the Viking Hotel, Jack Bouvier packed up his unworn formal clothes and prepared to return to New York. Perhaps he knew that word of his "indisposition" was already traveling the gossip grapevine to Newport, East Hampton, and New York society. Perhaps he knew that it would be difficult to go back to his old haunts and his old way of life. Perhaps, as he headed for the railroad station, he even felt it might be better this way.

Jack and Jackie honeymooned in a pink villa overlooking the Pacific Ocean at Acapulco. One of the first things that Jackie did after their arrival was to write a letter of forgiveness to her father. Jack Bouvier showed it to his partner, John Carrere, with tears in his eyes. Carrere later recalled that it was one of the most compassionate and touching letters he had ever read, "one that only a rare and noble spirit could have written."

When Jack Kennedy brought Jackie back from Acapulco, one of his first thoughts was to make Jackie his insurance beneficiary. Mary Gallagher and Evelyn Lincoln, his secretaries, were witnesses.

Jack and Jackie moved into a rented house on Dent Street, N.W., in Georgetown. It was quaint and narrow, like so many of the old houses in the area, and for the first time Jackie was able to indulge her knack for making a house into a pretty and livable home.

Marriage to Jack must at first have seemed like an undreamed of birthday present or holiday for Jackie. For the first time since her parents' divorce, she was truly part of a family again, a big happy family whose members loved each other and cherished their loyalty. The united

Kennedys were a far cry from the contentious Bouviers, the rigid Lees, and the demanding Auchinclosses. It must have seemed like the best days at Lasata, before the Bouviers had begun to quarrel and peck at one another.

Not the least of the advantages of Jackie's new life was the Kennedy wealth and generosity. All her life, Jackie had moved among very rich people and yet she herself was often the poor girl at the party. For years, her allowance from Jack Bouvier was a steady $50 a month. He paid for her tuition, travel, and medical expenses, it's true, but even though these expenses were formidable, Jackie herself never saw the money. She had her charge account at Bloomingdale's —but her father supervised that strictly. Her mother, though the wife of one of the richest men in America, had some firm old-fashioned ideas about the value of money. She quite sincerely believed that it would build Jackie's "character" if she attended expensive schools with rich girls, and had little spending money of her own. As a matter of fact, at the time she married Jack, Jackie was making $56.75 a week from the *Times-Herald*, and that was the most money she had ever been able to call her own.

CHAPTER FOUR
Married Life

As a Kennedy, Jackie swiftly found that there was no such thing as a money problem. This gave her, for the first time, the chance not only to indulge herself in shopping, but to carry out the sort of thoughtful gesture that became one of the Jackie trademarks.

For example, as a surprise for Jack, she had the huge sailfish he had caught on their honeymoon in Acapulco mounted and delivered to his office. Later Jack was to have this hung in what had been called "The Fish Room" at the White House since FDR was President. When she and Jack were invited to dinner at some Washington home, she always sent a graceful thank-you note by messenger the next day, often accompanied by some little gift—a terrine of *pate de foie gras*, perhaps, or a bouquet of fresh flowers. Being rich makes it easier to be thoughtful.

Jackie was pleased that her new husband and

her father got on well. Every once in a while, Jack Bouvier would visit the Kennedys in Washington, and occasionally Jack Kennedy had to go to New York, where his father-in-law would treat him to lunch at the Stock Exchange Luncheon Club, and proudly take him down on the trading floor. Jack Bouvier's strong capitalist/Republican sentiments were nowhere near as strong as his love for his daughter, and his pride in her handsome, able husband.

But not too long after his marriage, Jack Kennedy's back began bothering him again. He had suffered a ruptured disc while playing football at Harvard. This had been aggravated during World War II when his PT-boat 109 was struck by the Japanese. He was forced to come to his office on crutches, trying to appear his normal self, but actually in great pain. He hid the crutches when his constituents came calling, and forced himself to walk as if there were nothing at all the matter.

It was obvious that something must be done about his back. Jackie begged him to drop everything and go into a hospital immediately, but Jack insisted on hanging on until Congress adjourned that fall.

At last, in October 1954, he went into The Hospital for Special Surgery in New York for a lumbar-spine operation. It was a serious operation, but not normally a dangerous one. In Jack's case, however, infection set in. Jackie spent long nights at his bedside wondering, with the doctors, whether her husband would live. For two months, it was touch and go, but finally Jack was well enough to be flown to the Kennedy home in Palm Beach for Christmas—on a stretcher. Afterward, he was flown back to New York for still another operation, not to leave the hospital until February 1955.

At about the same time, Jack Bouvier was coming to the sad, inevitable decision to retire. He sold his seat on the stock exchange for a mere $90,000 (in 1929 they went for $625,000 and in 1968 would sell for as much as $515,000), and retired with a capital of about $200,000. He was in poor health: in addition to his slipped spinal disc he suffered terribly from chronically inflamed sinuses, and his much-abused liver was giving him trouble.

With the two most important men in her life seriously ill, Jackie's life darkened, but she fought her depressions. She took a course in American history at Georgetown. She gave Jack a set of oil paints and he produced a couple of paintings while hospitalized. She brought her husband endless stacks of books to keep his mind occupied. When he was finally released from the hospital, and the couple went to Palm Beach once again, Jackie arranged for the Library of Congress to send Jack still more books; she could tell that an idea was forming in his mind.

The book, which Jack wrote while confined to bed, won him the Pulitzer Prize. It was believed at the time that the fine hand of Joseph Kennedy had guided the decision of the judges. Nothing in the years between has been revealed to offset that impression.

It was titled *Profiles in Courage*, and it was inspired, Jackie recalled later, by the story of Senator Edmund Ross, who risked his political life to follow his conscience, casting the one vote that kept President Andrew Johnson from being impeached.

These years, from 1954 to 1957, were extremely difficult for Jackie. Besides Jack's painful back trouble and her father's declining health, she was beginning to see that marriage to the glamorous young senator was not going to be all wit and elegance. For Jack Kennedy was a superbly political creature, who rejoiced in the rough-and-tumble of Democratic party politics even as he delighted in the competition and striving within the Kennedy clan. He enjoyed sitting up late, smoking cigars, and talking politics with Massachusetts cronies whom Jackie found drab and dreary.

But Jackie was prepared to go the route with Jack, and was in fact looking forward to becoming a wife and mother in the tradition of Rose Kennedy. Her first pregnancy ended with a miscarriage in 1955, but, undaunted, she and Jack had bought a huge white house in Virginia: Hickory Hill. This was later to become the home of Bobby and Ethel Kennedy and their brood when Jack and Jackie took up residence in the White House. But for now, it was to be the scene of happy Kennedy family reunions, and the home for the big family that Jackie was certain she would raise. She set about decorating the nursery as soon as she discovered that she was pregnant again, in 1956.

Her doctor allowed her to accompany Jack to the Chicago Democratic Convention. She spent most of the time with her sister-in-law, Eunice, in their air-conditioned hotel room, seeing Jack only briefly when he stopped on his way to another caucus or convention session.

But then it developed that Jack had a chance for the vice-presidential nomination. One wonders how serious he was when he let his name be put in nomination. Shrewdly political, he probably doubted that Adlai Stevenson could make much headway against the enormously popular incumbent, Dwight D. Eisenhower. And he knew full well that a smart politician avoids associating with losers. It's likely that Jack and his floor manager, Bobby, decided to make a bid for the vice-presidential nomination just for the invaluable experience of waging a floor fight. They knew it would be worth a lot later—maybe even as soon as the 1960 convention.

But it suddenly looked as if Jack had a serious chance, and Kennedys love to win. Jackie went to dinner with Jack the night of the voting for the vice-presidential nominee, and then to his headquarters.

The results were tragic and disappointing. Jack lost the nomination to Estes Kefauver, his senate colleague. And Jackie lost her baby. The stillborn girl was buried in the Kennedy family plot in Brookline, Mass. Jackie couldn't bear to return to Hickory Hill, the scene of too many poignant memories, so the couple moved into another rented house, at 2808 P Street, N.W.

It was while the Kennedys were living at P

Street that Mary Gallagher came to work for Jackie. Having been a secretary in Jack's office before her marriage, she had recently begun a part-time job with Jackie's mother, Mrs. Auchincloss, at Merrywood. Most of the time, Jackie was away from Washington, once again pregnant, and taking it very easy. Her young marriage had turned out to be a series of emotional crises, and she wasn't very happy.

The bitterest blow of all during this time was the death, in August 1957, of Jack Bouvier. By this time, Lee was living in London, and Jackie was very much caught up in her husband's political and family life. Jack Bouvier treasured the visits and phone calls from his daughters more than anything else in his confined life, but such contacts came less and less often. In fact, when Jackie became pregnant for the third time, with Caroline, her father learned about it only from reading an item in the paper.

When Jack Bouvier entered Lenox Hill Hospital in July, Jackie was surprised. Preoccupied with her own life and her own problems, she hadn't realized that her father was so sick. He had cancer of the liver, and died a week later, at the age of sixty-six.

Inwardly shattered, but much in command of herself, Jackie flew to New York from the Kennedy compound in Hyannis Port, and quickly took charge of the funeral arrangements. She and Jack stayed at Jack Bouvier's apartment on East Seventy-Fourth Street, and from there she directed every detail of his burial. It was Jackie's show, Jack merely offering comfort and support;

perhaps he, like the other members of the family, was surprised at her ability to handle a multitude of details at a highly emotional time. Her Bouvier flair for doing the correct thing in an individualistic way must have impressed Jack greatly. If he had ever had any doubts about her ability to bring zest and style to the official functions at the White House, they were dispelled.

She dispatched her aunts to choose the casket, and she herself conferred with florists. She wanted to avoid the standard funeral atmosphere, she said, and rejected the usual lilies and chrysanthemums because she could never associate her dashing, vital father with the mournful fact of death. She chose daisies and bachelor's buttons, in little white wicker baskets, and garlanded his casket with summer flowers. "I want everything to look like Lasata in August," she told her aunts. And so the atmosphere was anything but somber when Jack Bouvier's funeral mass was sung at St. Patrick's Cathedral. It was bright and lovely, just as her father would have wanted it, more like a wedding, in some ways, than a funeral. There were few mourners —his family, his dedicated maid, Esther, two dozen associates and friends. But in the back row, there was a group of women, dressed in black and wearing veils so thick that it was impossible to see their faces—if there had been anybody so insensible as to want to know who these ladies were.

Jack Bouvier was buried in East Hampton, in the Bouvier family plot, and Jackie went back to

Washington to await the birth of Jack Bouvier's first grandchild.

Jackie's first child was a daughter, born November 27, 1957, and named Caroline Kennedy —no middle name, perhaps to avoid family squabbles. Caroline, you recall, was the unused first name of Jackie's sister, Lee, who, in turn, had been named after Caroline Maslin Bouvier, wife of John V. Bouvier, Sr.

The baby was born by Caesarean section— with Jackie's history of unsuccessful pregnancies, the doctors wanted to take no chances. Jackie has the kind of lean-hipped, flat-chested body which sends fashion editors into ecstasies, but which causes furrowed brows among obstetricians. Some women are physically unsuited to bearing children, and Jackie is one. Of the five known pregnancies in her life, she has only two surviving children.

Jack, of course, was delighted to be a father— so pleased, in fact, that he bought a new house for Jackie, at 3307 N Street. A three-story, redbrick house, bigger than the one on P Street, it was the Kennedy's home during the 1960 Presidential campaign.

At this time, Nurse Maud Shaw came to take care of Caroline. A cheerful, sensible Englishwoman, it was she who eventually bore most of the practical responsibility for caring for the two Kennedy children.

After Caroline's birth, Jackie began building up a little universe of her own within the limits of her world as Jack's wife. She began taking a more serious interest in fashion, for one thing.

Since she could easily have made it a career, and since as a fashion editor or designer she would have had considerable impact on the world of fashion, it came naturally to her. She did not have to strive very hard to develop her instincts for dress—they were always there. She read fashion magazines and *Women's Wear Daily*, and did not begrudge the time, effort, and expense required to build a superb, highly individual wardrobe.

As concerned with her environment as with her personal appearance, Jackie dove enthusiastically into the project of decorating the new house. She was constantly fixing up one room or another, Mary Gallagher reported. She was never satisfied with the arrangement of her furniture, the paint on her walls, the rugs on the floor. Jack, like most husbands, was not much concerned with the way the house looked, so long as there was a comfortable corner for him to settle in. Once, while Jackie was in the throes of another rearranging spree, he bellowed, "Dammit, Jackie, why is it that the rooms in this house are never completely livable all at the same time?"

In the study, for example, Jackie switched the wallpaper three times in less than six months.

She continued her keen interest in riding, going out to Merrywood to ride, or to Middleburg, Va., to hunt with the Middleburg Hunt. She swam and sailed at Hyannis Port during the summers, though she never could be persuaded to join in the Kennedy family touch-football games like her sister-in-law, Ethel. She discovered a marvelous hairdresser named Kenneth, then working at Lilly Dache's salon in New York, and she made frequent visits to New York to have her hair tended to.

Meanwhile, back at the house on N Street, the household carried on. Maud Shaw looked after Caroline; Mary Gallagher handled the bills and the correspondence; Providenzia Paredes, Jackie's devoted personal maid, took care of Jackie's wardrobe to the extent of ironing her stockings and changing the sheets when Jackie took her afternoon naps. After a succession of cooks who couldn't get along with Jackie's requirements, Pearl Nelson took over the kitchen. There was also a great problem in keeping maids—Jackie was constantly sending to Mrs. Pauwels of the Eugenia Pauwels Employment Service for replacements.

If you've gotten the impression that Jackie was not actively involved in the day-to-day routine of her household, you're absolutely right. She was the field marshal who directed the efforts of her small army of servants and assistants, never making a bed, cooking a meal, or changing a diaper herself.

It was not that she considered herself too good for such mundane tasks. They simply had no place in her upbringing. In the rarefied days of Jackie's childhood, there were always servants to do the disagreeable work. Even when Janet Bouvier was living in straitened circumstances after her divorce, Jackie and Lee were cared for by governesses, and they never saw their mother wash a dish or even answer the door herself. Set down in the kaffee-klatching world of house-wives in suburban subdivisions, Jackie would have withered as quickly as an orchid in a cornfield. She had been schooled for a queenly role in life, and it was the only one she knew how to play. She learned early to be a star, but she never acquired the folksy touch that a politi-cian's wife is supposed to have.

Her father had taught her to play hard to get with her Bouvier relatives in order to make her company more desirable. He told her to act very cool with men who wouldn't respect her if she were too friendly. Jackie grew up to be a woman who was warm in public, cool in private, and completely ignorant of the traditional skills most women acquire at an early age from their mothers. Jackie's mother was never as profound an influence in her life as was Jack Bouvier, and perhaps this is another reason for her total lack of interest in housewifely chores.

Outside of royalty, itself a vanishing breed, there are few women nowadays who were brought up as was Jackie Kennedy. And of those, many perceive the innate irrelevance and worth-lessness of their roles and rebel against the patterns imposed upon them. Not Jackie. She was ideally suited by heredity and temperament to live this kind of life, and though it baffled her associates and exasperated her husband, she actually had no choice in the matter at all. Jackie is as she is.

Jack Kennedy breakfasted alone from a tray in the downstairs library, going through the morn-ing *New York Times*. After Caroline had learned to walk, she would join him, toddling around the room, nibbling at his toast, lecturing him in solemn baby talk. There was a deep bond between Jack and his little girl, and he bestowed on her the nickname "Buttons."

Gradually, Jackie learned to deal with the basic differences between herself and her husband. His attitude toward his appearance was, to say the least, casual, even after he had married the meticulous Jackie. He was in the habit of sending his factotum, Muggsy O'Leary, out to do his shopping for him. Once, Mary Gallagher recalls, he "blasted" Muggsy for coming back with some shirts that were too expensive. They had cost $3.50 apiece.

Over the years, Jackie was able to educate Jack about clothes and grooming, finding him a good barber who razor-cut his hair with the talent of a Michelangelo, and putting him in the hands of George Thomas, his devoted valet, who kept him looking spruce. The days were over when Jack Kennedy could ask Mary Gallagher to take the lint off his suits with a piece of scotch tape and walk away feeling well groomed. As president, Jack was named "America's Best-Dressed Man of the Year," and, in private, he gave due credit to Jackie for the metamorphosis.

While Jackie liked formality and elegance in her life, Jack was much more casual. He was in the habit of bringing extra people home for dinner, usually without notice, and this became more the rule than the exception as events ground toward the 1960 election. To Jack, it was nothing—the cook could slice a cold ham or simmer up a simple New England fish chowder. But to Jackie, it was sometimes a great irritation. Jackie—who liked delicate French menus, with gleaming silver, fresh flowers on the table, a carefully considered guest list, and brilliant conversation—must have shuddered when Jack drove up at dinner time, or earlier, or later, with a carload of aides, advisors, speechwriters, and dependable political cronies.

After Jack's nomination as the Democratic candidate for president in 1960, the little house on N Street became a tornado of activity. Only the serene Jackie managed to shut herself off from the ringing phones, the constant stream of visitors, both powerful and trivial, and the total absence of routine, let alone elegance. She was pregnant again, and this time she must have been particularly grateful; it provided her with an always-respected excuse for not taking part in Jack's campaign activities.

Suddenly, Jackie had been transplanted from her private world to the public stage. In a sense, she liked the idea—it was an opportunity to shine. But this time it was not just another deb party, or even a wedding. People were not automatically on her side. She was subjected to vicious criticism as well as to gushing praise. People began writing to *her*, not just to Jack. Sometimes they were kind, asking for her photo or congratulating her on the impending birth of her child, but sometimes they were jealous and ugly. Her hairstyle, the first of the bouffant

73

bubbles, was roundly denounced. A few irate Republicans sent combs. One day, Jack asked Mary Gallagher, "How is the mail running on Jackie's hair?" "Heavy," was the reply.

The other Kennedy women, like the wives of the ancient Irish warriors, relished the political fray, and with their speaking ability and their afternoon teas and coffee hours, they were a formidable political weapon. Ethel, Eunice, Pat, and Jean, Jackie's sisters-in-law, gave unstintingly of their time and their energy to Jack's cause.

But Jackie was not much of a campaigner. Once her own mother had to bail her out of a political obligation by throwing a tea for Jackie at Merrywood. Jackie did condescend to give a couple of press teas at the N Street house, but Mary Gallagher observed that Jackie "prepared for these brief political soirees with the attitude of being inconvenienced." When observers were around, particularly photographers, Jackie stepped into the role of candidate's wife. Mrs. Gallagher recalls the time when Jackie asked her to "pour" at a reception, only to be dismissed and replaced by Jackie when it was time for the picture taking. Miffed, Mrs. Gallagher returned to her upstairs office.

And yet, in spite of her withdrawn, enigmatic presence, or perhaps because of it, Jackie did capture the imagination of the public in a way that the more conventional Pat Nixon, wife of Jack's Republican opponent, never managed to do. Perhaps it was because, years ago, (in an era of Democratic mink-coat scandals) Richard

Nixon had praised his wife as the possessor of "one good Republican cloth coat."

Jackie Makes "Best-Dressed" List

And strangely enough, it was Jackie, rotundly pregnant, who had it all over the perky, wasp-waisted Mrs. Nixon. Fashion writer Eugenia Sheppard praised Jackie for managing to look chic while *enciente*. "Take Jacqueline Kennedy," wrote Eugenia in a column lambasting the maternity smock, "who swept to the head of the best-dressed list in her maternity clothes. Never caught napping in a smock, she wore nothing but one-piece dresses, slim at the sides. . . ."

But Jackie's personal elegance came dangerously close to being a political liability for Jack. *Women's Wear Daily* cheerfully noted during the campaign that Jackie and her mother-in-law had spent $30,000 a year in Paris haute couture alone, and Nan Robertson of *The New York Times* asked Jackie to verify it. It was the occasion for one of Jackie's most-quoted quips: "I couldn't spend that much unless I wore sable underwear." In one graceful stroke, Jackie had transformed her image from that of a profligate clotheshorse to that of a wit. Nevertheless, in her book, *First Lady*, Charlotte Curtis calculated after exhaustive research that Jackie alone had managed to spend upward of $50,000 on clothes in the first sixteen months of the Kennedy administration.

But when Jackie made her infrequent appearances at her husband's side during the final weeks of the campaign, it was always in the same conspicuous red wool coat. Newsmen were grateful to her—the color was unmistakable and it was always easy to spot Jackie in a crowd. It was discreetly announced that the coat, which became as famous as either Jack or Nixon during those days, was a copy of a Givenchy original. Jackie had bought her copy at thrifty Ohrbach's in New York. For the time being, at any rate, her image as a fashion plate was balanced by her reputation as a dollar-watching young wife.

PART TWO

CHAPTER FIVE
Jackie In The White House

In his campaign speeches, Jack Kennedy had promised the voters that, if elected, he would "get the country moving again." And it was true that after his election, the handsome young president infused the nation with a spirit of youth and adventure which it hadn't known, some observers said, since the days of Teddy Roosevelt. It was exciting to be alive in the days of Jack Kennedy's presidency, but "to be young was heaven." And to be Jacqueline Bouvier Kennedy was to be totally in your element. If ever a First Lady had been born to the role, it was Jackie.

During the weeks immediately after the election, Jack spent more time at home, with his staff, advisors, and with his brother and confidant, Bobby. The focus of the nation's attention shifted from the White House, where President and Mrs. Eisenhower were packing up and preparing to retire to their farm in Gettysburg, Pa., to the red brick house on N Street from which Jack was issuing his daily announcements of government appointments.

Curious crowds gathered outside every day, and Jack, who loved contact with the people, broke into his affairs of state several times a day to go outside and smile, wave, shake a few hands and say hello. Jackie remained totally aloof from such things, unless Jack urged her into it. The Secret Service men, who were sent to guard the president-elect and his family as soon as the election had been decided, were objects of disdain to Jackie, until she realized that they were able to control the crowds outside her house. Her attitude toward them softened considerably after that.

Soon after the election, Jackie began planning her spring wardrobe, looking forward to getting out of maternity clothes and back into haute couture. The problem was, however, that First Ladies traditionally patronize American designers—Mrs. Eisenhower's "official" designer had been Mollie Parnis of Seventh Avenue. Jackie's tastes were decidedly different, and yet she had to stick with American clothes. Her solution was to designate Oleg Cassini her personal designer. Cassini had never been particularly popular with the fashion writers since he opened his house in 1950. Known as a creator of "sexy" clothes, he toned down his flamboyance somewhat, letting Jackie's predeliction for Givenchy classicize his work somewhat. Later on, Jackie reverted to her favorite European designers for some of her more spectacular gowns, but Cassini's association with her as "court dressmaker" had already raised his stock inestimably.

Jackie also named Letitia Baldridge, a bright young woman who used to work for Ambassador Claire Boothe Luce, as her social secretary. There was a brief flap over Tish Baldridge's ill-advised press conference, in which she said that Mrs. Eisenhower had not yet invited Jackie to inspect the living quarters at the White House: "The invitation has not been extended yet—but we hope it will be."

But it was the birth of her baby which occupied most of Jackie's attention. Already, innumerable gifts were pouring in from all over the nation. Most of them were blue, as if everyone wanted Jackie's child to be a boy. And most of them were donated, anonymously, to various charitable institutions in Washington.

On Thanksgiving Day, 1960, the president-elect and Caroline flew down to the Kennedy Thanksgiving celebration in Palm Beach. Jackie, on doctors' orders had to stay behind. It was three weeks until the baby was due, and it would have been foolish to take chances. At around midnight, Jackie was taken to Georgetown Hospital where she gave birth to a premature baby boy. When Jack received the news, he was enroute to Palm Beach aboard the Kennedy plane, the *Caroline*. He gave orders for the craft to turn in midair and head back to Washington.

During the twelve days she was confined to the hospital after the birth of John F. Kennedy, Jr.,

Jackie was visited by her husband twice a day. Secret Service agents were stationed in a room directly across the hall from Jackie's. Mary Gallagher came to Jackie's bedside every day, after Jackie had begun to recover, to keep up with the correspondence that flowed in faster than ever. And Louella Hennessy, the nurse who took care of all the Kennedy mothers after their babies were born, was brought in.

While her mother was in the hospital with her new brother, Caroline Kennedy enjoyed perhaps the happiest time of her young life. She had her indulgent Daddy all to herself, accompanying him almost everywhere. Her press coverage was almost equal to his. She was an extroverted, friendly child, fond of attention, but too winsome to be called a brat.

Jackie was discharged from the hospital on December 9, and two Secret Service men made a chair of their hands to carry her up the long flight of steps to the front door of the house on N Street. It was a big day for Jackie. Later that afternoon she would finally pay a visit to the White House, and in the evening board a plane for Palm Beach.

Her visit to the White House was friendly enough, but she despaired over the "dreary" appearance of its rooms. The Eisenhowers were people of unsophisticated tastes, who preferred their farm at Gettysburg to the White House anyway. The dismal, potted-palm decor of the Executive Mansion, Jackie remarked to a friend later, "almost sent me right back to the hospital with a crying jag."

Palm Beach, with its sunshine and activity, was supposed to be an antidote to Jackie's post-childbirth blues. But the swarm of politicians, press people, and other strangers was too much for Jackie, who remained sequestered in her room most of the time. One day, Rose Kennedy asked Mary Gallagher, "Do you know if Jackie is getting out of bed today? You might remind her that we're having some important guests for lunch. It would be *nice* if she would join us." Jackie took the message from her mother-in-law in high spirits, singsonging in imitation of the elder Mrs. Kennedy, "You might remind her we're having important guests for lunch . . ." The important guests, Mrs. Gallagher reports, arrived and departed without a glimpse of the elusive Jackie.

While in Palm Beach, Jackie stayed in her bedroom except for specific appointments that involved her alone, such as an interview with *Time* magazine. She broke her seclusion again when the fitters from Bergdorf Goodman arrived to fit her gown for the Inaugural Ball. Jackie had designed it herself—a sleeveless floor-length gown of silk crepe, with a bodice embroidered in silver thread. Over it went a white chiffon overblouse, also sleeveless. There was a long cape of white crepe, standing high at the neck with a little mandarin collar. Her Gala gown was being designed by Cassini.

She kept Mary Gallagher hopping with orders to deal with this designer and that, instructions to be relayed back to her staff in Washington, and endless phone calls and correspondence.

She wasn't sure which hat she would wear to the Inauguration ceremonies, and arranged for her milliner, Miss Marita, at Bergdorf's, to make two versions of the same "pillbox" design. She had arrangements to make concerning horses for the Middleburg, Va., house she and Jack had rented as a retreat. She wanted a "gentle" horse for her husband. There was liquor for George Thomas, the butler/valet to order.

Tiffany Diamond Flak

And most interestingly, through Tish Baldridge and without Jack's knowledge or consent, Jackie was arranging with Tiffany's to borrow the fabulous diamond pin and diamond pendant earrings which she wanted to wear to the Inaugural Ball. "Tell Tish," Jackie said to Mary Gallagher, "that if it gets in the newspapers I won't do any more business with Tiffany's. If it doesn't we'll buy all the State presents there." Jack had already gotten wind of Jackie's plan, and had forbidden her to go through with it. But Jackie requested Tiffany's to back up her story that she'd borrowed the gems from her mother-in-law.

Jackie wore the Cassini gown to the pre-Inaugural Gala, along with an emerald necklace and earring set which Jack insisted she wear. The Gala was preceded by dinner with the Philip Grahams, of the *Washington Post*, then the traditional pre-Inaugural concert at Constitution Hall. On January 20, Inauguration Day, Jack rehearsed his magnificent Inaugural Address downstairs while Jackie readied herself. She was to wear a fawn-colored wool coat with a sable collar and a matching muff, with a fawn-colored domed pillbox hat which was to become known as the "Jackie hat" when women across the nation began demanding it in stores. At noon, Jackie was still applying her makeup, while her husband fumed downstairs. "For God's sake, Jackie," he howled. "Let's go!"

The ceremony was held on Capitol Hill, in blazing sunlight and biting cold. The snow which had blanketed Washington made walking hard, and television viewers were happy to see that Jackie was wearing high-heeled, fur-trimmed boots. That night, at the round of Inaugural Balls, Jackie wore her white chiffon-and-crepe gown. At the end of the achingly long day, Jack Kennedy was the thirty-fifth President of the United States, and Jackie was undisputedly First Lady, not only of the country but of the entire world of fashion. As one writer described her, Jackie looked "yummy."

The first few weeks after the inauguration were as hectic for Jackie as the weeks before, as the new First Lady fought to see her demands met for a perfect wardrobe. In his book *In My Own Fashion*, Oleg Cassini called these weeks "the frantic period. . . . There were constant letters and phone calls: 'Hurry, hurry, I don't have any clothes.'" Cassini and a specially assembled staff conducted fittings, sewed sample garments, and searched France and Italy for the finest fabrics. Cassini estimated that they created more than 100 dresses in the first year of Kennedy's presidency, and 300 during the course of the administration—an incredible number. Many were designed and produced at breakneck speed to satisfy Jackie's need to have the "perfect" outfit to wear on every occasion. For a visit from Krushchev, Cassini remembered, he took a taxi from Union Station to the White House in the middle of a raging snowstorm, carting twelve boxes of Jackie's clothes.

While working at superhuman speed, Cassini had to adhere to Jackie's flawless sense of style and specific demands. Incredibly, the designer passed Jackie's tests with flying colors, creating remarkable designs, but not sensational outfits, which could make her appear to be "the Marie Antoinette or Josephine of the 1960s," Jackie told Cassini.

Jackie's impact on American women was so profound that they will probably never be quite the same again. In her book *The Beautiful People*, in which Jackie figures prominently, Marilyn Bender of *The New York Times* wrote, "Jacqueline Kennedy, the superconsumer, redeemed fashion from the Puritan ethic of sin. She not only disabused the French of some of their cherished misconceptions about American-style backwardness but she infused the national consciousness with a Gallic appreciation of fashion. Since Jacqueline Kennedy, there is no longer much status in Anglo-American dowdiness."

Perhaps the most important lesson she had for women was the elegance of simplicity, the power of understatement. The little-nothing dresses and the plain cloth coats had been the uniform of uppercrust ladies for some time. But when Jackie stepped into the world spotlight, they became worldwide fads. It's important to point out that Jackie is not much of an innovator of new ideas. She lets other women do the trail-blazing, then, at the point when styles are appearing in the fashion magazines but when average consumers have not yet worked up their courage to try them, Jackie adopts them and the public at last accepts them.

Most of her fashion decisions are based on her immense knowledge of the field, her uncanny instinct for what is timely and becoming to her, and her innate flair for achieving a tasteful but highly individual look. But sometimes it's based on more mundane considerations.

Take that famous pillbox hat, for example. She has a problem head size—a larger-than-normal head and dislike of slicked-down hairdos, add up to a whopping twenty-four inches on the tape measure. Thus, she has trouble finding ready-made hats which fit, and, more often than not, is seen hatless. This disturbed the sagging American millinery industry, which noticed that Jack Kennedy wasn't the world's greatest hat wearer, either. Jack prevailed upon Jackie to at least *try* to find some hats, and Jackie contacted Marita O'Connor at Bergdorf's about her problem. Miss Marita brought a Christian Dior hat with a narrow front and a wider back, but it looked better backwards on Jackie so they simply reversed it. It became an international craze.

While the fashion industry has never been

notably political, it's a safe bet that after the Democratic Convention in 1960, every rag-trader in the world was rooting for Jack Kennedy, because they were swift to realize that in Jackie they had what Marilyn Bender called "the greatest merchandising gimmick since Shirley Temple dolls." Window mannequins were quickly fitted with bouffant brunette hairdos, their eyes repainted with the wide-spaced "Jackie" look. Jackie rode in a gold cart with the president while wearing big-lensed horn-rimmed glasses; moments later, it seemed, women were besieging optometrists for the "Jackie sunglasses." Even her pregnancy became a fashion force. Following Eugenia Sheppard's attack on the butcher-boy maternity look, stores had trouble keeping the one-piece chemise-style maternity dress in stock. Lane Bryant used the phrase, "First Lady Maternity Fashions" in their ads—The Lilly, a simply cut, no-waistline dress designed by Mrs. Lilly Pulitzer of Palm Beach, and done up in a variety of custom silk-screened cotton prints, was an echo of Jackie's maternity shifts. The Kennedy women practically lived in Lillys during their vacations in Palm Beach, and before long what had started as an interesting hobby for Mrs. Pulitzer had burgeoned into a multimillion dollar business. Even Quaker Oats boosted sales by offering "Jackie and Caroline" mother-and-daughter outfits as premiums.

Another area which has held Jackie's consuming interest for years, ever since she made her first European trip with her three Vassar chums, is travel. Unlike Mrs. Franklin Roosevelt, who traveled thousands of miles as a personal emmisary from her husband, Jackie undertook her numerous overseas jaunts purely for the pursuit of pleasure. Her glamorous trips made good copy for the feature writers and the fashion pages, but they were—like her expenditures on clothes—a potential political liability for Jack. Early in 1961, while working on a crucial message to Congress concerning the U.S. balance-of-payments problem, Jack explained to a friend that in the year before, U.S. tourists had spent over a billion dollars more overseas than foreign tourists had dropped in the U.S. This sum was the preponderant item in the American deficit in international payments. Jack's friend asked the obvious: Why not try to discourage foreign travel by U.S. citizens?

"Well, I've considered asking Americans to stay home next summer," Jack answered ruefully, "but how on earth can I do that when I can't even keep my own wife from going abroad?"

Jackie started out globe-trotting that same year in the spring after the Kennedys moved into the White House with a State visit she and Jack made to the major capitals of Western Europe. It was a time of considerable international tension —U.S.-French relations were not at their best, with the testy Charles de Gaulle heading the French government.

There was the balance-of-payments problem, and the touchy balance of power with the Communist bloc countries. The world was biding its time before making up its mind about Jack

Kennedy—how he performed on this first major round of talks with world leaders could affect the course of history. And the performance of his wife on this critical junket would also weigh in the world's judgment of the new American president.

CHAPTER SIX
Jackie Charms the World

They arrived at Orly airport in Paris on May 31, and the crowds cried *"Vive Jacqui."* Perhaps it was because they knew of her French ancestry, perhaps it was the chic picture she made in her plain wool coat and the famous pillbox hat; but whatever the reason, it set the pattern for the entire visit. Everywhere the Kennedys went, it was *Jacqui* who got the ovations. She met a distantly related Bouvier at a reception given by President de Gaulle. She wore a Cassini-designed gown to the State dinner, and the next day the French press was raving about its asymmetrical style which bared one shoulder. She made a graceful concession to the French fashion industry by wearing a Givenchy gown to another State dinner in the Hall of Mirrors at Versailles. This one was white satin, with a bodice of red, white, and blue. Invitations to that particular dinner were so prized that there were members of Paris's haute monde who left town quietly, rather than bear the ignominy of having been left out. At the end of the visit, Jack gallantly told his hosts, "I am the man who accompanied Jacqueline Kennedy to Paris."

From France, the Kennedys went on to meet the Khruschevs in Vienna—an almost surrealistic encounter between two old, peasant-bred Russian Communists and two young aristocrats from the most powerful capitalist nation in the world. The meeting went surprisingly well, as did the Kennedys' State visit to London to visit Queen Elizabeth II and Prince Philip. In her slim, simple floor-length gown, Jackie made her royal hostess look dated and dowdy . . . at least, by America's new standards.

Afterward, Jack returned to Washington, but Jackie joined her sister, Lee and Lee's second husband, Prince Stanislaus Radziwill, on a nine-day unofficial visit to Greece. While there, a Greek friend of Lee's, a shipowner named Aristotle Onassis, stopped by the villa where the party was staying to say hello to Jackie.

At this point, it's appropriate to take a closer look at Caroline Lee Bouvier Canfield Radziwill, Jackie's only sister and closest friend. As sisters who may have felt themselves to be competing for the love of their absentee father, the two had a contradictory relationship while they were growing up. Jack never praised the one at the expense of the other, never compared them within earshot of either one. But he did, understandably, enjoy it when the two little girls tried to outdo each other in their demonstrations of

affection. There was rivalry between the two—
and yet there was a deep bond, the sort that
cannot really be understood unless you have
seen your parents divorce, and have acquired a
stepfather after many dull, deprived years. Occasionally, it must have seemed to Jackie and Lee
that the entire adult world was conspiring
against them. Thus, in spite of their rivalry, they
were drawn toward each other as allies.

Jackie was the smart one, the brave one, the
witty one. Lee, three years younger, was more
pliant and tractable. And more beautiful. Jackie
had a unique, highly identifiable look which
people called beauty because she had the force
of personality to go with it. Lee's delicate fea-
tures and more conventional prettiness bespoke
a more approachable nature. It wasn't an accident that Jackie did things like spending her
junior year in France, winning the Vogue Prix de
Paris, and going to work for a daily paper,
accomplishing things which called for intellectual ability and personal initiative. Lee, on the
other hand, was married at nineteen, after one
year at Sarah Lawrence, to exactly the sort of
young man you would have expected, and
seemed more suited to an old-fashioned, somewhat passive role in life. As they grew older, they
came to lean more and more upon each other,
even though Jackie was said by all to be smarter,
and Lee was generally held to be prettier.

Lee's husband, Michael Canfield, was assigned to the staff of Winthrop Aldrich, the
American Ambassador to Great Britain, and
thus Lee went to London. She fell in love with

the city and even after her childless marriage to Michael Canfield disintegrated, she was a confirmed Londoner. In 1959, she married Prince Stanislaus Radziwill, scion of a noble Polish family who had made a fortune on London real estate after fleeing Poland. Since the Catholic Church did not recognize Lee's divorce from Canfield, she was, technically speaking, a sinner in the eyes of the church, even though by the time Jackie and Jack made their London visit, they had two children. Since this could become an embarrassment to the first Catholic President of the United States, Jackie was dispatched to Italy on a mission to obtain an official annulment from the Vatican for her sister. It was all handled with almost overwhelming discretion. The two sisters lolled on the yacht of Fiat industrialist Gianni Agnelli, off Ravello, while the emissary was ferried back and forth from Rome by motor launch. Secret meetings were held between intermediaries, and, as the yacht skipped from port to port in an effort to elude reporters, the arrangements for Lee's annulment were hammered out.

Carping criticism for Jackie's Italian journey had barely begun to simmer down when it was announced that Jackie and Lee were to undertake a long journey through Asia in the fall of 1962. A lot of people were upset when Jackie missed Thanksgiving and her children's birthdays in order to travel to such outlandish places as Udiapur, Shalimar, and Delhi—even if the President of Pakistan, Mohammed Ayub Khan, did act as her personal guide. But the two sisters were as happy as schoolgirls, and perhaps while they were taking an elephant ride together, Lee may have mentioned to Jackie that she was becoming really good friends with that swarthy little Greek billionaire, Aristotle Onassis.

But Jackie was not only preoccupied with seeing something of the rest of the world. Back in Washington, she embarked on her most ambitious undertaking and perhaps what will be remembered as her most enduring contribution to the Republic: the restoration of the White House.

Refurbishes White House

Actually, it was not the building itself that needed restoration, that having been accomplished quite thoroughly when the mansion was gutted and rebuilt during the Truman administration. At that time, the old building was found to be so decrepit as to be unsafe. The interiors were lovingly dismantled, new internal reinforcements were built in, and the corners adjusted to proper right angles again. When it was completed, the White House retained its old majesty, but stood with a new stability that permitted its occupants to breathe easier.

Jackie pronounced it "dreary"—the strongest condemnation possible in her vocabulary—and set out to reform things. First there was the seemingly insignificant matter of flowers. Jackie abolished the stiff formal arrangements of gladioli and chrysanthemums which had been constructed by commercial florists (and looked it), substituting the natural informal look of blossoms brought in from a country garden. She loved daisies, apple blossoms, poppies, freesias, and tulips, and used red and purple anemones so much that people very nearly learned how to pronounce the name.

But Jackie was after a more lasting and comprehensive change in White House decor. She asked Henry Francis DuPont, creator of the renowned Winterthur Museum in Wilmington, to be advisor to her project. Jackie is one of those women who, even when they know a lot about a subject, insist on the advice and guidance of the best specialists and experts. A White House Committee on Fine Arts was created, with David Finley as Chairman. Congress passed a bill making the White House a national monument, preserving it forevermore from the personal whimsies of presidential families (such as Harry Truman's still-controversial balcony). The position of White House curator was instituted, and the White House Historical Association was founded "to enhance the understanding, appreciation, and enjoyment of the Executive Mansion."

There were those who began yelling "politics!" when the project was undertaken, seeing in it some kind of plot to turn the White House into a Kennedy family monument. But they were soon refuted when they realized that this was, indeed, the personal activity of the First Lady, and a temperamentally nonpolitical one at that. Amusingly, many of the most active contributors and supporters of the White House restoration were Republicans.

The critics also railed about government extravagance, but again, Jackie was precisely the right woman for the job on this count as well. Using her almost incredible persuasiveness—which she had exercised on her grandfather years before when she wheedled him into sending her horse along when she went to boarding school—Jackie charmed many of the nation's outstanding museums and private collectors into lending or giving outright some of the greatest gems of American furniture. Among them were a mahogany library table donated by Mr. and Mrs. Douglas Dillon (Jack's Republican Secretary of the Treasury), a Hepplewhite mirror with a carved frame that included the likeness of George Washington and which had once graced historic Fraunces Tavern in New York, and furniture that had once belonged to Washington, Lincoln, James Madison, and Daniel Webster. Two Empire chairs, in maple, which had been made by her ancestor, Michel Bouvier, were a gift of Mr. and Mrs. Henry T. McNeill of Pennsylvania.

Under Jackie's aegis, and under the expert hand of David Finley and the White House Committee, the Blue Room was restored to the way it looked at the time of James Monroe; the Red Room was totally redecorated in the French and American Empire style; and by the time Jackie was finished, the only room in the White House which had been left untouched was the Lincoln Room. This may have been because of a special reverence for Lincoln, but it's more likely that it was because that was the bedroom Jack used. Jackie called upon John Walker, director of the National Gallery, to assist in preparing a guidebook to the White House, which is still the standard guide to the White House. While there was some question about the propriety of *selling* such a book, the fact that the proceeds were devoted to financing the continued restoration and upkeep of the White House seemed like a thrifty and sensible measure.

Jackie's knack for charming private donations in order to make White House elegance possible extended to her entertainments. The Kennedy years are remembered today with fondness and nostalgia—it was a time when the White House was the social center of the nation, not merely the place where the Chief Executive and his family lived. In the past, private rich ladies like Perle Mesta and Gwen Cafritz, or the French or English Ambassadors were the most sought-after hosts in the capital. Bred to the tradition of entertaining on a grand scale, Jackie decided to change all that. One of her first, and, naturally, most controversial parties was the State dinner given President Mohammed Ayub Khan of Pakistan.

Perhaps she was inspired by the State dinner and ballet performance the French government had staged when she and Jack had visited France earlier in the year. Jackie conceived the idea of holding a banquet at Mount Vernon, George Washington's home, on July 11, 1961. The spe-

cial tent pavilion was contributed by the Philadelphia firm of William H. Vanderherschen; the
National Symphony Orchestra donated a magnificent concert; and even Lester Lanin sent a
trio over for incidental music, gratis. Display
designers from Tiffany's and Bonwit's did the
decorations. White House chef Rene Verdon
prepared the food at the White House, almost as
usual, except that it was shipped down the
Potomac in U.S. Army field kitchens, and the
guests were transported from Washington
aboard the Presidential yacht and four smaller
Navy vessels. It wasn't nearly as expensive as it
looked at first, and what is perhaps more important, it gave the American public the sense that
their country was not only as rich and powerful
as any, it could also match any other in elegance
and imagination.

There were other noteworthy parties and
events conceived by Jackie and flawlessly executed in every detail, which enhanced not only
the American image abroad but its self-esteem at
home, and which helped to build the myth of the
famous "Kennedy Style." There was the State
dinner for President Abboud of Sudan on October 4, 1961, followed by a program of Shakespeare from the American Shakespeare Festival
Theatre, and the State Dinner for Governor and
Mrs. Munoz Marin of Puerto Rico, followed by a
concert of Pablo Casals. The Casals concert was
attended not only by the diplomatic corps and
the usual roster of important guests, but also by
such distinguished American composers as
Elliot Carter, Walter Piston, and Samuel Barber.

A State dinner for the Shah and Empress of Iran featured a ballet performance by the Jerome Robbins troupe.

There was the altogether unique dinner on April 29, 1962, to honor Nobel Prize winners, not only from the U.S., but from the entire Western Hemisphere—the flowers of science, literature, and diplomacy. Scientist Linus Pauling made the singular gesture of first picketing the White House with a good-natured group of Ban-the-Bomb advocates, then going inside to dine with his colleagues and the president. Both Jack and Jackie were delighted by Pauling's puckish lack of hypocrisy.

Of course, it's inaccurate to imply that Jackie managed all this by herself. Her life-style and her accomplishments would have been impossible without the dedicated, sometimes exasperated, work of a large staff. As is customary among women of Jackie's social stratum, the care of her children was the responsibility of a nurse, the redoubtable Maud Shaw. Her social secretary, Tish Baldridge, later replaced by Jackie's old roommate from Miss Porter's, Nancy Tuckerman, was in charge of guest lists, invitations, and the zillion details of her social life as First Lady. Pamela Turnure dealt with the press, helping to set up the famous televised White House tour in which Jackie was the "star," sending out the latest biographies and news releases, and dealing with the press' questions and requests for interviews with Jackie.

The much-put-upon Mary Barelli Gallagher was Jackie's personal secretary. She worked in an office within the White House itself, handling Jackie's personal correspondence and whatever else was not attended to by the press or social secretaries. On occasion, this included babysitting, and on Jackie's trip to Dallas in 1963, Mary Gallagher even filled in for Jackie's regular personal maid.

That completely devoted servant, Providenzia Paredes, was in charge of Jackie's fabulous wardrobe, seeing to it that each garment was cleaned, repaired, and stored where it would be instantly accessible, although Jackie never wore anything more than a few times. As a rule, garments she no longer wore were sold through a discreet New York thrift shop, or occasionally given to friends or employees. Mary Gallagher wore a gown of Jackie's to the Inaugural Ball.

Kenneth Battele, Jackie's favorite hairdresser, came down from New York regularly to arrange the First Lady's hair; at other times Jean Louis substituted. The Kennedy masseuse, Miss O'Malley, kept her in shape. Master chef Rene Verdon ran the White House kitchen, assisted by cooks from the U.S. Navy. But even with this small army of helpers, Jackie's life as Mrs. Kennedy was busy and exhausting. She napped every afternoon to appear fresh and sparkling for the big social events of the evening, and she relaxed by riding at Glen Ora, the estate which she and Jack had rented in Virginia. After a year or so in the White House, the Kennedys decided to build a retreat of their own at Atoka, on Rattlesnake Mountain in the Virginia countryside.

In January 1963, Jackie told Mary Gallagher and Tish Baldridge that she was "taking the veil"—retiring from public activities—giving as her reason that she saw too little of Caroline and John-John. It was, in fact, because she was pregnant.

Jack's pleasure at the news did not mitigate his irritation with Jackie's spending habits—which husbands, typically, seem most concerned with when each new year begins. In 1962, Jackie had spent a staggering $28,000 on clothes, food, liquor, beauty, and such. In 1963, perhaps because of Jack's frequently expressed displeasure and perhaps because she was pregnant and not in the market for expensive clothes, she spent only $16,000.

During pregnancy, Jackie, like most mothers-to-be, was at the mercy of moods and outbursts: sweet and reasonable one minute, a petty tyrant the next. During the spring of 1963, she was angered by the well-intentioned doctor at Walter Reed Hospital who kept bugging her about the decor of the rooms she was to occupy when the baby was born. She blasted her staff for throwing away her memos. She was bothered by the notebooks the press ladies carried at White House social gatherings, and wanted to keep reporters from mingling with her guests. She said that having them come in after every dinner made her feel like some social-climbing hostess who invites a columnist to every party. She overspent in furnishing Atoka, and incurred Jack's formidable wrath again. She chastised her staff for sending a selection of White House menus to British Prime Minister Harold Macmillan, who was worried about what to serve the president on a forthcoming visit. She recalled with impatience, rather than her characteristic amusement, that while she was visiting in India, her hosts flew in planeloads of bread from Beirut, Lebanon, because someone had heard that Jackie liked cream cheese sandwiches for lunch. She used her pregnancy as an excuse not to attend a dreary brunch for Congressional brides, yet she had managed to make it to the ballet the night before.

Piqued By Berlin Trip

Perhaps Jackie was disgruntled because, for once, her husband was going off on a big European trip without her. Her pregnancy prohibited her from accompanying him on what was perhaps the most dramatic trip of his administration—the historic visit to Germany when he made his famed *Ich bin ein Berliner* speech in West Berlin.

Instead, Jackie flew to the secluded house on Squaw Island where she and Jack had spent their Hyannis Port summers since his election. This time, Mary Gallagher accompanied her, performing her usual secretarial chores and also helping out with a joint birthday party for Caroline and her mother at the end of July.

Jackie dashed off memos to her staff back in Washington, never to be accused of overlooking any details simply because she wasn't there to look after them herself. She told the White House guards to be "hawk-eyed" about wear and tear on the furnishings and ravages of souvenir hunters. She wanted the housekeeper, Anne Lincoln, to work out with chef Rene Verdon new wording for the menus, so that one could understand what each course was even if one couldn't read a word of French. It wasn't a classical approach, but a practical one.

Until August 7, 1963, Jackie was busy and for the most part, happy. Now that she was in the final stages of pregnancy, her short temper and depression passed, and she looked forward to the birth of the baby. On the morning of the 7th, however, Jackie's Secret Service man called for a helicopter to bring Jackie to Otis Air Force Base. Her baby was arriving dangerously early.

At Otis Air Force Base, an ambulance took Jackie to the hospital. There was no time to take her to Walter Reed, where the hapless military doctor and his newly painted room were waiting, but the Secret Service and Jackie's physicians had prepared a contingency suite of rooms for her at the base hospital.

Jackie, really frightened, kept murmuring, "This baby mustn't be born dead!" At 1 P.M. she was delivered of a baby boy, who, though premature, was normal and healthy in every way. The president flew in from Washington at 1:30 P.M., looking wan and worried, and took off for the delivery room. His sister, Jean Smith, joined him soon after. As the afternoon progressed, it became evident that something was dreadfully wrong with his new son.

Jackie was kept unaware of the crisis. She knew her son was premature, but she assumed the hospital had any problems under control. In a matter of hours, she was dictating memos to Mary Gallagher, who had accompanied her to the hospital.

The baby's trouble was diagnosed as hyaline syndrome, a respiratory problem to which premature babies are especially susceptible. The baby—Patrick Bouvier Kennedy—was flown to Children's Hospital in Boston for intensified special care. The president flew to Boston to be with his son in the morning, then flew back to Jackie, then once again to Boston that night. He was there when the baby died just two days later, on August 9, early in the morning.

Other members of the family arrived to console Jack and Jackie—Bobby and his brother, the Auchinclosses, and the Kennedy staff.

When little Patrick Kennedy was buried, his father placed inside his little coffin a silver money clip with a St. Christopher medal—a gift to him from Jackie. From her hospital bed, Jackie instructed Mary Gallagher to get a replacement for Jack—"Get in touch with Tiffany's"—not knowing that in only a few months she would be thinking once again of the St. Christopher medal, in the midst of an even greater tragedy.

CHAPTER SEVEN
The Last Autumn

Jackie's youth and basic good health helped her to recover physically from Patrick's birth, but it would take longer for her to recover psychologically from his death. At this highly emotional time in her life, a man reappeared whom she had met before. His name was Aristotle Onassis.

"Twice in his life, Aristotle Onassis had been linked with two sisters, and twice he has married the one nobody was watching," wrote Doris Lilly. And, in truth, there are many parallels between Onassis' courtship of the beautiful, spoiled Livanos sisters, and the beautiful, spoiled Bouviers.

Since 1959, Lee had been married to Prince Stanislaus Radziwill, the descendant of Polish kings. But, as Miss Lilly points out, "the family emerged from the Russian Revolution and World War II with nothing much left but a glorious history." The Radziwills lived in the lovely London suburb of Henley and it was probably in London that Onassis met Lee Radziwill. By 1963, they were very good friends. The prince—"Stas"—as he was nicknamed years ago, accompanied Lee to Athens, where she boarded the *Christina* and stayed aboard for most of the summer. The Prince was stashed, somewhere, and Maria Callas was nowhere in sight. But an object as big as the *Christina* is a little difficult to hide, and gossip ran wild. Drew Pearson opined that Onassis aspired to be the President's brother-in-law, unintentionally making one of the few understatements of his career.

At this point, Jackie was busying herself with plans for the White House social schedule for the following fall, and asked Nancy Tuckerman for the dates of the winter's State visits. As possible entertainers, she suggested Margot Fonteyn and Rudy Nureyev, Lunt and Fontanne, and either Leontyne Price or Maria Callas.

Callas?

Apparently, when she thought better of it, Jackie had second thoughts, to say the least, and followed up with a note to Nancy. If she hadn't sent Callas a letter, she was to forget it and ask Leontyne Price. Two days later, Nancy called Mary Gallagher to say that everything was fine. Maria Callas couldn't come.

Sheer preoccupation is the only explanation for this unlikely lapse of Jackie's sure-footed instincts as First Lady. In the late stages of pregnancy, perhaps she was thinking of other things. Otherwise, one cannot conceive of her coming so dangerously close to so huge a *faux pas*—if it was meant sincerely. On the other hand, it may have been intended as a kind of joke, a dig at her sister's rival, which Jackie reconsidered almost immediately.

They had gone to considerable trouble to arrange for Lee to be remarried to Stas in a Catholic ceremony after annulling her earlier marriage to Michael Canfield. If Lee should leave Stas in order to marry a divorced non-Catholic who had been maintaining an open liaison with a married opera star, it could mean not only embarrassment for the Kennedys—it could mean the end of Jack's career. The narrow margin of the 1960 election haunted him. The slightest tip of the scales could make a difference. If enough voters in the right states had been irreparably outraged by the gossip about Lee and Onassis, perhaps the damage had already been done.

But those wagging tongues were stilled in August 1963, with the birth and death of little Patrick. It's one of the sad truths of human nature that the cycle of scandal, gossip, and speculation can be broken only by an event of such proportions.

In view of this, it's interesting, to say the least, that Jack allowed his wife to accept Aristotle Onassis' invitation to cruise with him and both Radziwills aboard the *Christina*. The presence of Franklin D. Roosevelt, Jr., then Undersecretary of the Department of Commerce, and his wife, was hardly enough to dispel the aura of scandal.

Onassis was, after all, shipping oil to Communist China and Castro's Cuba in his tankers. He was unwholesomely friendly with Egypt's Nasser, Haiti's Duvalier, and Argentina's ex-dictator, Juan Peron. He had also been indicted by the U.S. government for some tanker dealings during the war. If Jackie had lapsed a bit, earlier in the summer, by almost inviting Maria Callas to the White House, what did Jack think he was doing in allowing her to join Onassis aboard his yacht?

It's been suggested that he took the risk because he had delegated Jackie to break things up between Lee and the shipping king. Washington columnists believed that Jack thought that Jackie alone could bring the association to an end. This theory, if true, opens up an alarming number of new possibilities.

On the other hand, it could well be that after Jackie's ordeal, Jack could refuse her nothing. She loved the sea, and Onassis promised a lot of fascinating excursions to ancient sites. It would do her good to be with Lee—at such times, a woman needs to be with another woman, and Jackie had few close female friends.

In *Death of a President*, William Manchester does an intriguing rearrangement of the supposed facts: "She (Jackie) had wanted to stay with him and the children. Normality, routine— it seemed the best way to cure her depression. He had a different plan: she should forget herself in other lands. Politically, she suggested it was unwise . . . but his mind was made up." It's interesting to picture Jackie giving cool political advice to Jack, who, supposedly, was eager that she join the cruise aboard the *Christina*.

Enter Ari Onassis

The squat, dark man who kept turning up with such uncanny regularity at the crises in Jackie's life deserves a close look. Aristotle Onassis was born on January 20, some say in 1906; others insist earlier, and not in Greece but in Smyrna, then an important commercial center in Turkey. Since Constantinople had first fallen to the Muslims, the Onassis family, like a large number of Greeks, had been subjects of the sultan of Turkey. Like some other minorities, they were regarded with a mixture of suspicion and grudging admiration by the ruling classes; this attitude was exacerbated by the unbridgeable gulf between the Greek Orthodox religion and that of the ruling Turks. Greeks dwelling in Turkey learned the arts of survival first. They had to outthink their rulers, and so were considered devious.

They had to be twice as good as the ruling class of Turks in order to get to the top of the business and professional world. The Turks considered themselves the warriors and the aristocrats (a Greek word, incidentally!) but it was the Greeks who kept the country going as its businessmen and administrators. They were admired, not liked.

The situation was not too different from the way it was in Boston, between the moneyed Brahmins and the scrappy, able Irish.

Aristotle Onassis learned the competitive spirit from his father, Socrates Onassis, a fairly successful tobacco merchant in the predominantly Greek town of Smyrna—since ancient times, an important port on the Mediterranean. Other Greeks were constantly embroiled in the Greek cause in Turkey, but unlike others in the Onassis family, Aristotle was indifferent to politics. His first love was the sea.

His mother died when Aristotle was six, and soon afterward, his father found a handsome stepmother for him and his older sister, Artemis. Two more daughters were born—Merope and Calirrohe. As was customary among the Anatolian Greeks, the children were given names from Greek classic mythology. Mainland Greeks named their children after Christian saints.

This is not to say that the Onassis family was irreligious in any way—far from it. Every year, the children's paternal grandmother, "Yia Yia," made a pilgrimage to Jerusalem, returning with religious souvenirs, stories of the Holy Land, and large religious lithographs.

"I remember particularly one scene that showed a meadow with lambs and happy children dancing above the face of the devil spitting fire," Onassis recalled, years later. "When I asked her what it meant, she told me that this was a representation of heaven and hell, and if I was a good boy I would go to the higher place, if I was bad I would go down below.

"To tell the truth, I still don't know where I am going," he concluded.

Whatever his destination in the next world, Onassis was headed straight for the top in this one. His spirit was tempered during World War I, when Turkey sided with Germany, while Greece, his true homeland, fought beside the Allies. The Greeks of Smyrna rendered outward allegiance to the Turkish sultan's cause, but within their churches they prayed for an Allied victory. Onassis and his schoolmates at the Evangeliki Scholi—a Greek Orthodox school for boys—were forced to wear the Turkish fez instead of the English-public-school cap normally prescribed by the school. Greeks of all ages were considered potential saboteurs. Young Aristotle Onassis learned to find his own ways around authority, a skill he used with great success in his adult life.

But when the war ended, Greek troops occupied Smyrna and its Greek population enjoyed the experience of lording it over the Turks who had ruled them until that moment. The mood was expansive and optimistic for families like the Onassises. The restrictions on exporting tobacco were lifted, prosperity reigned in the Onassis family, and Aristotle went sailing in the harbor in his own boat, and joined a sailing club which, in Smyrna in the 1920's, passed for "fashionable."

Then, in 1922, the brief happy respite ended. Turkish nationalist troops swept into Smyrna, with countless Greek refugees fleeing before them. It all happened so fast that there was no time to escape. Greek agitators were lynched in the streets. Except for a small area around the U.S. Consulate, which was guarded by Marines against both Turkish troops and Greek fugitives, the city was in ruins.

Except for one uncle, a political activist who just managed to slip away to Athens in time to save his own life, the Onassis family felt the full impact of the vengeful Turkish resurgence. Socrates Onassis went to prison, to await summary trial as a political offender, while sixteen-year-old Aristotle, his mother, and the girls were sent to a euphemistically named "evacuation center" to await deportation to Greece. Things looked bleak—but only on the surface.

Bright, well educated, unfailingly polite, Ari had a lot going for him besides his incalculable drive and his sense of self-preservation. Contrary to legend, he didn't grow up on the streets, but he knew what it was to be oppressed, and the risks necessary to overcome the odds. As a rich man's son, he possessed the requisite good manners and self-confidence to deal with those temporarily in power. He was only a boy, and a smallish, plain one, at that, but he was well equipped to rescue his father, salvage what was left of the family fortune, and set matters up for a new start for the house of Onassis.

When the Turks came to their house, he addressed the commander of the Turkish soldiers in impeccable Turkish, helpfully answering their questions and expressing his regrets that no, he didn't know where to find any liquor. In the shambles of his young life, Onassis had the presence of mind to make friends with a Turkish general and a subordinate, and was granted the right to move around the devastated city. To a lad in his position, that was all the working capital he needed.

When an American vice-consul stopped by, also looking for a drink, Onassis volunteered to drive through the city in the consulate's Model T in search of booze. His father's friends came up with bottles of ouzo, raki, and brandy (for a price), and the American diplomat was delighted. He awarded the boy a single bottle, which he shrewdly gave to the Turkish general. Everybody was happy—the two men went their separate ways with their respective refreshments, and the boy was left with an American I.D. card admitting him to the U.S. Marine Zone, and a Turkish Army pass which allowed him to move in and out of the shattered city. The goodwill of the American vice-consul led to the release of the Onassis women from the detention center, and their passage aboard an American ship to sanctuary in the Greek Islands.

Though most of the other men of the family had been killed in the crisis, Socrates Onassis was still alive in prison. He could be set free, but it would take a lot of money. There was enough in the family safe in his office, but getting to it was another problem.

A Turkish friend of the elder Onassis wanted to retrieve a packet of papers and valuables he had left in the Onassis' family office safe. Using his various passes, and escorted by a Turkish army guard, Aristotle and the Turkish businessman wound their way through the ruined city to the office, which, although it had been wrecked, had not yet been looted. After all the proper papers were signed, the Turk happily left with his parcel, and young Aristotle had a brief, private conference with the guard. In the end, he was allowed to empty the safe of the family fortune.

Unquestionably, Aristotle Onassis saved his father's life. When it became evident that money alone was not enough to rescue him, Aristotle increased the pressure by organizing a delegation of fifty Turkish businessmen, who marched to the prison protesting the imprisonment of their friend, Socrates Onassis. This was at a time when each night a few more prisoners were taken to a midnight "trial"—at which nobody was ever declared innocent, and from which nobody ever returned. Socrates Onassis might have been next. Though his father was still imprisoned, he had been saved from the "midnight trials."

At seventeen, according to the Turkish military edict, Aristotle would have to register for deportation to Greece. Both his father and his American friend urged him to flee to Athens before his next birthday. Laden with messages for friends and relatives in Greece, and with most of the family's cash, Aristotle went to the prison for a good-bye visit with his father. For the first time in all his months of visiting the prison, he was stopped and led to the office of the commandant for "questioning." But he slipped away from his guards and sauntered casually through the gate, waving to the sentries who had come to recognize him.

He fled to the American consulate, where his friend the vice-consul dressed him in an American sailor's uniform as a disguise. Three weeks later, young Onassis led his womenfolk from an American ship onto the soil of mainland Greece. Then he went to Constantinople, enlisting the aid of his father's friends, and pleaded with the right officials for his release. It was a delicate task that would give a seasoned diplomat pause, but the sixteen-year-old Aristotle flattered the right people, greased the appropriate palms, and obtained his father's release.

What happened next probably went a long way to shape the man. When the whole family was reunited in Athens, they criticized the boy for spending too much money in his efforts to free his father. Even Socrates Onassis chided him for the way he handled the negotiations. It didn't seem to matter that the man's life had been saved, or that the boy had risked his own again and again, or that the family had trusted in him enough to assign him the task in the first place.

He'd done a man-size job and succeeded, and now he was being scolded like a baby. It taught Aristotle a bitter lesson about gratitude and loyalty, and obliterated any traces of sentimentality in his character. Angry and resentful, he turned his back on his family and resolved to trust no one ever again. He also resolved to show them a thing or two about his ability with money.

He decided to go to Buenos Aires, but refused

to accept more than fifty Turkish pounds (about $200) from his family. He spent fifteen of them on a special travel document, and began the voyage in the indescribably squalid hold of an Italian steamer. It was too much for him, but he couldn't afford to transfer to the relative comfort of a cabin, so he bribed an officer to let him stay on the deck. For twenty-one days he stayed topside, sleeping on the coiled stern lines, and arrived in Argentina on September 21, 1923.

He was still bruised from his family's unfeeling ingratitude, and to make up for it he came on as an aggressive, cocky, pushy kid with an eye for every angle. What made it worse was that he took many risks—but he landed on his feet almost every time.

He wasn't afraid of work—construction labor, dishwashing, working for the telephone company for 25¢ an hour. On the side, he peddled cigarettes on the street, with the thought of perhaps someday becoming a tobacco merchant like his father.

Worked As Dishwasher

He had managed to retain a sentimental streak. Some of his Greek friends recall when Aristotle, working as a dishwasher, washed a glass used by Carlos Gardel, the great singer of tangos. He boasted of it for weeks.

And he made mistakes. To get a work permit, he added six years to his age. Since he was a Greek refugee from Turkey, he was technically a stateless person, so he said he had been born in the Greek mainland city of Salonika. These were small liberties with the truth, but they'd cause him trouble in the future.

His father sent him some tobacco samples, hoping to get some Argentine customers. Eventually, Aristotle made his first sale to Juan Gaona, a cigarette manufacturer, for $10,000. Other sales followed, and with his commissions, Onassis wasn't poor anymore.

Aristotle's business principles were evident even in this first venture, and would remain with him throughout his life. First, he didn't use his own money for capital. He used it as collateral, borrowing against it. Years later, this was how he built his empire. Second, he was willing to start small. He wasn't satisfied with a modest share of the luxury field. The cigarettes were hand finished, some of them tipped with rose leaves, and only two workers were required for his entire company.

And third, he had no scruples. He gave his cigarettes the name of Bis—despite the fact, or more probably because of it, that there was already a very popular Bis cigarette selling in Argentina at the time. It was even made by another Greek! Onassis was sued, of course, settled out of court, and ceased to use the Bis name. But he'd turned a handsome profit in the meantime. This has been his attitude toward the countless lawsuits that have been filed against him over the years.

Onassis prospered, and began sending money home to his widowed aunts, and paying for the best schools for their children. He and his father had reconciled in their letters. At twenty five, he was a millionaire, dealing in hides, grain, and, of course, tobacco.

In 1929, Greece announced an exorbitant new tariff on goods from countries with which it had no commercial agreement. Though the move was not directed against Argentina, Argentina fell into this category. Onassis knew that, in retaliation, Argentina would raise its tariffs on Greek goods, such as the tobacco he was selling. He decided to go to Athens to argue with the authorities.

He argued so successfully that the Greeks not only exempted Argentina from the tariff decree, they made Onassis their representative in trade negotiations with the Argentine government. Shortly after his return to Buenos Aires, he was made the Acting Consul General for Greece. It was an important post, for Greece was a seagoing nation, and Buenos Aires one of the most important ports in the world. A thousand Greek ships put in there yearly. Onassis wielded an enormous amount of official clout, and on the other hand he had his own business interests to look out for. His competitors cried "foul!" but he held the post till 1935. By that time, of course, he didn't need it anymore.

Like the canny Joe Kennedy, Onassis foresaw the world economic crisis precipitated by the 1929 crash. Quietly, he converted many of his holdings to cash and prepared to ride out the storm. But to a man in a good cash position the depression was a time of opportunity, if you had a good business mind. Onassis had one of the best, and he was quick to see that the trade crisis had knocked the bottom out of the shipping business. Old ships were selling for the same prices for which they could be sold for scrap. But most were in good condition, and their earning capacity could pay back an investment in as little as a year.

For $120,000 cash, Onassis bought six 9,000- and 10,000-ton freighters from the Canadian National Steamship Company. Established Greek shippers told him he was crazy to buy ships when there were no cargos to transport. Their dire predictions didn't bother Onassis, but having to spend his own money on them did. He'd have preferred to borrow, pay interest, and keep the money. For two years, he kept the ships in mothballs, then, when the depression began to ease, he put them into service one by one.

Again and again he slashed through red tape and cut corners to widen his profit margin. He registered most of his ships in Greece, not out of patriotism but because wages for Greek seamen were the lowest in Europe. But when Greek regulations got in his way, he devised an ingenious out. He registered his ships in Panama, thus inventing the "flag of convenience"—regardless of the nationality of its owners, the ship flies the Panamanian flag, is subject to infinitesimal Panamanian taxes, and conforms to Panamanian safety standards, the lowest that insurance companies allow.

Even in his days as one of the world's youngest millionaires, Onassis was anything but handsome. He never was much at repartee and bright conversation, though he had a certain charm when he cared to use it. He was not interested in culture, charity, or good manners. And yet he always had a strong attraction for women, and when he wanted one badly enough to make an effort, he always succeeded. To his credit, he loved them one at a time, and his serious relationships lasted for years.

His first was Ingeborg Dedichen, a Scandinavian beauty he met on one of his trips to Europe in 1934. They remained together for ten years, traveling constantly. Aristotle learned from Ingeborg the fine art of showering gifts on a lady. He acquired a taste for the high life, and for surrounding himself with the best that money could buy.

And he learned to his dismay that there were things money *couldn't* buy, a fact which continued to frustrate him for years. The man who taught him this hard truth was another, slightly younger Greek, named Stavros Niarchos. They met in Athens, where Niarchos was a dashing, good-looking, polished member of Athens society—who drove a borrowed Bugatti and worried about his bills at the tailor's. Family reverses left him penniless, with nothing but his breeding and snobbery to protect him. He envied Onassis his wealth, but put him down as a bumpkin from Smyrna. He even implied that Onassis had somehow betrayed Greece in the process of getting his father out of the Turkish prison. The apparent surface liking between the two men faded fast; Niarchos entered the shipping business, and the two men became bitter personal enemies as well as business competitors.

In Buenos Aires, the large German and Italian populations were supporting Hitler and Mussolini, and the officially neutral Argentine government was leaning somewhat toward the Axis. Onassis, as a businessman, wanted to maintain good relations with everybody. He did nothing to offend the Argentine government, while he hoped to earn a share of the millions the U.S. was spending on shipping war material.

But someone in Argentina quietly told the FBI that Onassis had "expressed sentiments inimical to the United States war effort," and FBI Director J. Edgar Hoover saw fit to inform Rear Admiral Emory S. Land, of the War Shipping Administration, that Mr. Onassis' activities and movements in the U.S. should be "carefully scrutinized."

Despite the suspicion, Onassis did enough business with the U.S. government to bring his personal fortune up to an estimated $30 million by the end of the war. Because he was an Argentine citizen, and his ships were registered under the Panamanian "flag of convenience," almost every cent of his war profits was out of the reach of the U.S. Bureau of Internal Revenue.

His astonishing luck had held. Of all the Greek shipowners, Onassis alone lost not a single sailor nor ship during the war. Two of his ships had been sunk, but not until after Onassis had sold them both to the Japanese—just before Pearl Harbor.

Richer now than he'd ever imagined, Onassis decided to wait out the postwar reconstruction period in New York. He had his eye on some government-owned tankers and Liberty ships that would probably be up for sale, and he also had his eye out for a wife. He had never had any intention of marrying Ingeborg, who accepted this as a fact of her existence. But he was now in his forties, and he wanted a son.

He had his eye on the two young daughters of Stavros Livanos, another Greek shipping magnate, and as he phased Ingeborg out of his life, he began courting the elder Livanos daughter, Eugenia. But, amazingly, when he proposed marriage, she refused. Onassis, ever the pragmatist, remained friends with Eugenia and turned his attentions to her seventeen-year-old younger sister, Athina, or Tina. They were married in 1946, and as a wedding present her father gave Tina a town house in New York. Onassis spent a million dollars decorating and furnishing it, and the couple moved in and began a lively social life. Eugenia eventually became the wife of Stavros Niarchos, Aristotle's rival.

One oil executive recalls that during this period, every time he turned around, Onassis or a subordinate was inviting him to a party. Onassis could see that the big money in shipping was going to come from transporting oil, and he intended to get it. Without putting forth a cent of his own, characteristically, Onassis then commissioned the construction of the five largest oil tankers in the world, at a cost of $40 million. His collateral for the loans was a contract with the Mobile Oil Company to carry their oil—in tankers he didn't have yet!

U.S. Indicts Onassis

In the mid-fifties, Onassis was indicted by the U.S. government for buying surplus ships through a dummy American corporation. It was just what a dozen other Greek shippers had done, but Aristotle Onassis was the big target. He hired 375 lawyers and began preparing his defense. In an incident which rankled Onassis for the rest of his life, he was arrested at the Colony restaurant in New York; the considerate agents allowed him to finish his lunch. In Washington, D.C., the Attorney General read him the charges, and Onassis was escorted to jail.

He pleaded not guilty, posted a $10,000 bond, and was released after only a few moments in custody, but Onassis was not a forgiving man. A year later, the tangled case was resolved when Onassis paid $7 million in compensation and agreed to build 198,000 tons of tankers in U.S. shipyards. Onassis felt that he had in fact done a lot for the U.S. shipping industry, and that if he'd done as much for the British, "I would have been knighted. In America, I was indicted." Again, Onassis felt that instead of gratitude for his efforts, he was being punished. It was like his family's reaction to his rescue of his father from prison.

In his domestic life, too, there was ingratitude and bitterness. Young Tina was bored and lonely within her gilded cage. Two children, Alexander, born in 1948, and Christina, born in 1950, were small compensation for a husband much older, set in his ways, whose friends were mostly dull businessmen. Even the couple's more interesting acquaintances, like Cary Grant, Margot Fonteyn, and Aly Khan were not the friends Tina Onassis would have chosen for herself.

She loved horses and skiing—Ari couldn't have cared less. Gossip columnists began reporting that Tina was seen dining and dancing with young men of the international set every evening that Onassis left her alone.

Onassis was hard at work sewing up a deal with the Greek government which would give him a government-sponsored shipyard and the national airline. But the powerful Queen Frederika wanted the plums to go to a good friend of hers, who often entertained the Greek royal family on his yacht. His name was Stavros Niarchos, and when Onassis found out, he made the legendary wrath of Achilles look like a restrained pout. The Greek premier, Constantin Karamanlis, effected a compromise whereby Onassis got the airline and Niarchos got the shipyard.

Onassis won another prize in 1957—but it cost him a lot more. Onassis' yacht, the *Christina*, was the scene of a gala party in Venice, honoring the Greek dramatic soprano, Maria Callas. Her combination of vocal artistry, dramatic ability, and exotic beauty had made her an international celebrity as well as an operatic prima donna. Onassis toasted her again and again as Tina's smile faded.

They met again in Milan and in London, where Onassis took a huge party of guests to hear her sing the opera *Medea* at Covent Garden. Afterward, he threw a party at the swank Dorchester Hotel. Tina did not look her best.

There was a brief respite when the Onassises entertained Aristotle's aging friend, Sir Winston Churchill, aboard the *Christina* in the harbor at Monte Carlo. Onassis heard that the former U.S. Ambassador to England was entertaining his son and daughter-in-law nearby, and invited the young couple to come meet Sir Winston at cocktails. While the son of the ambassador had a long chat with Sir Winston, Aristotle Onassis showed his yacht to Jacqueline Bouvier Kennedy. They met again when Jackie went ahead to Greece after she and Jack made their 1961 State visit to London.

Onassis' marriage to Tina ended on a cruise aboard the *Christina* that summer. The guests included Sir Winston Churchill, Maria Callas, and her industrialist husband, Giovanni Battista Meneghini. At the end, Callas announced that she was through with Meneghini—Meneghini announced that he was through with Callas. Tina began issuing terse statements through her lawyer and Onassis began a lot of vulgar jabbering. In Venice, he was quoted as saying that he was, after all, a sailor, and sailors always have a girl in every port. In 1959, Tina filed suit for divorce in New York State, proudly citing as correspondent an anonymous "Mrs. J.R." and not mentioning Callas at all.

Callas and Onassis lived together openly for the next ten years, mostly aboard the *Christina*. When they met, Callas was unquestionably the leading operatic soprano in the world. But with the scandal surrounding the two of them, her bookings fell off sharply. It might have been that opera houses were relieved to have an excuse not to hire her—her temper was formidable and she had many enemies among other singers and musicians. Her career declined, and for a while she concentrated only on recording. Gradually, she worked less and less and finally gave it up completely. Her life with Onassis was more important to her.

By and large, Onassis was faithful to Callas, as such things go. She accepted his absences philosophically, and if his lesser flirtations bothered her, she didn't show it. She was serenely confident that he'd come back to her in the long run. And on that score, he never disappointed her.

Jackie's Trip To Lesbos

When Jackie boarded the Onassis yacht in Athens in 1963 every flag in the harbor was raised in her honor. Asked about the destination, Onassis replied with graceful evasion, "To this or that island. Mrs. Kennedy is the captain." And since she would understandably want privacy, the press was unusually gentle.

Barefoot and windblown, she rode in a speedboat along the coast of Lesbos—the island where Onassis had paused in his flight from Smyrna as a boy. Accompanied by her host and a Secret Service man, Jackie roamed the ruins of the Palace of Minos. The UPI story said that she was particularly interested in "the Queen's apartment, where she admired the ruins of the ancient boudoir, bathroom, bedroom and vials in which the Queen used to keep her perfume." She oohed and aahed over 3,000-year-old jewelry and admired an ancient wine jug shaped like the head of a bull.

They stopped at Istanbul where, as usual, crowds turned out to cheer the most famous woman in the world. "I will return when my husband is no longer president," Jackie told them.

But back in Washington, Representative Oliver Bolton, an Ohio Republican, blasted Jackie for sailing with Onassis. He complained that Onassis owed the U.S. for an insured mortgage on one of his ships, and that he was due in a few days to make a $1,400,000 payment on another.

"If Onassis were an American shipowner, a clear conflict of interest question would be raised," Bolton complained.

After Pierre Salinger showed the story to the president, Jack was livid. Matters weren't helped much when the State Department reported that Athens was buzzing with rumors that Onassis invited Jackie to sail with him only because

Stavros Niarchos had had Princess Margaret as a guest aboard his yacht. Jack wasn't about to let his wife be used as a pawn in any ego-tripping status contest between two celebrity-hunting billionaires.

He put in a prompt radio-telephone call to the *Christina* and told Jackie, "Get off the ship, even if you have to swim to shore." But Jackie didn't leave.

According to Willi Frischauer's biography, *Onassis*, the shipowner was particularly careful not to embarrass Mrs. Kennedy by appearing with her in public when the ship was in port. He tried to keep out of sight when there were reporters or photographers around, leaving his sister, Artemis, to act as hostess. Jackie noticed this, and told Roosevelt to relay her appreciation to Onassis, and her insistence that he join them publicly when they went ashore. To all appearances, she couldn't care less whether her connection with Onassis was embarrassing to Jack. Probably she was irritated that Jack had suggested she cut her trip short, and this was a way of retaliating.

It was the kind of cruise that girls like Jackie dream about. The beautifully appointed yacht was stocked with every luxury and delicacy imaginable. Onassis, who knew a great deal about living, fell over himself trying to make Jackie as comfortable and happy as possible. Champagne and caviar, dried mullets packed in ice, cartons of canned hams, fresh fruits and vegetables from private farms, and seemingly inexhaustible supplies of long-stemmed red roses and colorful gladioli filled the ship's storage lockers. Not one, but two hairdressers and a platoon of musicians accompanied the party. Every night, the guests and their host gathered for a sea-going dinner party—Roosevelt and his wife, the Prince and Princess Radziwill, Aristotle Onassis and Mrs. John F. Kennedy.

On this cruise, Jackie caught her first glimpse of Skorpios, the gemlike island which was to be the scene of her second wedding. At that time, Onassis had owned it only briefly and instead of the palace he was to build, there was only a twenty-room bungalow standing amid the island's pines and olive groves. "It's simply magnificent," Jackie breathed.

Onassis then took her to the top of a hill where bulldozers were already at work leveling the site. There he described to her the 180-room replica of the palace of Knossos, Crete, which he intended to build, complete with hanging gardens.

That night, the party dined on Skorpios, with roast suckling pig and lots of piney-flavored *retsina*, the national wine of Greece. The next day, the *Christina* resumed its lazy, luxurious voyage until bad weather forced it to put in at Skorpios again. Jackie was delighted at having another chance to explore the island with the attentive Onassis.

As was his custom, Onassis presented the ladies with rich souvenirs of their voyage aboard the *Christina*. For Lee, there was what Doris Lilly described as "something nice in pearls," but for Jackie there was a blazing diamond and ruby necklace. In the light of the rumors that preceded the cruise, it would almost seem that Onassis had gotten the packages mixed up.

But that's the kind of mistake that Aristotle just didn't make.

After a quick trip to Morocco to visit King Hassan II, Jackie returned to Washington, tanned and glowing, to be greeted at the airport by Jack, Caroline, and John. From Onassis, she brought a gift of model whaling ships for Jack. Soon afterward, the family retreated to the new house at Atoka, where Jack outlined his plans for building up to the 1964 Presidential campaign, beginning with a fence-mending expedition to Texas in November.

Whatever passed between them on the subject of Jackie's cruise, her refusal to come home when summoned, or her public appearances with her controversial host is a tantalizing mystery that will never be solved. There's no doubt that Jack made his feelings clear to her—but already his mind was forging ahead to the next problem. Lee and Stash were back together—for the time being, at least—Jackie was back in Washington, and Jack couldn't afford to dwell on such matters when there were practical political matters pressing in on him. Apparently both Jack and Jackie put thoughts of Aristotle Onassis aside, and devoted themselves to immediate concerns.

Jackie returned to Washington October 17, set her social secretary to work sending out thank-you notes to her various hosts, and the children planned a party for Halloween.

Then Jackie turned her attention to the finishing touches on her new house at Atoka. The First Family spent the first two weekends in November there, and reports were that the president was not at all pleased with it. Mary Gallagher reports that Jack was annoyed at the "inconvenience of giving up his bedroom to overnight guests," but since the original plans for the house mentioned "five or six bedrooms," this observation, like so many of Mrs. Gallagher's, is perhaps questionable.

A few days later, the president was thrilled when the magnificent Black Watch pipers played on the lawn of the White House. No one could know that within the month, they would be playing again for him, for the last time.

CHAPTER EIGHT
Emerges From Despair

Jackie seemed to be emerging from the despair that followed Patrick's birth and death. Undoubtedly, the sea voyage had lifted her spirits. Her obstetrician, Dr. John Walsh, had pronounced her fully recovered, and although it had been announced after Patrick's death that Jackie would rest until January 1, Jackie felt that it was time for her to reappear. She seemed not only willing, but eager to be with Jack and attend to the duties of First Lady. Perhaps the tragedy of young Patrick had brought them closer together, or perhaps she was grateful to Jack for letting her make her trip aboard the *Christina*. Or, perhaps, she suddenly realized that an election was little more than a year away and that her White House privileges would last for another four years if she could help her husband get re-elected.

At any rate, she agreed to attend the Army-

Navy football game with him after Thanksgiving, though football bored Jackie almost to tears. Speaking of their immediate plans, she told Jack, "We'll just campaign. I'll campaign with you anywhere you want."

This was precisely what Jack Kennedy had wanted to hear. It wasn't going to be an easy campaign. Despite the excitement and vision of his administration, not too much had been accomplished. Important legislation like the Civil Rights Bill was stuck in Congress, and memories of the Cuban missile crisis, the Bay of Pigs fiasco, and the building of the Berlin Wall were altogether too fresh in the voters' minds. Jack wanted a resounding victory, a clear-cut vote of confidence, to give him the power to accomplish tangible results during the next four years. Of course, it never occurred to him that he might not win at all—might not live out his year. . . .

To set the stage for a Democratic victory in 1964, it was necessary to start laying the groundwork then, bolstering up state organizations, and whipping up enthusiasm among the electorate. And it was necessary to start immediately because there was a serious problem already in a key state.

The state Democratic party in Texas was split in two. Followers of conservative Democratic Governor John Connally and liberal Democratic Senator Ralph Yarborough had about as much affection for each other as the Montagues and Capulets. Theoretically, anyway, that was something for another Texan, Vice-President Lyndon B. Johnson, to settle, but in the all-out politics of

Texas, Johnson's unspectacular brand of political moderation had earned him no clout with either wing. As vice-president, without patronage to dispense or power to wield, he had become a hollow giant, a political nonentity in his own state. Thus it was up to the president to heal the division, or Texas' twenty-five electoral votes would surely fall to the Republicans.

Jack was not enthusiastic—he loved campaigning, but this was an awkward time. West German Chancellor Ludwig Erhard was coming to Washington at the end of the month, and Press Secretary Pierre Salinger was going to Japan to act as advance man for a planned presidential visit there in February. He and Caroline were studying French together; he was shopping for a fur rug as a Christmas present for Jackie; and his office was about to be redecorated, financed by the sales of Jackie's guidebook to the White House.

But it was decided that on November 21, the President, Mrs. Kennedy, Vice-President and Mrs. Johnson, and assorted aides, secretaries and Secret Service men would begin a brief tour of major Texas cities. It was the first time Jackie had been West since the 1960 campaign.

It would serve, among other things, as a kind of run-through for the Kennedys and their staff, a rehearsal for the many such trips they would have to make between now and election day, 1964. It would be a good opportunity to spot and to remedy possible problems in their procedure so that by the time the campaign was in full swing, all would be running smoothly.

Space prevented Jackie from bringing along both a maid and a secretary, so Mary Gallagher was called on to double as Provi's stand-in. Jackie and Provi planned in advance which clothes to take and where each dress would be worn. To make the scheme foolproof, Provi taped to each suitcase a list of the outfits within, and an itinerary of the events involved.

Unfortunately, one of the "bugs" in the planning procedure became evident almost at once. Relying on erroneous weather reports, Jackie chose an autumn wardrobe of light wools, expecting snappy weather. It turned out to be fair and mild throughout their trip, and Jack, irritated, ordered his staff to work out a better system for finding out the probable weather at their destinations.

The first stop was San Antonio, where Jack was to dedicate the new Aero Space Medical Health Center, and where they were met by the Johnsons, their hosts for the visit. Afterward, the party reboarded Air Force One and flew to Houston International Airport where Jack and Jackie were to attend a dinner in honor of Congressman Albert Thomas. At both airports, the crowds screamed, "Jack-eee" and brought flowers—the yellow roses of Texas. At Houston, they grasped her hands, almost dragging her over the railing, and the elderly Congressman Thomas and an equally elderly friend volunteered to run interference for Jackie between the landing area and the motorcade. For the gallant Congressman Thomas, it was a lifetime thrill.

To Jackie, Houston seemed "two blocks of Manhattan in the middle of a prairie." To Houston, Jackie was the attraction and the president secondary. When Jack asked Dave Powers to estimate the crowd, Dave replied, "For you? About as many as turned out the last time you were here, but a hundred thousand more have come to look at Jackie!"

After the couple refreshed themselves in their suite at the Rice Hotel in Houston, which had been thoughtfully redecorated for their visit, Jackie put on a black cut-velvet suit and accompanied her husband to a meeting of the LULACS—a Latin American organization—in the Grand Ballroom. There, after Jack had spoken about his Alliance for Progress for Latin America, Jackie gave a brief speech in carefully memorized Spanish. Her old-fashioned Castilian accent sounded quaint to her Spanish-speaking listeners, but they loved her. Afterward, Jack, who spoke no Spanish, collared a spectator and questioned him closely about Jackie's speech. Seemingly satisfied, he told Jackie that she had been "wonderful." Jackie knew that her performance had not been great, but she was touched by her husband's efforts to make campaigning a happy experience for her.

At 11:07, the presidential plane, with two other aircraft carrying the rest of the entourage and the reporters, landed in Carswell Air Force Base in Fort Worth, in an annoying light rain. Nobody thought there would be much of a turnout, considering the weather and the late hour. But as they drove to the city they found that the road was lined with cheering people, drenched from waiting in the rain. For the first time there were shouts of "Lyndon!" amid those for Jackie and the president, and the dour countenance of the vice-president brightened. The Johnsons, and Governor John Connally and his wife, were pleased by Fort Worth's welcome.

For the Kennedys, exhausted and strained, what seemed most important at the moment was a good night's sleep. But the hotel arrangements, as Kenny O'Donnell said later, were "all screwed up." The rooms at the Hotel Texas were small and down-at-the-heel; in one room the two staff members who shared it actually had to unpack one at a time because it was so small. Secret Service Agent Lem Johns lost his shaving gear in a wild luggage mix-up, but that was the least of his worries. What bothered him most was that the lobby of the hotel was full of boisterous Texans in ten-gallon hats, some of whom appeared to be toting shooting irons in the grand old Texas tradition.

The press badgered Jackie for interviews, but she retired upstairs, sending word through Pam Turnure that Thursday had been "a wonderful day," and that "Texas friendliness was everything I'd heard it to be."

Through another mix-up in the comedy of errors that was the Kennedy visit to Fort Worth, Mary Gallagher did not arrive at the hotel to tend to Jackie until long after the president and first lady had arrived. This irked the president, who told Mary to arrange to ride with the luggage car which traveled by a different route from that taken by the motorcade, and which arrived at hotels before the others.

"You were great today," Jack told his wife. "How do you feel?"

"Oh, gosh, I'm exhausted," sighed Jackie.

Jack's much-publicized vitality was waning, too. He was, after all, forty-six. But, already half asleep, he told her, "Don't get up with me. I've got to speak in that square downstairs before breakfast, but stay in bed. Just be at the breakfast at nine-fifteen."

That night, in the absence of her maid, Jackie laid out her own clothes for the morning—a light wool Chanel suit, the color of raspberries, with a navy-blue collar. A navy blouse, handbag, low-heeled shoes, and a pink pillbox hat completed her ensemble.

The twelve-to-eight shift of Secret Service guards took over outside Room 850, where the Kennedys were sleeping. Agent in charge Roy Kellerman inspected the parking lot which the Kennedy's suite overlooked, checked the car the president would use the next day, and went to bed. Unknown to him, nine of his agents, off duty, were relaxing at the Fort Worth Press Club with presidential aide Malcolm Kilduff; later they continued at a local club which, though it served no liquor, managed to hold their interest till the wee hours. Others had a few drinks back at the hotel despite the fact that they were to ride in the car following the president's. Nobody drank too much, and nobody was exactly hung over the next morning, but that crucial edge of alertness was not going to be there when it might have counted.

Dallas — The Queen City

Dallas was the big one on this trip, the queen city of Texas, the place where the money was. An insurance and banking center, it had grown fabulously wealthy in the past thirty years. In Dallas, men talked about football and politics and grew richer by the moment, leaving things cultural entirely to the ladies.

Women took lessons in china painting, men were steadfast Republicans, and kids went to S.M.U. and pledged fraternities. It was not the sort of city Jackie would feel at home in, nor was it the sort of city that would be sympathetic to the bold, liberal young president from New England.

In the 1960 campaign, a gaggle of Dallas housewives had spat at the Lyndon Johnsons. Only the month before, U.N. Ambassador Adlai E. Stevenson had been assaulted there on U.N. Day, and voiced to presidential assistant Arthur Schlesinger his doubts that the president should go to Dallas. The Secret Service, according to William Manchester, regarded Dallas as a "tough town" and were worried that Vice-President Johnson might be the target of abuse. Senator J. William Fulbright told Kennedy, "Dallas is a very dangerous place. I wouldn't go there—don't *you* go!" But concern about the presidential visit was strongest among those closest to the Dallas scene, while the supposedly clearer heads in Washington expected, at most, a few boos.

Nevertheless, Republican Senator John Tower of Texas declined an invitation to appear in Dallas on November 22, Congressman Bruce Alger canceled a banquet to be held in his honor there, and an Austin newspaper editor, speaking of Kennedy's visit, predicted, "He will not get through this without something happening to him."

The morning of November 22 dawned with a light drizzle. Kenny O'Donnell weighed the possibility that it might clear before the important Dallas motorcade, since fair weather brings out the crowds. He was aware that Jack wouldn't mind being rained on in an open-topped convertible, but on this trip Jack was being particularly solicitous about Jackie. If it rained, the bulletproof plastic bubble would have to be used on the blue Presidential Lincoln which had been flown down in a cargo plane from Washington. It wouldn't do to let Jackie get wet since she was clearly a major political asset in this tricky state.

That morning, the *Dallas Morning News* had carried an ugly hate-Kennedy ad, accusing the president of selling food to Communist soldiers who were killing Americans in Vietnam, of reaching a secret agreement with the U.S. Communist party, and of full responsibility for the imprisonment, persecution, and starvation of "thousands of Cubans." Members of Kennedy's party saw it in early editions of the paper, and began to feel a bit more nervous. Other papers dramatized the Democratic party split. The *Chicago Sun-Times*, however, had a cheering note: "Some Texans," it said, "have begun to think that Mrs. Jacqueline Kennedy may turn the balance and win her husband this state's electoral vote."

Jack woke to his valet's knock at 7:30, full of the "vigor" that seemed to be his chief quality. He looked through the papers, did not like what he saw—although he missed for the moment the inflammatory ad—and fired off orders that Senator Yarborough was to ride in the car with the Vice-President.

Then it was downstairs and out to the parking lot where he delivered a brief speech to a waiting crowd. As usual, there were cries of "Jackie!"

Jackie, meanwhile, was going through her slow morning ritual of dressing, arranging her hair, applying makeup, and gradually awakening. Unlike her husband, she was never exactly a shining morning person. "Oh, Mary," Jackie said to Mrs. Gallagher as she took inventory in the mirror, "one day in a campaign can age a person thirty years!" In her foggy early-morning state, she vacillated as to which pair of gloves to wear—long white ones, or short white kid ones that buttoned at the wrist. Finally she chose the short ones and allowed Mary to button them for her. All she was thinking of was Dallas, the crucial motorcade, and Jack's desire that she appear her very best before the eyes of Texas. To Jackie, that meant Dallas, and so it was a surprise to her when the elevator stopped at the mezzanine floor and she was brought toward the Longhorn Room where her husband was addressing the breakfasting Fort Worthers.

"Mrs. Kennedy is organizing herself," he had told them, explaining the delay. "It takes her longer, but of course, she looks better than we do when she does it."

When Jackie entered, the crowd went wild. She had trouble getting to her husband's side. There were presents—cowgirl boots for Jackie, a ten-gallon Stetson for Jack. Jack's speech had been a good rip-snortin' political one, but Jackie had clearly been the star of the show.

"When are you going to have her come out of a cake?" one anti-Kennedy newsman asked Dave Powers sourly.

"She's not that kind of bunny!" snapped Powers.

Back in their room, readying themselves for the flight to Dallas, Jackie was finally awake enough to perceive that the walls of their dingy little room were covered with a priceless assortment of art—including a Monet, a Picasso, a Prendergast, and a Van Gogh. They discovered a little catalogue which indicated that the exhibition had been arranged in their honor, and listed the collectors who had lent their works for the delectation of the president and his first lady. Impulsively, they phoned one of them, Mrs. Ruth Carter Johnson, to thank her for her thoughtfulness.

Moments later, Kenny O'Donnell showed them the ugly ad in the *News*, and Jackie's happy vivacity dissolved. "Can you imagine a paper doing a thing like that?" Jack said to O'Donnell. Then he turned to Jackie and said, dismissing it casually, "Oh, you know, we're heading into nut country today." Then he went into one of what Jackie called his "Walter Mitty" moods. "You know, last night would have been a hell of a night to assassinate a president. I mean it. There was the rain, and the night, and we were all getting jostled. Suppose a man had a pistol in a briefcase. . . ." Jack pantomimed, pointing his finger like a pistol, "Then he could have dropped the gun in the briefcase and melted away in the crowd!" It was a joke, his way of making light of the ad and of Dallas' record as a "tough town."

But after a brief visit from the vice-president, Jack was all steely seriousness. *"Get him in the car,"* he ordered O'Brien, referring to Yarborough. The Senator was to ride with the Vice-President, or else he'd have to walk. And Larry O'Brien managed it, even though it meant pulling Nellie Connally, the wife of the Governor, out of the car so that there would be room. Lyndon Johnson, Governor Connally, and Senator Yarborough rode from Fort Worth to Carswell Air Force Base together, proclaiming their brotherhood as Texas Democrats to the crowds that lined the streets.

It took only thirteen minutes for Air Force One to fly from Fort Worth to Dallas, and since the presidential party was already on the ground with plenty of cars and a good toll-road to Dallas, it seemed to fly in the face of common sense to reboard the three planes and fly that short distance. It would have been faster, counting the time spent in getting to and from the airports, to simply drive to Dallas.

The Secret Service raised this point, as did Ted Clifton, pilot of Air Force One. The answer Kenny O'Donnell gave was, "With two fields we have two landings, and for a politician nothing except weather is more important than a good airport landing."

The Secret Service doesn't meddle in purely political decisions. Its purpose is solely to protect the life of the president. But these men hate the thought of airport landings, crowded lobbies, and other public appearances where the president is an all-too-easy target for would-be killers. There is, after all, a limit to what even the Secret Service can do toward protecting their man. They often wish he wouldn't take such risks, but politicians thrive on contact with the public, and the Secret Service is resigned to the fact that presidents tend to put politics before safety. William Manchester put it, "Threats are like *Hail to the Chief;* they are part of the office." And, as the King of Italy said in 1897, just after an attempt on his life, *"Sono gli incerti del mestiere"*—those are the risks of the job.

PART THREE

CHAPTER NINE
Assassination

If it is possible for two hundred million people to participate in a four-day event and experience basically the same emotions, it happened between lunchtime on Friday, November 22, 1963, and the evening of Monday, November 25. Those four days are part of our national memory as days that bound the diverse American people together, uniting us in a way that prosperity and victory had not been able to do. And at the center of all this is the image of a thin young woman with dark hair, whose face was wracked with grief and transfigured by courage.

In the years that followed, Jackie's image has changed; many would say it has tarnished. People do not think of her the same way they did on that incredible weekend, or during her years in the White House. She is a different person, as all of us are.

But despite the passage of time, despite all the other hands raised in violence and all the other blood that has been shed, the heroine of our national tragedy remains Mrs. John F. Kennedy. It was the finest, most courageous hour of Jackie's life, despite criticisms leveled at her for some of her other actions. Anything else she had done, or may do in the future, cannot lessen or defile what she did during those endless hours when a nation watched her, on a million television screens, through its tears.

For Jackie, Friday, November 22, had begun as a promising day. When Air Force One touched down at 11:38, Central Time, there was a big friendly crowd waiting at Love Field. All the yellow roses were sold out, so a loyal Democratic lady thrust a bunch of red ones into Jackie's arms, hoping she wouldn't notice the departure from Texas custom. Liberal-minded citizens were going all-out to shout down the conservative majority in Dallas.

They might have been from Dallas, but they were also Texans, and they were determined to give the Kennedys a warm Texas-size welcome if at all possible. Conservative Democrats on the reception committee had excluded liberals, union representatives, and minorities from the official events, so they were paying tribute to the president in the only way they could.

The president's visit to Dallas was scheduled to last only a few hours, just long enough for the motorcade to the Trade Mart where he was to deliver a speech, then another motorcade back to the airport, whence the Kennedys were to depart for Austin and a visit to the vice-president's LBJ Ranch.

Police Chief Jesse E. Curry, well aware that tensions were high in his town, had deployed most of his officers around the Trade Mart, which seemed to be the most likely place for trouble. He anticipated some kind of ugly demonstration, and already his men had carted away three men with especially distasteful anti-Kennedy placards. There were 365 policemen at Love Field, sixty at the Mart, and lone officers scattered along the route.

Kennedy was certainly not loved by the Dallas establishment, but they were proud of their city and determined that its more extremist elements behave themselves. And it is possible that their actions were influenced by Southern chivalry and they hoped not to offend the sensibilities of the First Lady, whatever they may have thought of her husband.

The crush of people slowed the motorcade to twenty miles per hour, to fifteen, to ten, to seven. A motorcycle policeman, riding beside Jackie at the left of the Lincoln, was forced to drop back. Agent Cliff Hall sprang from the follow-up car to move alongside the president's car, shielding Jackie with his body.

At 12:21 P.M. the motorcade swung into Dealy Plaza, nearing the last leg of the journey to the Trade Mart. The route zigzagged from Main Street to Houston to Elm, and, along this stretch, spectators were relatively sparse. Photographs and films of the historic moments give no idea of the dimension of the welcome in other areas along the motorcade.

It reminded Jackie of Mexico, "hot, wild, loud, with the blazing sun strong in your face," with the sound of cheering washing over her like waves. Jack waved and grinned back at the crowds, and Nellie Connally heard him repeating, "Thank you, thank you," and wondered why he bothered, since they couldn't possibly hear him over the sound of their own shouting.

Jackie, in her pink wool suit, sweltered and tried to stay cheerful. In her lap were a pair of sunglasses with large lenses that Jack wouldn't let her wear, because people wanted to see her face. She saw a triple railroad underpass ahead, and yearned for its cool shadows as the blue Lincoln crawled ahead at 11.2 miles per hour.

There was a strange, sharp noise.

Jackie thought it was a motorcycle noise, Chief Curry thought it was a railroad torpedo, but the men in the motorcade who had done a lot of hunting recognized it as the crack of a rifle. But even the Secret Service agents of the White House detail did not recognize it immediately.

It was only when they saw the president lurch and grab at his neck that they realized what it meant. In the vice-presidential car, agent Rufus Youngblood caught the scent of gunpowder and yelled, "My God! They've shot the president!" He leaped over the back of the seat into the passenger compartment of Lyndon Johnson's car, pushing the vice-president to the floor, shielding him with his own body, and thinking wildly that this would be horribly embarrassing if he turned out to be wrong.

But he wasn't, and in fact he had grasped the situation before the agents in the president's car itself. If they had thought as quickly, and had moved as fast. . . .

Agent Roy Kellerman, in the front seat of the president's car, thought he heard him cry, "My God! I'm hit!" Aghast, Kellerman turned to see, and as he realized that the president *was* hit, the big car wobbled on its course. The momentary pause was tragically crucial.

At that moment, Governor Connally was hit. The car slowed still more, its driver frozen in panic. The Governor shouted, "No, no, no, they're going to kill us all." Dazed, Jackie thought, Why is he screaming? and turned to Jack. His face was quizzical. He raised his right hand toward his head as a third shot hit home. For a moment, there was no blood.

"My God, what are they doing? My God, they've killed Jack, they've killed my husband!" Jackie cried.

Jack's body pitched toward his wife, and Jackie, going into a deep primeval kind of shock, rose blindly, turned, and sprawled on the trunk of the car, as agent Greer finally stepped on the accelerator.

For a moment, Jackie was almost as close to death as her husband as she slipped and tried to keep her balance on the sloping trunk of the accelerating car. Agent Clint Hill dashed behind the car, grabbing at the special metal grip on the trunk, and planted his toe in the footstep beneath the bumper as the big car gathered speed. Jackie reached out, her hand grasped his, and, as William Manchester says, it is impossible to say who saved whom. She drew him up, and he pushed her back onto the back seat, which, though bespattered with her husband's blood, was at least safer. Agent Hill grasped the partly raised window on the left of the car, hooked his foot on the right side of the car, and hung on as the car sped to Parkland Hospital. The Secret Service had failed; Hill knew immediately that the president could never survive such a wound, and, in his anger, grief, and frustration, he pounded the trunk of the car with his free hand.

The police alerted Parkland Hospital, only a few blocks away, and the Lincoln arrived there three minutes later, at 12:36. There were not two, but three passengers in deep shock—the president, who was already moribund, the governor, comatose from his own massive wound, and Jackie, numb beyond comprehension. During subsequent interviews with both the Warren Commission and with author William Manchester, she was unable to recall more than bits and pieces of the sequence of events since Dealy Plaza. It is reported that she watched Abraham Zapruder's famed amateur movie of the assassination as if it had all happened to another woman.

The big Lincoln pulled into the emergency entrance of Parkland Hospital. Doors flew open, other cars pulled up, members of the hospital staff converged on the presidential car. But in the dreadful panic of the moment there were no stretchers or stretcher bearers. Angry agents barked, "Get us two stretchers on wheels" but the hospital for a moment did not respond. The shock was too unbelievable. So far as Jack Kennedy was concerned, however, delay no longer mattered.

The stretchers at last arrived, and the governor, who had regained consciousness, was transferred to one and wheeled away. Jackie remained in the drab hallway. The doctors knew their cause was hopeless. In fact, Manchester observed, Jack would almost certainly have been entered on the hospital records as DOA—dead on arrival—had he been anybody but the president. The throat wound was small, so small that it was originally assumed to be an entry wound; an assumption which was to lead to endless contradiction and speculation after the release of the Warren Commission Report some months later. But it wasn't the throat wound that killed Jack; it was the massive head wound, and the horrible bleeding which resulted from it, that killed him.

There was no blood pressure, no pulse at all, although his body was trying automatically to breathe and once in a great while his heart contracted in what might have been called a heartbeat. Though Jack's blood type was O, Rh Positive, he was given a transfusion of O, Rh negative blood, since the doctors knew that the question of possible reactions to a mismatched blood type was quite academic.

Other drugs were administered as a matter of routine, not because anybody had the slightest hope they might be effective, but to delay the moment when life had left Jack's body completely. They inserted first a breathing tube through his mouth, which didn't work because of the wound in his neck. Then they cut open a tracheotomy—a temporary breathing passage in the neck.

After waiting in the hall, Jackie entered the room where her husband lay. She had been certain he had been killed, and yet when she saw all the doctors and nurses running into the room, and heard them talking about resuscitation and fluids, she began to wonder whether there might be hope, after all. Could there be a chance? "God," said Kenny O'Donnell to Larry O'Brien, "it's a thousand-to-one chance he can live."

It was too much for Jackie; she had to be at Jack's side. A nurse tried to bar the way, but Jackie said firmly, "I'm coming in and I'm staying." The nurse tried to push her away, but Jackie said, "I'm going to be in there when he dies." Jack's personal physician, Dr. George Burkley, interceded for her. "It's her right, it's her right, it's her prerogative," he said, leading her into the room. A cardiac pacemaker was wheeled into the crowded room, and one of the doctors began massaging the heart through Jack's chest. Nothing was of any use.

Two priests from the nearest Catholic parish had been summoned, but winding through the dense traffic delayed them. Father Oscar Huber went directly to Jackie murmuring his sympathy. Her stockings were bloodied from kneeling on the floor of the little room. He placed purple and white ribbons on his shoulders and began the ancient ceremony. *"Si capax, ego te albolvo a peccatis tuis. . . ."* "If possible, I absolve you from your sins. . . ." Then, with Jackie and Dr. Burkley, he recited the *Hail Mary* and afterward, his stoic priestly demeanor collapsed. Shakily, he told Jackie, "I am shocked. I want to extend my sympathy and that of my parishioners."

Jackie, born and bred a Catholic, had one great question for Father Huber. What if Jack were already dead when the priest had administered the last Sacrament? Seeing her agonized concern, he told her, "I am convinced that his soul has not left his body. This was a valid last sacrament."

Jackie's head dropped. She had done all she ever could for Jack in this life. Now she teetered on the edge of fainting. A nurse brought a cold towel.

Lady Bird Johnson, who had been waiting elsewhere in the hospital with her husband, the new president, and their attendant Secret Service men, now went to Jackie through what Lady Bird described as "a hall of silent people." Beside her husband's body as a nurse worked on it, Jackie sat "quiet as a shadow," her eyes "great wells of sadness."

"Jackie," said Lady Bird, "I wish to God there was something I could do."

By this time, that was the forlorn wish of nearly everybody in the country. It had taken hours and in some cases, days for word of President Lincoln's assassination to spread across the nation. News of Jack Kennedy's death took only moments. Radio, television, and news-service wires carried it at first; afterward, it spread by word of mouth and by telephone, as total strangers walked up to each other on the street, saying, "Have you heard?" In minutes after the official announcement, the universal answer was a sorrowful, "Yes."

The tragic news reached the airplane carrying Pierre Salinger and most of Jack's cabinet as it was on its way across the Pacific. Dean Rusk, Secretary of State, announced, "Ladies and gentlemen, it is official. We have had official word— the president has died. God save our nation." The big plane turned majestically and doubled back toward Washington.

At this time, Dallas police were frantically combing the city in an effort to capture the assassin, or assassins. Nobody knew whether Jack's death had been plotted by an international Communist conspiracy, a local enclave of Dallas conservatives, some far-out group of anarchists or anti-Catholics, or by a lone tormented soul. Considering the tension in the air before the president's visit, the Secret Service was unwilling to take chances. They assumed the worst, that President Johnson and Jackie were in danger as long as they remained in Dallas, and they urged the new president to leave at once for Washington. President Johnson agreed to go back to Air Force One, but insisted on waiting at Love Field until Jackie and Jack's body joined them. He didn't trust Dallas anymore, either; in fact, ten months later he turned down an invitation to speak before a convention of American Legionnaires in Dallas, a practically unheard of thing to do at the height of a campaign.

Even though Jackie was now a president's widow, and the Secret Service men and Jack's aides, such as Dave Powers, Kenny O'Donnell, and Larry O'Brien should have followed Lyndon Johnson to the airport, they remained with her. She kept repeating, "I'm not leaving here without Jack."

She was thinking clearly, even though her body was seized by a physical weakness that left her faint. "You just get me in there, before they close the coffin," she told Kenny O'Donnell. But in the pathetic comedy of errors that followed the assassination, the coffin hadn't arrived yet, hadn't, in fact, been ordered. The Dallas Police put agent Clint Hill in touch with Vernon B. Oneal, a Texas undertaker, and Clint told him to "bring the best one you have out to Parkland, immediately." Oneal chose the bronze "Brittania" model, made by the Elgin Casket Company, and raced it to the hospital in his new white Cadillac hearse.

Ken O'Donnell brought Jackie down the passage to a door, and Pam Turnure saw her reach out quickly and make sure the door was unlocked. Jackie had guessed, correctly, what was arriving, and that they wanted to keep it a secret. A doctor appeared, and she asked him, "Please, can I go in? Please let me go back?"

The doctor refused, and Jackie leaned toward him. "Do you think seeing the coffin can upset me, Doctor? I've seen my husband die, shot in my arms. His blood is all over me. How can I see anything worse than I've seen?"

She wanted to put something essential in the coffin with Jack. The St. Christopher money clip she had given him when they were married would have been appropriate, but that was already in a tiny coffin buried in Brookline only a few months ago. The new one was too new to be really a part of him. Suddenly, she thought of her wedding ring, the plain gold band Jack had bought in Newport just before they were married. She asked a Dallas policeman to help her undo her bloodstained glove, and an orderly managed to work the small ring onto Jack's dead finger. Afterward, in the corridor, she asked Ken, "Did I do the right thing?" Ken told her, "You leave it right where it is."

"Please, Sergeant," Jackie said to a Dallas policeman, "why can't I get my husband back to Washington?"

Embarrassed, he couldn't explain to her that the Dallas authorities would not let Jack's body leave without an autopsy since he had been the victim of a homicide. Earl Rose, the Dallas County Medical Examiner, insisted upon enforcement of the Texas statues, even though he was prolonging the agony of a young widow, holding up the wheels of the U.S. Government, and delaying the first Texas U.S. President at the airport.

"There are state laws about removing bodies, and you people from Washington can't make your own law!" said Rose. A Justice of the Peace was brought in, while Dr. Burkley came close to tears of simple frustration, and Ken O'Donnell and his hardheaded associates tried to think of a way to bulldoze out of this macabre dilemma. "One side," growled O'Donnell, sensing that now was the time for direct action. Dave Powers backed Jackie into a cubicle—things were getting ugly and he wanted to protect her. Agent Kellerman began to pull the coffin on its wheeled base while other aides and agents pushed; the Dallas opposition at the door gave way to the sheer force of human muscle, and Earl Rose logged a "Burial—Transit, No. 7992" belatedly in his records, describing the "usual occupation of the deceased" as "President of the United States."

Jackie rode in the hearse to Love Field; true to her vow, she did not leave Jack's side until they reached Washington.

The coffin was placed in the plane's tail compartment, where seats had been removed to make room. Adjacent to it was the little bedroom where she and Jack had last been alone together, and Jackie started in. She stopped short. For lying on the bed, dictating to his secretary, Marie Fehmer, was the new president, Lyndon Johnson. Hastily, the two left without a word.

Sara T. Hughes, a Dallas judge, was rushed to the field to swear in the new president. While they were waiting for her, disagreements broke out between Kennedy staffers, who wanted to get back to Washington immediately, and Johnson people, who knew their chief wanted to be sworn in before departure. "We're not going back to Andrews Air Force Base until the president has been sworn," MacKilduff told Jack's military aide, Godfrey McHugh.

McHugh pointed toward the tail compartment and cried, "I have only one president, and he's lying back in that cabin!"

After Jackie had refreshed herself in the cabin, President and Mrs. Johnson came back to offer those useless necessary words that must be said. Lady Bird told her, "Oh Jackie, you know, we never even wanted to be vice-president and now, dear God, it's come to this!"

"Oh, what if I hadn't been there," said Jackie. "I was so glad I was there!"

"Well—about the swearing in," began Lyndon Johnson awkwardly.

"Lyndon," said Jackie, then caught herself, "oh, excuse me, I'll never call you that again. I mean—Mr. President."

As William Manchester pointed out, "Of all those who had been with her husband, she was the first to accept the future."

"I mean," she continued, "Mr. President."

"Honey, I hope you'll call me that for the rest of your life," said Lyndon Johnson, referring to a first-name friendship regardless of what the future held in store.

Right then, he was most concerned with the swearing-in, and with the photos and recordings that would preserve the moment for posterity. It was not so much a matter of Johnson's personal vanity, as a sense of the history of the moment itself. Though it took place in the midst of private tragedy, it was nevertheless a moment that belonged to the American people, and which transcended political boundaries. Lyndon Johnson wanted Jackie beside him when he took that oath, because in a sense, it was Jackie's moment, too. And because it would emphasize the continuity of American government at a time when very little seemed stable or lasting.

After the judge arrived, there was a tedious discussion about camera angles and how people were to stand. Afterward came the brief ceremony itself, with the new president being sworn in with his hand on Jack Kennedy's personal Bible. The photographer got his pictures, with Jackie's pained profile. Then the new president said, "Let's get this plane back to Washington."

It was 3 P.M. Jack had been dead for over two hours, and back in Dallas the police were beginning to question a ferret-faced young man named Lee Harvey Oswald, who had allegedly shot and killed Officer J.D. Tippitt just a little while after the president had been shot. To those aboard Air Force One, all they knew was that a suspect had been caught. In their grief and numbness, it hardly mattered.

Jackie sat in the aisle seat, one of two that had been left in when the others had been removed to accommodate the long coffin. People came back to kneel beside her and mutter a few words. Mary Gallagher wanted to bring soap and a wet washcloth, but Ken O'Donnell told her, "Don't do anything. Let her stay the way she is."

Then he asked Jackie diffidently if she'd like to change to another dress.

"No," she said fiercely, "Let them see what they have done." Similarly, she objected when MacKilduff proposed landing the plane and removing the coffin in such a way that no photographs could be taken. Again Jackie insisted, "I want them to see what they've done."

Ken brought Jackie a glass of Scotch. Everyone aboard the plane—except, of course, the crew—had emptied glass after glass, but, as often happens with people in deep emotional shock, it appeared to have no effect at all. They drank enough to anesthetize them—and stayed cold sober. Jackie had one drink, then another. Nothing happened to her, either. When they were met at the airport, one aide from Bethesda Naval Hospital was outraged that no one had thought to give these glassy-eyed survivors anything to drink.

Because Jack had been murdered, there would have to be an autopsy. Because he had been in the Navy, Jackie chose Bethesda to handle it. Dr. Burkley went with the coffin, assuring Jackie that "I'll stay with the president until he is back at the White House."

Jackie began to think about the funeral itself, at first thinking that it should involve no elaborate ceremonies, but gradually coming to the decision that a full State funeral, with all the dignity and pomp the nation could muster, would be appropriate. Meanwhile, Chief of Protocol Angier Biddle Duke was putting out a silver tray in which diplomatic envoys could leave their cards when they called at the State Department, and a book for them to sign when they made their condolence calls. Already, the formal pageantry was beginning to take shape.

The plane landed at Andrews Air Force Base, in the midst of blinding lights set up for the benefit of the television cameras. Jackie asked those Secret Service men who had been closest to Jack to carry his coffin off the plane. She requested that the man who had been driving the Lincoln when Jack was killed drive the hearse to Bethesda—a touching gesture on her part.

The television coverage and the subsequent newspaper and magazine photos made the arrival of Air Force One as familiar a piece of our collective memory as that bright Inaugural day had been. There are many who will remember Jackie not as the incredibly young woman in the pillbox hat and sable muff, nor the queenly figure in widow's weeds following her husband's body to Arlington, nor the jet-setter wife of Aristotle Onassis—but as the helpless, blood-stained woman who stepped off Air Force One and rode, incongruously, back to earth with a bronze coffin on the platform of a loading truck. Somehow, in those still-wounded moments, before the nation had begun to heal, she embodied the helpless grief of a bereaved nation.

CHAPTER TEN
The Longest Weekend

Bob Kennedy had rushed to Andrews Air Force Base to meet Air Force One. No one had noticed when he slipped aboard the airplane by a door out of camera range. When the bed of the trunk descended, he was at Jackie's side.

"There's a helicopter here to take you to the White House," he explained. "Don't you want to do that?"

"No, no, I just want to go to Bethesda," she replied. Spotting the waiting gray ambulance, she said, "We'll go in that."

The loading platform stopped five feet above the ground. The men could jump, the women needed help, and the heavy bronze coffin had to be wrestled down by a waiting honor guard which had been sent over from Arlington.

If the ensuing scenes, like some of those at Dallas, seem undignified, unorganized, and even unintentionally ridiculous, it must be remembered that the participants had no real plans and no precedents to go by. Much was left to chance and improvisation, and since everyone was still highly emotional, still coming to terms with the enormity of events, many of their actions were rough, illogical, and lacking in the polish that had characterized the Kennedy years. Protocol is for people who know the ropes, whose heads and hearts are cool, whose attention is riveted upon what they are doing. Grown men and women who feel lacerated and lost are not too adept at pomp and circumstance.

Clint Hill assumed Jackie would ride in the front seat of the ambulance and started to guide her there. "No," said Jackie. "I want to go in the back," and turned to open the rear door. It was fastened from the inside, and Jackie jerked at it. Columnist Mary McGrory, who was on the scene, wondered, Why doesn't somebody help her? Col. Jim Swindal ran over to help her, but at that moment the driver released the lock from the inside. Jackie opened the door for herself and scrambled in awkwardly. Bobby Kennedy joined her in the rear compartment beside the casket. Agents Greer, Kellerman, and Landis piled into the front seat; Dr. Burkley climbed in and sat on Landis' lap; and the ambulance started its forty-minute drive to Bethesda.

"I don't want any undertakers," Jackie told Bobby. "I want everything done by the Navy." She leaned on the casket and whispered, "Oh, Bobby, I just can't believe that Jack has gone!"

On the way to the hospital, she described the

motorcade, the moment of Jack's death, and the chaotic aftermath. It was an emotional ordeal for Bobby, but he listened silently for twenty minutes. Afterward, he said, "It was so obvious that she wanted to tell me about it that whether or not I wanted to hear it wasn't a factor . . . I didn't think about whether I wanted to hear it or not. So she went through all that."

But it was a purgative experience that Jackie needed in order to carry on, and as the new head of the family, Bobby recognized this. He would handle his own grief in his own way, dealing with it alone, inside himself. But Jackie needed to share hers.

The ambulance moved through downtown Washington, where already a party of workmen was laying television cable for coverage of the funeral. It appeared to Jackie's friend, Bunny Mellon, that "All Washington was being wired."

The approach to Bethesda Naval Hospital was lined with silent crowds come to catch a glimpse of the ambulance as it sped past. When it arrived, Jean Kennedy Smith was waiting for her sister-in-law in a suite in the tower of the hospital. Ben Bradlee, chief Washington correspondent for *Newsweek*, was waiting with her, and Jackie collapsed into his arms.

"There was this totally doomed child," Bradlee recalled, "with that God-awful skirt, not saying anything, looking buried alive."

"Cry, *cry*," he told her. "Don't be too brave."

Ben's wife said, "Here's your mother," and Mrs. Auchincloss stepped forward. "Oh, Jackie," she said. "If this had to happen, thank God he wasn't maimed!" Silently, Jackie kissed her mother.

Nancy Tuckerman was there. Jackie said, "Oh, Tucky, you came all the way down from New York to take this job, and now it's all over. It's so sad. You will stay with me for a little while, won't you?"

Nancy was stunned to realize that at such a moment Jackie could be concerned about *her*.

Bobby stood behind Jackie, looking, Ben Bradlee observed, "like the strongest thing you have ever seen. He was subdued, holding Jackie together, keeping everyone's morale up when his own couldn't have been worse. He was just sensational."

Bob drew Jackie aside and said, "They think they've found the man who did it. He says he's a Communist."

Jackie was staggered by the absurdity of it. She probably thought, *It even robs his death of any meaning.* She went back to her mother and said bitterly, "He didn't even have the satisfaction of being killed for civil rights. It had to be some silly little Communist."

Jackie's thoughts turned to Caroline and John-John. Caroline had been on her way to visit a friend, Agatha Pozen, when her father was shot. The accompanying Secret Service agent ordered the car to return to the White House, where Caroline spent the afternoon with her brother and Maud Shaw. Neither child had any idea of what had happened, nor did they sense anything out of the ordinary until one helicopter after another began arriving at the White House helipad, bearing various officials, all of whom wore strange, sad expressions. Fearful that the children might learn accidentally of the tragedy before their mother could tell them the news, the staff had whisked them to Mrs. Auchincloss' house on O Street in Georgetown. But when Jackie was informed of this, she said, "They should be in their own beds. Mummy, my God, those poor children, their lives shouldn't be disrupted now, of all times. Tell Miss Shaw to bring them back and put them to bed."

"Jackie," Mrs. Auchincloss asked her daughter, "are you going to tell the children or do you want me to, or do you want Miss Shaw?"

Jackie asked her mother what she thought.

"Well," she answered, "John can wait. But Caroline should be told before she learns from friends."

Jackie agreed. "*I* want to tell them, but if they find it out before I get back, please ask Miss Shaw to use her discretion."

Janet Auchincloss was glad her daughter had said that. It gave her the opportunity to do for Jackie the only thing which could have eased her lot in any way. Telling Caroline would be an intolerable burden for Jackie; it might cause her to lose control of herself and make the moment so painful that it would scar Caroline for the rest of her life. There would be enough demands on Jackie's courage in the days to come and enough pain for Caroline to bear in the years ahead.

And so Jackie's mother took things into her own hands, phoned Miss Shaw, and told her that Jackie wanted *her* to tell Caroline. Last summer, when Patrick had died, the president had been too grief stricken to tell his daughter that her baby brother was dead, and Jackie was in the hospital. So the sad duty had been thrust upon Miss Shaw at that time. Until the assassination, it had been the hardest moment of her life. She objected to Mrs. Auchincloss, "Please," she begged, "can't someone else do it?"

But in the end it was the firm, sensible, and altogether loving Englishwoman who told Caroline at bedtime that her father had been shot, and that God had taken him to heaven to look after little Patrick. Caroline turned her head into her pillow and wept. Nurse Shaw stayed with her until the little girl was asleep.

Back at Bethesda, Jackie, still in the horribly stained suit, was speaking compulsively, but coherently. Some of the people there urged a Navy doctor to give her a sedative, but he wisely answered, "If she doesn't want it, okay. Leave her alone, let her talk herself out." She repeated her memories of the assassination, of Parkland —and of the death of Patrick.

The devout Ethel Kennedy was there, telling Jackie that Jack had gone straight to heaven and that he was "just showering graces down on us."

"Oh, Ethel," Jackie said, "I wish I could believe the way you do."

Dispute Over Burial Site

The immediate practical considerations were beginning to loom. Should Jack be buried in the family plot in Brookline, or in Arlington? Or was there another place more appropriate than either?

The Kennedys, and in fact, everyone from Massachusetts, favored the Brookline site. On the other hand, Ben Bradlee and Secretary of Defense Robert McNamara felt that the presidency was not a local possession, and that Jack's body should be buried at a spot that symbolized how he belonged to all the people. Jackie couldn't decide at that point.

Bobby gently asked her what she thought should be done after they left Bethesda with Jack's body. Though both *Life* magazine and the Associated Press wrote that Jackie had made a series of quick decisions about the funeral at this point, William Manchester reports that all she did was refer him to an engraving of Lincoln's funeral catafalque which had been reprinted in the White House guidebook. It was really Bobby who was in charge, at this point.

He phoned the office of Ralph Dungan, one of Jack's most able aides. There Sargent Shriver, painter William Walton, and others were already forming tentative plans for the funeral. Bobby requested that a member of the Special Forces be included in the guard of honor, that the Navy Hymn be played, and that Jack's personal effects be removed from the West Wing of the White House so that they would not upset Jackie when she arrived home. (This is according to William Manchester, whose narrative does not always present President Johnson in a sympathetic light, and which is therefore, probably more reliable than Mary Gallagher's vindictive book. Mrs. Gallagher says this unseemly haste was ordered by LBJ.) Those who spoke with him told the press they were acting on Mrs. Kennedy's request. And so, in a sense, they were, for Jackie placed implicit trust in her brother-in-law.

Richard Cardinal Cushing would officiate. He was Jack's friend and admirer and the longtime spiritual advisor to the Kennedy family. Anybody else would have been unthinkable. The ceremonies would be planned in accordance with the definitive work, *State, Office, and Special Military Funeral Policies and Plans.* First on the agenda was the lying-in-state in the Capitol Building, regardless of whatever arrangements were made for burial. Dick Goodwin was put in charge of this, and he delegated Arthur Schlesinger, Jr., to find out about Lincoln's funeral. Schlesinger phoned librarians at the Library of Congress, who unlocked the great collection to look up some century-old magazines with sketches and descriptions.

The toughest question was the issue of religious services. There had never before been a Roman Catholic President, and back in the 1960 campaign this had been a worrisome topic. Jack had met it head-on by discussing his views on religion and the presidency before a group of Protestant clergymen in Texas—he had acquitted himself well and the dire prophecies of a hot-line between the White House and the Vatican had dissipated. The Kennedy family and the planners agreed that there must be a funeral Mass, though not in the White House, and not a long-drawn-out High Mass. The casket would be placed in the East Room prior to the formal lying-in-state, so that family, friends, and invited mourners could pay their respects and clergy from every faith would take turns kneeling at *priedieux* beside it. In fact, numerous clergymen of every denomination had already shown up at the White House to volunteer for this vigil, although there had been no announcement at all.

At Bethesda, the hours dragged on while in the morgue the doctors continued their autopsy. At midnight, the embalming hadn't even begun. George Thomas was sent to the White House to bring Jack's favorite suits and ties.

Ken O'Donnell had been bothered by the thought that Jackie's wedding ring would be buried with her husband. It didn't seem right, and when he suggested that he get it back for her, she agreed. Dr. Burkley worked the ring free, and insisted on giving it to Jackie personally. Deeply moved, Jackie gave him a red rose— one of two which Dr. Burkley had rescued from the bouquet she had carried, and which he had given to her back in Dallas. "This is the greatest treasure of my life," he said.

It was late. People began leaving, over the protests of both Jackie and Bobby who felt in desperate need of companionship. Jackie invited her mother and Uncle Hughdie to stay with her at the White House. But they couldn't leave until Jack was ready, and that would take several more hours. There was a final decision to be made that night. Would Jack's coffin be open or closed? His face was unblemished; an undertaker's cosmetician had already touched it up. Both Bobby and McNamara felt that the public would want an open casket, yet Jackie rebelled against this. "I want the coffin closed so badly," she insisted.

"It can't be done," they told her.

"I don't care. It's the most awful, morbid thing," she said adamantly. "They have to remember Jack alive." In the end, Jackie's wishes prevailed, and during and after the funeral, no one in the press and few in the public at large objected.

At the White House, a volunteer corps of friends and associates of Jack's had assembled to help decorate the East Room for the semipublic services the next day. William Walton was in charge; helping out were a couple of dozen people ranging from Arthur Schlesinger and Sargent Shriver to six White House butlers and the man who had trained the late president's dogs.

Actually, Lincoln's funeral was a poor model, occurring as it did at the height of Victorian sentimentality and the American tendency to overdo. Walton decided that restraint was in order; instead of swathing the chandeliers entirely, he opted for swags of black crepe. Louis Arata, the White House upholsterer, luckily had a good supply on hand and knew where to get more. The catafalque, a replica of Lincoln's, arrived without any decoration at all. Walton ordered it masked with magnolia leaves cut from the trees Andrew Jackson had planted around the White House. Lincoln's funeral had been graced with a crucifix, an odd item for a free-thinking President in a then predominantly Protestant country. But it was entirely appropriate for Jack, and after rejecting several crucifixes offered by various funeral homes and churches, Walton settled on an austere Benedictine cross from Sargent Shriver's home.

A guard of honor was roused from the nearby Marine barracks to await the president's body on its final arrival at the White House. It was 5 A.M., and at long last the president's body was ready: dressed in a blue-gray suit, reposing in a new, flag-draped mahogany casket, which replaced the one from Dallas which had been damaged in transit. In a hearse from Gawler's Funeral Home, Jackie and Bobby accompanied Jack's body on the drive to the White House.

Along the route, working people, mostly black men and women on their way to work on the early shift, lined the streets. And when Jackie looked behind her, she saw that a long procession of automobiles had assembled behind them, following the hearse in tribute to her husband.

The "casket team" from Arlington took the coffin from the hearse and bore it into the East Room. Godfrey McHugh laid a bunch of flowers against the casket and the men and women who had done the decoration slipped away silently, leaving Jack's family to their grief. Jackie knelt beside the American flag and buried her face in the Stars and Stripes. Then she left, leaving

Bobby Kennedy alone with Godfrey McHugh and Gawler, the funeral director. They opened the casket and Bobby looked on his brother's face.

He called the others in, one by one: McNamara, Schlesinger, Nancy Tuckerman, Bill Walton, and the rest. He asked them whether the casket should be open for the lying-in-state, or not. The consensus was that while Jack's face looked presentable enough, it was too made-up, too waxen. "It is appalling," said Schlesinger. "You musn't keep it open, it has no resemblance to the president," said Walton.

Jackie said, after seeing his face the next day, "It wasn't Jack, it was like something you would see at Madame Toussaud's." The casket remained closed—not because, as *Time* magazine gratuitously put it, "the president had been deeply disfigured," but because of the artificiality of his appearance and the growing feeling encouraged by the book, *The American Way of Death*, that open caskets were morbid and in bad taste.

Tributes had begun to flow in. Andre Malraux cabled Jackie from France, *"Nous pensons a vous et nous sommes si tristes . . .";* and Richard Nixon, Jack's opponent in 1960 and a man who admired Jack intensely, wrote a gentle note speaking of the role of fate in making the two men enemies. Echoing Kennedy's own *Ich bin ein Berliner* address, an unknown Englishman wrote in the American Embassy in London, "With the death of President Kennedy, every man in the Free World is a Kennedy."

It was nearly daylight before Jackie stumbled into Provi's arms. She had gone for nearly twenty-four hours without a moment's sleep—a powerful sedative administered at Bethesda hadn't even slowed her down. Now she was ready for a bath and rest. Dr. John Walsh gave her an injection of a half gram of Amytal, enough to knock out a pro football player. Jackie was out for perhaps an hour, when she woke and asked Provi for some orange juice. Then she fell back into unconsciousness for another two hours.

A private Mass for family and close friends was scheduled for the family dining room at 10 A.M. Jackie entered in her only black dress—the one she had worn when Jack had announced his candidacy for the presidency, and at John-John's christening. Instantly she saw that the little room was too crowded for the Mass to be conducted in anything approaching dignity, and insisted that the portable altar be moved to the East Room where Jack lay. It was a deeply emotional and intensely personal time, the last time when those who had known and loved Jack for himself, and not as a public figure, would have him to themselves. After this, he became the possession of all the American people.

Caroline sat at Jackie's side, restless and perplexed at first, then gradually grasping her mother's grief and need. Toward the end of the service, Caroline took Jackie's left hand in her right hand, and gave it an encouraging pat.

Afterward, Jackie stood at the main door of the East Room, shaking hands with the parting guests, thanking them, and giving each a few affectionate words. Later, she and the chief White House usher made a slow tour of the mansion, stopping briefly at the newly decorated presidential office where staff members were already packing up Jack's things. "Mr. West," she asked softly, "will you be my friend for life?" The normally correct Mr. West was unable to respond.

A long stream of invited guests began calling at the White House as soon as the family had left the East Room. Television cameras recorded their arrivals, which seemed like a parade of all the power, wisdom, and vitality of the world. They included former Presidents Dwight Eisenhower and Harry Truman; dying Senator Clair Engle of California came in a wheelchair; and an incongruous contingent of Southern governors, including Ross Barnett—many of them men who had opposed Jack Kennedy with all the might at their command. The Supreme Court Justices came, and Barry Goldwater—who had differed vehemently from Jack politically but who had been warmed by his vital personality, and who had valued his friendship. Late in the day, the men and women who admired Jack most of all came to pay their respects: the Washington press corps, who had relished his wit and enthusiasm even as they criticized his lack of hard accomplishment. Bobby Kennedy returned, wearing dark glasses to hide his swollen eyes.

Meanwhile, Jackie sat in her bedroom upstairs overlooking the Rose Garden. She covered pages of paper with doodles, notes to herself, addresses and phone numbers, and the names of people she wished to contact personally. She was keeping her mind busy with the here-and-now—good therapy for a newly widowed young woman who could not sleep.

And as is to be expected of Jackie, she was preoccupied with what to wear. Black stockings, of course; Mary Gallagher was sent to buy some from Garfinckel's department store. Jackie wanted an old-fashioned mourning veil, the kind that covers the entire head. Mary gave the stockings to Provi and mentioned that she would shop for the veil, but Provi, according to Mrs. Gallagher's book, said that there was no need as Jackie already had two that she had evidently forgotten about. Provi showed Mary two long black mantillas, saying that Jackie would decide later in the day which one to wear. Mary, still skeptical, checked back with Jackie. A mantilla —usually a lacy, frivolous affair and not at all the sort of thing to wear to an American funeral —was not what Jackie wanted. William Manchester says that a "White House seamstress" had to make a proper veil; Mary Gallagher says that Lucinda Morman, who was indeed the White House seamstress, borrowed one from Rose Kennedy.

There was a question of music. Recalling Jack's delight with the Black Watch pipers, she asked if they could be persuaded to play *Hail to the Chief*—which had originated as a Scottish ballad tune. She was persuaded that American listeners might take it amiss, and the idea was scrapped. She wanted a Navy chorus to sing during the funeral Mass, but the church insisted on using its own choir. Even a chorus composed of entirely Catholic midshipmen was unacceptable.

Jackie Chooses Church

There remained the question of where the Mass was to be held. The diocese of Washington was immensely proud of its romanesque Shrine of the Immaculate Conception, which seated 2,500. Jackie detested the name, had never attended a service there, and was generally apathetic to the idea. St. Matthew's Cathedral was close to the White House, and though it was nowhere near as grand as the costly Shrine, it was what she and Jack had come to think of as their own church in Washington.

Bobby Kennedy later recalled, "The priests insisted on Immaculate Conception, but she was very insistent about St. Matthew's." He told Jackie, "I think it's too small. It only seats eleven hundred."

Jackie didn't care whether the mourners stood in the streets, and said so. "I just know that's the right place to have it," she said.

Besides, she had another reason. She had decided to follow her husband's casket on foot, not "in a fat black Cadillac," and the Shrine was too far away to walk there from the White House. At first everyone was appalled at the suggestion. Angier Duke instantly pictured a nightmarish tangle in which diplomatic ranks and protocol would be forgotten. The Secret Service and FBI shuddered at the impossibility of protecting all those foreign heads of state, when, after all, Jack himself had just been gunned down on a street in a supposedly civilized city. Bobby Kennedy was worried about the number of aging and infirm dignitaries who would have to walk farther in a few minutes than they might otherwise walk in a normal week.

Jackie's idea may have had its roots in the French Catholic custom, in which the mourners traditionally follow the casket on foot. Or maybe it was because she knew that similar processions had honored Washington, Lincoln, Grant, and Theodore Roosevelt. She did not know that the Joint Chiefs of Staff—in fact, nearly all the military planners—were in agreement with her. It is a time-honored military custom to march behind the caisson of a fallen Commander-in-Chief.

She capitulated a little. Instead of making the entire journey on foot, she would let them drive her all the way except for the stretch between the White House and St. Matthew's. Those who could not make it on foot would be driven to the church in advance. "Nobody has to walk but me," she said, but she would walk, alone if necessary. "What if it rains?" they asked her. "I'll walk anyway," she said.

The big question of the burial site was settled that afternoon. The Kennedys and the "Irish Mafia" all felt that any site outside of Massachusetts was unthinkable. They would have settled for Boston Common. But Jackie had an effective ally in Secretary of Defense McNamara, who felt the president ought to be buried on federal property. The national cemetery at Arlington fell within his domain, and early Saturday morning he went there and inspected it for possible appropriate sites. After the Mass, he took Bobby, Jean Smith, Pat Lawford, and Bill Walton to Arlington. Despite the dismal rain (which ruined Bill Walton's last dark suit and forced him to wear tan gabardine to the rest of the ceremonies), all the visitors were surprised and pleased with the site. Bill Walton found a spot fittingly located right on the line connecting the magnificent Custis-Lee Mansion at the top of the hill with the Lincoln Memorial across the river. When they returned to the White House, Jean Smith, who had anticipated that Arlington would be a grim and dreary place, greeted Jackie with, "Oh, Jackie, we've found the most wonderful place!"

Later, they took Jackie out to Arlington, and, in her words, "We went out and walked to that hill and of course you knew that was where it should be." Bill Walton drove a tent stake to mark the spot.

Meanwhile, Lee and Stas Radziwill were flying over from London. The captain of their plane came into the passenger compartment and sat down with Stas. "I understand that your wife is Mrs. Kennedy's sister," he said, then commenced to weep. The Radziwills arrived late that afternoon and someone in the White House remarked to Lee that it was nice of her to come.

"How can you say that?" she said. "Do you think I wouldn't have?"

Others were on their way, or making plans to come. At first, the State Department issued directives to its overseas envoys to discourage foreign dignitaries from attending. Besides the security problems, the protocol-sensitive diplomats felt that the presence of some heads of state might embarrass those of others. Confrontations and contretemps would be likely. But the outpouring of popular sentiment overseas was too much to ignore. Charles de Gaulle had had differences with Kennedy, had been told not to try to come, and originally planned to remain in Paris. But apparently his people were mourning for Kennedy like one of their own, and he changed his mind. "They are crying all over France," he told a friend. "It is as though he were a Frenchman." Eamon De Valera, president of Ireland, was coming. Queen Elizabeth was awaiting the birth of a child and could not attend, but she sent Prince Philip as her personal envoy. Ludwig Erhard of West Germany had been planning to come Monday for a State visit. His plans were unaltered, but in a tragic new context. In all, eight heads of state, ten prime ministers, and nearly all the surviving royalty in the world made their way to Washington.

That night, while Jackie remained alone, there was a family dinner for twelve in the private dining room at the White House. The atmosphere was desperately lighthearted—at one point someone snatched Ethel's wig from her head and plopped it on the pate of the balding McNamara. Jack would have enjoyed that bit of horseplay. But as if suddenly reminded of him the guests returned to a serious mood, more in harmony with their real feelings. One by one they slipped into the silent East Room to say, as Mary McGrory had said earlier that day, "Good night, sweet Prince."

The rain had ceased during the night, and there was sunlight to brighten Sunday's procession from the White House to the Capitol. During the last moments that Jack's body remained in the East Room, Jackie instructed Caroline and John-John to "write a letter to Daddy and tell him how much you love him." With a ballpoint pen on blue stationery, Caroline wrote a simple note in her best first-grade printing. John-John's was only a scribble but it was heartfelt.

Jackie and Bobby went down to the East Room where the casket was opened for them. She placed her own letter and those of the children inside, and with them a pair of gold cuff links she had once given Jack and which he had prized, and a piece of ancient whale tooth scrimshawed with the presidential seal. This had been another present she had given to him—it had remained on his desk all his thousand days in the White House. Bobby put a silver rosary in Jack's hands, then took off his PT-109 tiepin and put in inside the casket.

Mary Gallagher and Dr. Walsh saw Jackie as she left the East Room, and both worried about her ability to keep on. "I had never seen her look worse," said Dr. Walsh.

At 11:47 Central Time that morning, Jack Ruby shot Lee Harvey Oswald while the president's alleged assassin was being transferred to another prison. Millions of television viewers watched, horrified, as the nondescript little man whipped out a gun and killed Oswald before the television cameras. But to those deeply immersed in their grief over Jack's death, the news was almost irrelevant, or, at most, anticlimactic.

The nation had thought that with the sudden bloody loss of its leader, there could be no worse wound. Sunday morning taught them that there were indeed wounds more grievous, and slower to heal. Lee Harvey Oswald allegedly had killed a president; Jack Ruby killed something in America's sense of itself.

Even as pandemonium reigned in the Dallas Police Headquarters, Jackie and her children stepped sorrowfully but serenely out of the North Portico and watched as Jack's casket was placed on the gun carriage for its long last journey to the Capitol. Behind it walked a Navy seaman, carrying the presidential standard which was to follow the caisson through the ceremonies to come. And then the terrible sound of muffled drums began.

Instead of the traditional honor guard of military men, the thirty-six aides who had been closest to Jack, lined up on the east steps of the Capitol, including Dave Powers, Arthur Schlesinger, Dr. Jerome Weisner, and Ted Sorensen.

At Jackie's side was Bobby Kennedy, staunch

and strong in bearing, inwardly tortured by his own feelings. They and the children rode in a limousine with President and Mrs. Johnson, behind the procession. Members of the family followed in other cars and behind them all was an anonymous mass of plain citizens who had quietly broken through police lines to follow the dead president. There were, by some estimates, a hundred thousand of them—mostly young people.

When the casket arrived at the Capitol, a twenty-one gun salute was fired, the guns sounding every five seconds, and the Navy band played ruffles and flourishes, then "Hail to the Chief"— not in the rousing march time normally associated with it, but as a dirge, and then the Navy Hymn. It is practically impossible to hear these slow strains without recalling the events of November 1963.

Within the Rotunda, the original Lincoln catafalque had been set up, and the pallbearers set the almost unbearably heavy casket down. The numerous floral offerings were massed in areas away from the Rotunda—their sight was too depressing and their fragrance too overbearing for the bereaved family to contend with.

Speaker of the House John McCormack spoke first, in his gritty Boston accent, an echo of Jack's own. Chief Justice Earl Warren denounced hatemongering and violence. Some thought his remarks inappropriate, others felt he said things that needed to be said. Mike Mansfield, majority leader of the Senate, delivered a controversial masterpiece which, in the impossible acoustics of the Rotunda, went largely unheard. Frankly emotional, it was a tribute to Jackie as well as to her slain husband and there were those who thought it needlessly cruel. Jackie thought it magnificent. "It was the one thing that said what had happened," she said later, and afterward, she was thrilled when the Montana Senator walked over to her and gave her the manuscript of his speech.

The new president walked forward to the catafalque to present his huge wreath, then stepped back. John-John, too little to be expected to behave at so solemn an occasion, had been taken off by Miss Shaw but Caroline remained with her mother. The two advanced to the casket, Jackie explaining, "We're going to say good-bye to Daddy, and we're going to kiss him good-bye, and tell Daddy how much we love him and how much we'll always miss him." Caroline watched her mother, imitating her movements, and, with closed eyes, they leaned forward to kiss the flag. Caroline's tiny, white-gloved hand moved beneath the flag to touch the casket itself. When they turned to leave, the faces of the Joint Chiefs of Staff were wet with tears.

Plans and preparations continued. After the initial shock of the assassination, people had begun to rally spiritually, and like the friends, relatives, and colleagues of the slain president, everyone suddenly wanted to "do something." Arthur Schlesinger, Jr., said later, "I had never understood the function of a funeral before. Now I realized that it is to keep people from going to pieces."

Well-meaning mourners, and that included the majority of the population of the country, all wanted to pitch in somehow. Tish Baldridge flew in from her new job in Chicago to plan an elaborate floral bower for the grave site, which was never used, and to recruit the fife and drum corps of the Virginia Old Guard to play during the funeral procession. Tenor Luigi Vena, who had sung at the Kennedy's wedding, flew in to sing at Jack's funeral—and innocently included in his suggested repertoire *When Irish Eyes Are Smiling* and *Anchors Aweigh*. The Army Engineers, with their usual hydraulic preoccupation, thought a little artificial waterfall would look nice beside the president's grave and offered to build one. Jackie mentioned that the Irish Army had a special rifle drill which was performed in honor of fallen warriors. Someone phoned the Irish Ambassador, who was delighted to have something to do, and promptly arranged for a squad of Irish cadets to be flown over to drill for Jack Kennedy.

Those handling the arrangements, who decided what was to be included and what was not, began to get the feeling that "a kind of lunacy" was beginning to take over. Bill Walton, in the end, was the man who decided such questions of taste and the fitness of things, responsible only to Jackie and Bobby, who were the final arbiters.

After calling the three eulogists to thank them, Jackie consulted with Ethel concerning the Mass Card to be given to those attending the funeral Mass. Ethel suggested some traditional prayers to be printed on it, but Jackie swept them aside. "I'm not going to be pleading with God to take Jack's soul to heaven!" she exclaimed. Then she sketched what she wanted —a black-bordered card bearing the words, "Dear God, please take care of your servant John Fitzgerald Kennedy" on the back. The cards were printed overnight on a press belonging to the CIA (to the astonishment of many in the government who didn't know that the spies *had* a press).

Eternal Flame—Too Showy?

"And there's going to be an eternal flame," said Jackie, who later explained, "the thing just came into my head," and noted that everyone else was "rather horrified." To many, it seemed too showy and ostentatious, and besides, wasn't there an eternal flame at the Tomb of the Unknown Soldier? Checking revealed that there was not—a common misconception, perhaps confusing the eternal flames at Gettysburg and at the tomb of the French Unknown Soldier in the *Arc de Triomphe*. Reluctantly at first, the staff set about obtaining a gas-fueled flame that could burn perpetually, which could be lit by Jackie after the funeral.

Funerals mean, inevitably, flowers. In this regard, Jackie meant to exercise the same tasteful restraint she had used after her father's funeral. "Jack loved flowers, and that's why he hated the way flowers are used at most funerals," said Jackie to Bunny Mellon, who was in charge of the floral department. Jackie went on to describe those "awful purple wreaths and gold ribbons all around, looking like Harlem or Coney Island." The only flowers Jackie wanted at the grave itself were to be picked from the Rose Garden Jack had loved, and arranged in a simple wicker basket. That night, in the dark, Bunny cut a few white roses, hawthorn branches, chrysanthemums, and blue salvias, arranged them in a small basket and, at Jackie's suggestion, tucked in a little personal note to the dead president.

At the end of the long day, Jackie, Lee, and Bobby had supper together in the sitting room; Rose Kennedy and Stas Radziwill dined by themselves; and the rest of the Kennedys ate in the family dining room with the house guests, including Robert McNamara, Phyllis Dillon, and Aristotle Socrates Onassis. According to Manchester: "They badgered him unmercifully about his yacht and his Man of Mystery aura." Bobby came down later and drew up an imposing document saying that Onassis would give half his incalculable wealth to help the poor of Latin America. "It was preposterous (and obviously unenforceable) and the Greek millionnaire signed it in Greek," Manchester recounts. It has been impossible to ascertain just whose idea it was that Onassis should be a guest at the White House at this time—it might even have been that the accommodating Stas Radziwill and his wife had brought him along.

After dinner, various members of the family went to the Capitol again. They were amazed and profoundly moved to see the sidewalks swollen with crowds of people who had come to pay their last respects to Jack. In all, it is estimated that 250,000 people filed past his casket. The Capitol was originally scheduled to be open until 9:00, but the mourners kept coming, and it was decided to keep it open all night. Rich and powerful waited patiently in line with the poor and humble. Pierre Salinger's 15-year-old son waited fourteen hours; members of Jack's PT-109 crew went to the end of the line voluntarily; and aging boxing champ Jersey Joe Walcott waited eight hours in the cold night. They were a subdued multitude, gentle and polite with each other. There was no pushing or impatience. Sometimes they sang, songs of the freedom rides like *We Shall Overcome* and *Last Night I Had the Strangest Dream*. A German lad sang *"Ich hatt' ein Kameraden"*—a student song about a fallen comrade—and some seamen sang, "He's Gone to Be a Sailor in the Navy of the Lord." Columnist Mary McGrory sat beside a kid with a guitar and they sang, *Won't You Come Home, Bill Bailey?*—which had been Jack Kennedy's favorite song.

Jackie was given another injection of Amytal to get her through the night. Meanwhile, the mourners continued to file silently through the Rotunda, while, throughout Washington, lights burned all night as hundreds of men and women worked on the final preparations for the most elaborate State funeral the nation had ever held.

Cardinal Cushing began a discussion with the Papal Delegate which, in the Cardinal's words, developed into "a hassle." As a Catholic head of state, Jack was entitled to five absolutions at his funeral, and that—said the Delegate—was what he ought to get. Cardinal Cushing at last told him sharply, "If there are going to be five absolutions, you'll have to say them yourself. I won't do it because they'll last twice as long as the Mass itself. In the popular parlance, this family has had it!"

The cream of the FBI and the CIA was checking out St. Matthew's. Many of the foreign dignitaries—understandably nervous about U.S. security—had brought their own agents, and the place swarmed with Scotland Yard and *Surete* men, as well as Japanese and Germans. Oddly, no Russians were in evidence.

At Arlington, the team of casket bearers was performing a bizarre ritual. Fearful of the delicate task of trundling the heavy coffin down the Capitol steps, they had loaded an empty Army coffin with sandbags and were practicing carrying it up and down a flight of stone steps. There must be no mishaps with Jack's casket tomorrow.

At the French Embassy, where there had been threats on de Gaulle's life, locks were checked on the doors and windows.

In the morning, by 10 A.M., the Cabinet, the Congressional leaders, the White House staff, personal friends of the dead president, and prime ministers, heads of state, and the majority of the surviving royalty of the world gathered at the White House. It was, mercifully, a perfect day.

Every one of the distinguished mourners wanted to make the short walk with Jackie—including, to the utter dismay of the U.S. security men, the new president. Anonymous threats had increased. But Lyndon Johnson angrily told his military aide, who tried to talk him out of it, "You damned bastards are trying to take over. If I listen to you I'll be led to stupid, indecent decisions. I'm going to walk." Bobby's life had also been threatened, but he told CIA head John McCone, "Talk to someone else." Chief Justice Earl Warren, object of much vituperative scorn from segregationists, simply refused to listen to talk about safety. Charles de Gaulle's answer to the suave Angier Duke, who suggested that "it would be a courtesy to Mrs. Kennedy if he would not endanger his life," was a Gallic "Pfft!" Irish President Eamon De Valera, blind, and in his eighties, also insisted on walking, though his son had to be at his side to guide the old statesman, with a hypodermic syringe in his pocket in case the exertion should be too much. They all felt that if Jackie could pay this last homage to Jack, they could, too.

The family went to the Capitol in limousines, where the casket was brought down and buckled to the caisson. The Marine Band began a slow march, and the various elements of the long sad parade fell in. When the caisson arrived at the White House, Jackie and the family disembarked from the cars to begin the walk to St. Matthew's. Jackie nodded to de Gaulle, and saw him "sort of nodding and bowing his head, his face just stricken." The Black Watch pipers began a shrill, keening march, and for a moment Jackie felt close to tears again. Then with Bobby on her left and Ted on her right, she began her slow last walk behind her husband. Maybe she remembered that contrary to etiquette for everybody else, the president's wife always walks behind her husband.

The London Evening Standard wrote, afterward, that "Jackie [had given] the American people from this day on the one thing they [had] always lacked—majesty."

Behind the three chief mourners came Jamie Auchincloss, Sargent Shriver, and Steve Smith. Five yards behind them were President and Mrs. Johnson (surrounded by a convoy of agents), and behind them, a limousine bearing Caroline, John-John, and Miss Shaw. Then came the foreign delegation, twelve abreast, in sixteen ragged rows. Interspersed among them were various armed escorts, their minds not on the solemn proceedings but on the life-or-death task of protecting the men and women to whom they were assigned. First Deputy Secretary of the U.S.S.R., Anastas Mikoyan, was completely obscured by them, as were the Kennedy sisters, and the Radziwills.

Behind the foreign dignitaries came the Supreme Court Justices and the Cabinet, in firm straight lines, then the presidential assistants, Kennedy's personal friends, and the White House servants. "What friends he had," wrote McGeorge Bundy later, "and how much they cared."

At the cathedral, Cardinal Cushing stood on

the steps in his red and black vestments, a tall white miter on his head. "He looked . . . so *enormous*," Jackie remembered. He kissed her, then, breaking his own rules about the separation of Church and State, allowed her to kneel and kiss his ring. It was a perfectly proper gesture for a Catholic, but not, the Cardinal generally felt, for a First Lady in public. But this was an awesomely different occasion.

At this stage, Angier Duke's marvelously detailed preparations began to break down. For one thing, in gauging the seating capacity of St. Matthew's he had forgotten to allow for the fact that most of those present would be wearing the heavy overcoats which they had worn for the cold walk to the cathedral. In addition, some of the royal visitors were wearing ceremonial swords, which took up even more room. Duke jammed the dignitaries into pews, urging them again and again to move over and make room for another in the row.

John-John—"Where's My Daddy?"

The Low Mass was brief and simple, and Cardinal Cushing, with his voice roughened to a harsh rasp by asthma and emphysema, was intent on making it easy for the Kennedy family he loved so dearly. To some listeners, he seemed to hurry through the ritual—if this were so, there were plenty of good reasons. John-John asked, "Where's my Daddy?" and had to be taken out by an agent. Rose Kennedy was near collapse. Jackie found it all unbearably full of reminders of happier times that could never be repeated. She began to cry uncontrollably, her one real loss of composure in public. "There was everything going," she said. Agent Clint Hill, sitting behind her, gave her his handkerchief, and compassionate TV cameramen concentrated on the Cardinal. At Ethel and Bobby's request, Communion was offered; only the family and some friends participated. Then Auxiliary Bishop Philip Hannan, a churchman Jack had admired, read some of Jack's favorite Bible passages, and an abridged version of his classic Inaugural Address.

Suddenly, the old Cardinal burst into English, his aching voice full of the anguish the mourners and the watchers felt themselves. "May the angels, dear Jack, lead you into Paradise. May the martyrs receive you at your coming. May the spirit of God embrace you, and mayest thou, with all those who made the supreme sacrifice of dying for others, receive eternal rest and peace. Amen."

He hadn't planned it—later he compared it to "an inspiration, like Pope John calling the Ecumenical Council. . . . Suddenly, I wanted the human touch." Lady Bird Johnson later recalled, "It wasn't just a ceremony anymore. He was saying good-bye to a man."

The casket team brought the casket down the aisle, and through the doors. The band played *Hail to the Chief* for the last time for John F. Kennedy. The agent brought the restless, bewildered John-John back to Jackie as she stood with

Caroline on the steps. Keeping the little boy under control was a problem and to distract him momentarily, at least, Jackie bent and told him, "John, you can salute Daddy now and say goodbye to him." In the past, John-John liked to pretend he was a soldier for his father, and liked to give Jack a childish imitation of a military salute. It had been a source of affectionate amusement to Jack; as Jackie described it, John-John's little-boy efforts at saluting had been "sort of droopy." But that day—perhaps because he had seen so much solemnly precise saluting going on all around him that weekend —John-John's arm was smartly bent at just the right angle, his shoulders square, his chubby chin tucked neatly in. His salute to his dead father would have done credit to a West Pointer. Watching him, Cardinal Cushing remembered, "Oh God, I almost died."

An overzealous White House aide commandeered the first limousines for Jack's staff, thereby upsetting Angier Duke's carefully correct transportation arrangements for the hundreds of people who had jammed St. Matthew's. It was every man for himself after that; even heads of state were reduced to hitchhikers. Former President Dwight Eisenhower—who had, after all, planned the Normandy Invasion—had prudently brought his own car and driver, which he had already arranged to share with former President Harry Truman. Their old feuds buried, the two elder statesmen rode off together to Arlington, behind the coffin of a man young enough to be the son of either of them. After the funeral,

Truman invited Eisenhower to Blair House for a drink.

The trip across the Potomac to Arlington took over an hour and a half. Waiting there were a squad of riflemen, the Irish drill cadets, a group of pipers from the U.S. Air Force, a platoon from each branch of the armed services, and many spectators, including one who had to be brought down from a dogwood tree by MPs. Fifty jets flew overhead as the casket approached the gravesite, then as it was lowered onto the metal frame over the grave itself, Col. James Swindal, pilot of Air Force One, flew the big jet over the crowd of mourners in final graceful tribute to the man it had carried so many miles. Air Force observers called it the most exquisite maneuver they had seen. The Irish drill cadets, rifle butts reversed, went through their precise drill and marched off to a cadence counted in Gaelic.

Cardinal Cushing stepped forward, and, once more improvising brilliantly out of love for the man he was burying, conducted the prayers in English. "Oh God, through Whose mercy the souls of the faithful find rest, be pleased to bless this grave and . . . the body we bury herein, that of our beloved Jack Kennedy, the thirty-fifth President of the United States, that his soul may rejoice in Thee with all the saints, through Christ the Lord. Amen." Other prayers and blessings in English followed, then the mourners joined him in the Lord's Prayer. He sprinkled Holy Water on the coffin, then stepped back while the rifle squad fired a final salute. A baby in the crowd began to wail, and there was a curious rightness to the sound at that moment.

The Bugle Sobs

Then the Arlington bugler, Sergeant Keith Clark, began to sound taps, pointing the bell of his horn at Jackie. It was his feeling that, at funerals, the bugler should play only for the widow. On the sixth note of the calm, familiar melody which he had played daily at Arlington for four years, Sgt. Clark's clear tone broke, like a sob. Like the baby's cry moments before, like Cardinal Cushing's spontaneous prayers in English, like John-John's salute and Caroline's small hand on her father's coffin, that broken note seemed to have a place in this incredible sequence of events. It was, a reporter wrote, as if the trumpeter's lip had trembled for all humanity.

The trumpeter's trembling lip on the final strain of taps was neither an emotional reflex or a flubbed note. He was following tradition. The phrase is intended to be broken when taps is sounded for a general who has been killed in action. As Commander-in-Chief of the Armed Forces, John Kennedy's death at an assassin's hand had to be equated with death on the battlefield. Kennedy historians generally overlook this explanation of the faltering note.

PART FOUR

CHAPTER ELEVEN
Transition in Washington

As Jackie saw it, her responsibilities to the nation Jack had led ended at his grave in Arlington. But she had chosen of her own free will to carry on a little longer, by receiving the foreign emissaries at the White House. Simultaneously, President Johnson held a reception of his own at the State Department.

Buffets were set up in the dining rooms, and members of the Kennedy family set up an informal receiving line while Jackie went to her room, removed her long black veil and the black beret she had worn all day, and combed her hair. She had told Bobby that she would like to speak privately to four of the foreign guests—Prince Philip, De Valera, de Gaulle, and Emperor Haile Selassie.

She received the Emperor in her Oval Study, she spoke in French as the Emperor's English was limited, and she brought John-John and

Caroline to see the friend who had visited the White House the previous summer.

"Look, John," she said, pointing to the rows of decorations on the Emperor's chest, "he's such a brave soldier. That's why he has all those medals." John gingerly touched one. Then he and Caroline ran off to bring back the ivory toys he had given them on his last visit. They spoke no French, and the Emperor did not try to communicate with them in English, but, as Jackie said, "He had this thing of love, and they showed him their little presents."

The next person she saw was de Gaulle, and, as befitted the austere Frenchman, she made the conversation more formal. She brought him to a couch, and sat beside him, talking about "this French, American, English thing." Everyone, she noted, was becoming bitter over the differences between the three countries, "Everyone except Jack." Then she led him out into the hall saying, "Come. Let me show you where your beautiful commode is," and showed him the beautiful antique French chest which he had sent her and Jack. She drew a flower from a bouquet of daisies on it and gave it to him. "I want you to take this as a last remembrance of the president." The stern old warrior went downstairs with her flower in his hand, and after Jackie's exercise in personal diplomacy, it doesn't seem peculiar in the least that he was seen chatting later with Prince Philip over a cup of tea.

Bobby Kennedy brought Eamon De Valera upstairs to Jackie, and stayed for their brief, highly emotional meeting. They talked of Mrs. De Valera, whom Jack had met on his visit to Ireland and whom he liked, and of Irish places, legends, and poetry. It was too much for all three—the old man was weeping, Bobby could not maintain his gallant facade, and when the two left through the adjoining bedroom, Jackie, too, was sobbing.

She opened the door to the hall—only to find herself looking down on a nonplussed Prince Philip, who had been squatting on the floor with John-John, sharing a laugh. Jackie executed a swift curtsey, just as Angier Duke approached with Sir Alec Douglas-Home, Prime Minister of Great Britain. As the Duke of Edinburgh stood, he explained that John-John reminded him so much of his own son at that age that he couldn't resist abandoning protocol. "John, did you make your bow to the Prince?" she asked. "I did!" John cried triumphantly.

Angier Duke had seen Jackie make a curtsey to Prince Philip, and recalled the time she had asked him, when the Kennedys made their state visit to England, whether she was expected to curtsey to the queen. Duke had told her that the wife of a head of state never curtsies to anybody. When he asked her about her encounter with Prince Philip, she explained that she had bent her knee in a curtsey "because I'm not the wife of a head of state anymore."

Duke was anxious for Jackie to make an appearance downstairs, and asked Jackie whether she would prefer to mingle informally with the guests, or have a receiving line. Prince Philip came to her aid. "I'd advise you, you know, to have the line. It's really quick and it gets it done."

No one really expected Jackie to appear at all after the day she had been through. They were surprised and grateful when she did come down, and thoughtfully they passed through the line as quickly as possible. They paused only when Jackie had a special word for one or another of them, sometimes in their own language, sometimes through an interpreter.

To Ludwig Erhard she said, "You know, you and I were to have had dinner this very evening. I had ordered German wine and German music, and just now you and I would be getting dressed."

As Mikoyan, Deputy Premier of the Soviet Union, approached, it was evident that he was in a highly emotional state himself. Jackie could see that he was trembling and she reached for his hand. "Please tell Mr. Chairman President that I know he and my husband worked together for a peaceful world, and now he and you must carry on my husband's work." The interpreter translated, Mikoyan's eyes blinked back tears, and he stumbled away, his face in his hands.

When the last distinguished guest had passed through the line, Jackie rode upstairs in the elevator with Angier Duke. There was nothing left in her, and nothing left for him to say. He kissed her on the cheek and left her standing alone in the hall, weeping.

Meanwhile, Jackie was the principal subject of discussion at President Johnson's reception at the state department, where the foreign guests had made their way after greeting Jackie. Mikoyan, especially, was seeking people out and telling them about Jackie's words to him.

State Snubs Willy Brandt

Watching the State Department reception on television, Jackie learned that Willy Brandt, the dauntless mayor of West Berlin and a man Jack had admired greatly, was there. She hadn't seen him in the receiving line because, as the emissary of a city, he wasn't considered important enough for the State Department to send him through. But the day before, it had been announced that Brandt had renamed the square where Jack had told 150,000 West Berliners that he, too, was a Berliner. "I want to see him," she told Bobby, and a White House car was dispatched to fetch him. When Jackie and Bobby greeted him, he burst into tears.

After Brandt had left, the family and friends ate ham and chicken sandwiches, and Dave Powers told one funny story after another about his years with Jack and led the children in close-order drill up and down the long corridors. Life had to go on. And that day, tragically and ironically, was John's third birthday. He and Caroline sat together at a little table, with their family around them, and a cake with three candles was brought in. There were presents and ice cream, and the mood picked up. Jackie impulsively suggested they sing some of the songs Jack had liked. They sang *That Old Gang of Mine*, and then *Heart of My Heart*. It was an unbearable moment for Bobby, for these were songs the three brothers used to sing together, and he left the room quickly. But the others continued.

After everyone had gone home, Bobby Kennedy remained with Jackie asking her quietly, "Should we go visit our friend?"

It was nearly midnight. Jackie took some lilies of the valley from a bouquet, and they drove out to Arlington. A white picket fence had been erected around the new grave, the vault had been sealed, the grave filled in and covered with evergreen boughs. On top of them, a green beret of the Special Forces had been placed. The officer who had left it said, "He gave us the beret and we thought it fitting to give one back to him." A buff strap and Old Guard cockade had been left, and an MP had given his black and white Brassard. A heap of chaplets and other offerings, with bright ribbons, almost hid Bunny Mellon's tasteful little basket from view. The flame flickered in the wind. Bobby and Jackie knelt together and offered their prayers and, as she rose to go, Jackie put her bouquet on top of the grave.

CHAPTER TWELVE
"She Held The Nation Together"

Neither Jackie nor the nation could have anticipated the role she would play during the days immediately after Dallas. As Jackie moved through the drama of public ritual and private grief, she became the surrogate who acted out the feelings of millions. She gripped the public attention, and in their spellbound fascination with her, Americans discovered a balm for their souls. In Mary McGrory's felicitous phrase, "She held the nation together while she broke its heart."

If Jack Kennedy's sudden death had transformed him from an intriguing but largely unproven politician into a martyred hero, it had also transformed Jackie from a decorative but unnecessary public figure into a heroine worthy to be his widow. The word that journalists, and ordinary people, tended to use with reference to Jackie was "sublime." "She taught the world how to behave," said Charles de Gaulle, never an easy man to please, and that was one of the more restrained comments at the time. In show business parlance, Jackie's conduct that weekend was "a very tough act to follow."

After Dallas, of course, everything that followed was likely to be some kind of anticlimax. As David Brinkley of NBC observed: "The events of those days don't fit, you can't place them anywhere, they don't go in the intellectual luggage of our time. It was too big, too sudden, too overwhelming, and it meant too much."

The events that "meant too much" had stripped Jack Kennedy of all his human faults and enlarged him to superhuman size, and they had left the public with the idea that his widow was some kind of demi-goddess. And just as Lyndon Johnson found himself in the extraordinarily difficult position of having to govern a nation which kept comparing him to their idealized notions of his predecessor, so Jackie quickly discovered that she would always be measured against what people remembered she was like during the last days of November 1963.

The emotional emergency had driven her back to the most fundamental levels of feeling. She was, first of all, most deeply concerned with her children. Perhaps not the most enthusiastic or deeply committed mother in the normal course of things, she drew John-John and Caroline to her after Jack's death, and from them she took as much consolation as she gave. Similarly, she became closer to the Kennedys than she had ever been before, and her relationship with Bobby deepened into warm friendship. Jack's aides and friends rallied about her, and the attention and concern of the most brilliant and powerful men in the nation gave Jackie a different kind of reassurance; her own father was not alive to offer sympathy and support, so she had to rely on the substitute consolation of older men. In return, they had the satisfaction of knowing that they had helped in some small way the noble young woman whom they revered at least as much as everyone else.

Toward her employees, staff, and servants, Jackie was less noble, less consistent. But under the circumstances, they willingly put up with her difficult nature, her moods and blasts. Working long hours organizing and packing the Kennedy possessions was a form of therapy for everyone. For their own sake, as much as for Jackie's, they gave more than the last full measure of devotion to their tasks.

Toward the man who was now president, and toward his family, Jackie behaved, especially at first, with dignified and thoughtful courtesy. Johnson had sorely wanted to be president. But instead of winning the prize gloriously, as he'd hoped, he had felt it drop, tarnished and tainted, into his unwilling hands. Jackie sensed President Johnson's particular anguish, and Lady Bird's pain, and went out of her way to do what she could to make their lot easier. Jackie exercised her gift for the beautifully appropriate gesture toward those whom fate has handled roughly.

Although, as Jack's wife, she had no political power, and as his widow had not even an informal place in the government, Jackie realized that she could help smooth the transition of power. Whether she felt it was something she owed to Jack, or a favor to Lyndon Johnson in his unenviable position, or a harmless demonstration of her own importance at the moment, she was on hand in the East Room on the Monday after the funeral when President Johnson addressed a group of Latin American envoys, promising continued support for the Alliance for Progress. She wrote him encouraging notes and telephoned him several times, which he appreciated as much as her show of public support. But he was baffled and, no doubt, a little hurt that she persisted in calling him "Mr. President," and never Lyndon.

Wisely, Jackie kept herself busy. At first, of course, there was the welter of details concerning the funeral arrangements. Instead of letting up afterward, she pushed herself further. Though President Johnson had told her that she and the children could remain in the White House as long as she wished, Jackie understandably wanted to leave as soon as possible. For herself and the children, there were simply too many memories and associations. For the staff of the incoming Johnson household, and the outgoing Kennedy people, there was just not enough room to function without coming into occasional conflict. The nerves of all had been laid bare; Johnson's staff was tense and overzealous, while the Kennedy staff was exhausted, drained and hypersensitive. The quicker the new Administration was allowed to move in and set up, the quicker the wounds of all would heal. Thus, Jackie's first self-imposed goal was to leave the presidential mansion.

But first, Jackie and the children went off to the Cape for Thanksgiving with the Kennedy family, who focused all their attention and love upon them. Old feuds and irritations were forgotten as all the Kennedys drew closer together. From the Cape, Jackie telephoned President Johnson on Thanksgiving Day. It was an act which moved him deeply. "How could you possibly find that extra moment—that extra ounce of strength to call me Thanksgiving evening?" he wrote. "I only wish things could be different—that I didn't have to be here. . . . You have for now and for always our warm, warm love."

Meanwhile, the staff and servants at the White House worked through the long weekend. There was a kind of comfort in plain hard work during that bleak Thanksgiving. McGeorge Bundy assigned office space in the Executive Office Building for Jackie's use, and Mary Gallagher immediately began bundling Jackie's files and papers into her new headquarters next to Evelyn Lincoln's office. As she observed in her book, "There was no time for turkey or for tears."

It was probably during that weekend that Jackie decided to accept Mr. and Mrs. Averell Harriman's offer of the use of their house on N

Street, in Georgetown, until she made more definite long-term plans. The Harrimans moved into a hotel. When Jackie returned to the White House, the first immediate task was to transfer her personal things, and those of the children, into storage or to the Harriman house.

There was also the question of what to do with Jack's belongings. All his personal possessions and clothes were brought up to the third floor of the White House, put on racks and laid out on furniture. With Mary Gallagher, Jackie decided how to distribute personal mementos to Jack's closest aides and friends. His neckties were given to T.J. Reardon, Kenny O'Donnell, Larry O'Brien, Dave Powers, and Muggsy O'Leary. His cigar case went to Pierre Salinger. The famous rocking chair was a special gift from Jackie to Jack's loyal valet, George Thomas. She had a bronze plaque made for it with the inscription: *For George Thomas—The Rocking Chair of John Fitzgerald Kennedy—35th President of the United States. It was always in his bedroom—I knew he would want you to have it. JBK*

Unpredictable—Capricious

If Jackie was at times unpredictable and capricious in her distribution of Jack's effects, she can surely be forgiven. When Maud Shaw, the children's nurse, approached her directly and begged for some remembrance of the president —"like cuff links, or a tie clip that could be a keepsake"—she handed Miss Shaw one of Jack's shirts. And it was months before she thought to give Mary Gallagher anything at all, finally presenting her with a gold medal that the president had been awarded by B'nai B'rith.

"She wrote me not to forget him," said one of her correspondents during those days. "As though I could pass a single hour without remembering!" Perhaps, in her own shock and grief, Jackie underestimated the ability of the country to remember her husband. At any rate, she was determined to make sure that he had left his mark. From a truckload of priceless art from six New York galleries, she selected a painting to be donated to the White House in his name—a dreamy Monet of water lilies. And, most touchingly, she placed a plaque over the fireplace in the Lincoln bedroom which Jack had used. It read: *In this room lived John Fitzgerald Kennedy with his wife Jacqueline—during the two years, 10 months, and two days he was President of the United States—January 20, 1961 —November 22, 1963.*

On December 6, exactly eleven days after the assassination, Jackie and the children left the White House for the last time. For Lady Bird, she left a bouquet of lilies of the valley, and a tender note of encouragement.

At the Harriman house, Jackie at last gave way to the depression which she had been keeping at bay since Dallas. She seldom left her second-floor bedroom, leaving her correspondence to Mary Gallagher, the children to Maud Shaw, and the running of the house to the Harrimans' housekeeper. Two Navy men, on loan from the

Staff Mess at the White House, prepared the meals. Every day, John-John received a two-hour visit from Dave Powers, during which they told each other stories, played games, and acted out heroic adventures in which the little boy was always the hero, and the big Irishman was always the bumbling sidekick. Caroline continued in her school—which had been moved to the British Embassy—and both children spent a great deal of time visiting their cousins at Hickory Hill.

Jackie's first acts were, characteristically, kindly gestures of compassion. To Marie Tippitt, widow of Dallas police officer J.D. Tippitt, she sent a photograph of the Kennedy family inscribed: "There is another bond we share. We must remind our children all the time what brave men their fathers were."

She also wrote to Secretary of the Treasury Douglas Dillon, praising the Secret Service men who had guarded her family, and advising him that the president had always said that, before he left office, he was going to see that the highest possible recommendations were put into each man's file, with the suggestion that they be given opportunities to advance. She closed with the typically Jackie suggestion that they should all be made Ambassadors in the Diplomatic Service because they had always been so tactful. And it was at Jackie's insistence that Clint Hill, as well as Rufe Youngblood, received the Treasury Department award for bravery.

By this time, bales of letters and telegrams of sympathy and condolence had begun to arrive.

Over 800,000 eventually were delivered to Jackie, to whom the Congress assigned a secretarial staff to help handle them. Nancy Tuckerman and Pamela Turnure struggled to keep up with them, sorting them into file folders when the tide became too great to handle immediately. The fattest folder was that labeled "Especially Touching." The vast majority were sympathetic and sincere, but there were cruel exceptions. William Manchester cites a letter written to Jackie by a group of Dallas businessmen, upset by declining out-of-state trade and begging her to sign a testimonial to Dallas hospitality. Manchester says, "She passed it along to Robert Kennedy, who managed to forget what he did with it."

Jackie's sure social instincts told her that a public statement from her was in order, and she went on nationwide television from Bobby's office at the Justice Department to thank those who had sent condolences and to promise them that they would all be answered in time. "The knowledge of the affection in which my husband was held by all of you has sustained me, and the warmth of these tributes is something that I shall never forget," she said. "Whenever I can bear to, I read them. All his bright light gone from the world." She announced that these letters would be placed with Jack's papers in the Kennedy Library, to be erected in Boston.

There began the flood of requests to name and rename things after the late President. It may have begun with Jackie's request to Lyndon Johnson to rename Cape Canaveral, the Florida rocket center which everyone had trouble pronouncing, anyway, after Jack. Then the international airport at Idlewild, New York, was renamed John F. Kennedy Airport; Congress renamed the National Cultural Center the John F. Kennedy Center for the Performing Arts; and so on, right down to the Tobay Wildlife Center in Oyster Bay, N.Y., renamed the John F. Kennedy Memorial Wildlife Sanctuary. Canada named an unclimbed mountain after him, and his brother Bobby would be a member of the first expedition to scale it.

Dealing with these public matters could not possibly occupy enough of Jackie's time or emotional energy. It was a desperately unhappy period of her life. She told Mme. Nicole Alphand, wife of the French ambassador, that she felt like "a wounded animal. What I really wanted to do is crawl into a corner and hide."

But hiding was out of the question. Life had to go on, and while Jackie was deeply grateful for the Harrimans' understanding and generosity in lending her their house, she realized that she must begin to create some kind of life for herself and her children. She wasn't ready to make a drastic move, though quite possibly the idea of moving to Europe or perhaps back to Newport crossed her mind. But the welfare of her children was uppermost in her mind, and she knew that too many dramatic changes in their lives all at once would be bad for them. Growing up without their father would be difficult for them, but if they were in touch with his friends, such as Dave Powers, and their vigorous young uncles,

Ted and Bobby, they would be able to keep his memory alive. And their lives would include some healthy masculine influence. Jackie decided, for the time being, anyway, to remain in Washington, and she bought the fawn-colored house of the James McMillan Gibsons, across the street from the Harriman house, at 3017 N Street. The price was $175,000.

The prospect of moving into a new home and the excitement of decorating it revived Jackie's spirits a little. She hired fashionable decorator William Baldwin to come down from New York to do the interiors. Both her sister, Lee, and her sister-in-law Pat, decided to remain in Washington to be near her through the winter.

The children's lives had continued with as few changes as possible. Caroline had gone back to school the morning after the funeral, and her teacher had wisely plunged the class into preparations for a Christmas program, with a Nativity play, carols, and Bible readings. Both children busied themselves, under Maud Shaw's guidance, with Christmas shopping, and with making lists for Santa.

Jackie, Lee, and the children spent that Christmas with the Kennedys at Palm Beach, where a private Christmas Mass was held at the home of the Ambassador. During her holidays, Jackie came out of seclusion only once, to receive the Princess Lala Aicha of Morocco, sister of King Hassan of Morocco. They had entertained Jackie briefly during her Mediterranean cruise only two months before. The princess told Jackie of the king's gift to Jackie—a 100-year-old house in Marrakesh. It took a large van and a small truck to carry all the presents that Jackie and the children had been given.

The Kennedys returned to N Street on Monday, January 6, and it was then that Jackie had her first taste of what life was going to be like as Jack's widow. There were 400 spectators lining the sidewalks as she hurried into the house on Ted Kennedy's arm.

January was a busy month for Jackie, since there were other matters in addition to the new house. A special memorial Mass was held on January 18th in Boston. With Bobby Kennedy on a trip to Southeast Asia, Jackie flew up aboard the *Caroline* to join Rose Kennedy at the ceremony.

At about the same time, Bobby and Ted jointly announced that the Joseph P. Kennedy, Jr. Foundation was donating one million dollars toward the establishment of the John F. Kennedy Library, to be built on land given by Harvard University, for the purpose of giving "future generations insight into the issues, mood, and accomplishments of John F. Kennedy's life." Eugene Black, the retired head of the World Bank, was chairman of the library's board of trustees. By act of Congress, the National Cultural Center was renamed the John F. Kennedy Center for the Performing Arts, with Jackie as honorary chairperson. While Jackie's role in these activities was to be indirect, she knew that the weight of her name would help with fundraising activities, and she was interested in helping.

But for the most part Jackie kept to herself, so much that she probably was less aware than anyone else of the great proprietary interest that was being taken in her. During the funeral, those involved in it had been too numbed by grief and too absorbed in their tasks to realize the size of the audience which had sat in on the national tragedy. "It was weeks before they realized that for every spectator in the District that Monday, a hundred others had been watching in the fifty states, and it was months before the implications of this sank in," wrote Manchester. Two months later, the sidewalks outside the Harriman house were still crowded with well-wishers and those simply curious, wanting a glimpse of Jackie or the children.

In her first weeks of widowhood, Jackie did not notice this, or if she did, perhaps the implications were lost on her. But they finally did sink in toward the end of January, when for the first time since her return from Dallas she was persuaded to make a small step toward a normal life. Jackie and her sister Lee dined very quietly in a fashionable Georgetown restaurant with movie producer George Englund and actor Marlon Brando. When the story broke, certain elements in the press chided Jackie for gallavanting about in public with movie stars so soon after Jack's death. Brando, trying to be gallant, denied that he had so much as seen Jackie, and insisted that he was in Washington for the sole purpose of doing some research on a documentary about the American Indian. But, unluckily, a photographer had snapped a picture of the group in the restaurant, and in the end Pamela Turnure had to confirm that Brando, a close friend of the Kennedy family, had indeed dined with Jackie.

Crack In Flawless Image

This incident was a tempest in a teapot, most people said. The common-sense reaction was that if anything could help Jackie learn to smile again, she was certainly entitled to it. The incident was quickly forgotten, but it was the first hairline crack in the flawless image of Jackie which the public had come to cherish—even though it was only the product of its own over-zealous imagination.

Jackie had let it be known that she would observe a year's mourning for her husband. This custom used to be strictly formalized, to the point where widows were expected to wear either all-black or all-white ensembles for deepest mourning, and the addition of a black handbag to a white dress, or a white belt to a black one meant a transition to the less formal "second mourning" stage, but in modern times the custom has become much less rigid. Emily Post wrote in 1957, "Most of us merely do the best we can to continue to keep occupied, to make the necessary adjustments as best we can, and to avoid casting the shadow of our own sadness upon others." In other words, even the doyenne of Western etiquette would allow that in Jackie's case, as with any other widow, mourning could mean just about what she wanted it to. As a rule, a widow does not attend balls or formal social affairs, or take a leading part in purely social activities, but this is a matter of her personal preference and her own style of adjusting to life. Nowhere is there any prescription for the way the widow of a president ought to dress or conduct herself.

And yet, simply because Jackie *was* the widow of a president, the public felt that she was, in a sense, their property. In countries with monarchies where the taxpayers foot the bill for the royal family, there is, perhaps, something to be said for this attitude. But as a self-sufficient, independently wealthy young woman, Jackie could hardly be said to owe anything to the nation.

For a long time, there were no photographs of Jack anywhere in sight in Jackie's new house. Photo albums and folders of unmounted snapshots were left stored in boxes, pushed out of sight. Jackie knew that one day she would have to deal with them, but it took a long time for her to gather her courage to unpack them. Then one day she asked Mary Gallagher to stay with her while she went through some of the material on Jack. "It's so much easier doing it while you're here, than at night when I'm alone," Mary Gallagher quoted Jackie as saying.

During this period, the house was quiet and lonely. In the morning, during Dave Powers' daily visits with John-John, there was laughter and romping, but the rest of the time Jackie cut herself off from all but her staff, family, and most intimate friends. There were few guests, no parties, and reporters were strictly forbidden. This understandable need for privacy only served to whet the appetite of the sensational press and its patrons. News photographers hovered outside, attracting knots of onlookers while they waited in hope of a picture of Jackie or the children. After one enterprising photographer snapped a photo of Jackie through a window, she kept the curtains drawn. She was particularly protective of her children, and made it a practice to take them to the seclusion of the house at Atoka on weekends. Much of their time on weekdays was passed at Hickory Hill with the children of Bobby and Ethel.

This time marked the intensified friction between Jackie and her personal secretary, Mary Gallagher. This led, in time, to Mary's leaving Jackie and may have contributed to the bitchy tone of her book, *My Life with Jacqueline Kennedy*. According to the book, Jackie had originally suggested that Mary arrange to be paid out of Jackie's $50,000 appropriation granted her by Congress. Mary put in for $12,000 a year, a not–too–exorbitant figure for a professional secretary willing to work more than full-time for Jackie. But Jackie felt this was too much, what with all her other expenses, and the matter wasn't resolved until Jackie moved to New York later in the year and dispensed with Mary's services entirely.

To say the least, Jackie was not at her best during her stay in the house on N Street, and it is perfectly understandable. It is a lot easier to rise nobly to an emergency, as Jackie did after Jack's death, than it is to make the transition to a new life. Personal problems she may have had with Jack, little remembered slights and disappointments she may have harbored, possible deep-seated guilt she may have had for remaining alive when he was dead—these are all things that any bereaved human being must work through. It is never an easy, nor a happy process; it requires vast amounts of psychic energy, and it distracts one's attention from one's living friends and associates. But it is psychologically necessary to go through the valley of the shadow of one's own sorrow. While it is hard on family and associates, it is infinitely more painful for oneself. Jackie may not have been easy to get on with during this time, but it was surely not any easier for her.

Political bigwigs attended the wedding reception of Senator John Kennedy. Here, Speaker of the House Joseph Martin congratulates JFK and his bride.

Wily Joseph Kennedy and his wife, Rose, on election night, 1960. A dream comes true! His son, John F. Kennedy, has been elected President. Jackie will be the First Lady.

Harry Truman had reservations about "that Kennedy boy," but returned to the White House as a guest of the Kennedys after eight years of being snubbed by Eisenhower.

Jackie Kennedy was definitely not the girl next door! As First Lady, she lived an extension of her years as a socialite—fox hunting was one of her many activities.

Jackie proved both a decorative and diplomatically effective
First Lady when, on a trip to France with JFK, she charmed
irascible Charles de Gaulle. Paris adored her.

Jackie was always warmly received in England by Queen Elizabeth. With children Caroline and John-John, she attends unveiling of memorial to President John F. Kennedy.

Jackie Kennedy at an audience with Pope John XXIII. Many believed the meeting was arranged to enlist John's help in annulling the first marriage of her sister, Lee.

Dallas was the Queen City on JFK's Texas trip to shore up support in the '64 election. Jackie and the President were radiant just minutes before the fatal shots rang out.

Aristotle Onassis wandered in and out of Jackie's life long before their marriage. The Greek millionaire had the knack of being there in her crises when Jackie needed him most.

Robert Kennedy and Jackie, at the funeral of President Kennedy. Five years later, the Kennedys would lose Robert to an assassin's bullet; Jackie would lose a good friend.

In spite of sibling rivalry, Jackie and sister Lee Radziwell have remained firm friends over the years. They're seen here on a sunny day while visiting London.

A rare public photo – Jackie jogging in Central Park.

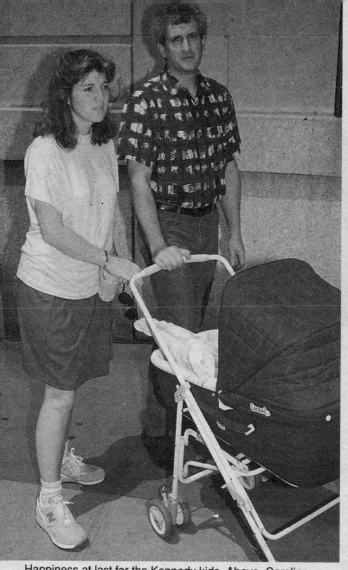

Happiness at last for the Kennedy kids. Above, Caroline Kennedy and husband Ed Schlossberg take their daughter Rose for a stroll in Manhattan.

John Jr. earned himself a reputation for being a ladies' man in the image of his father. Before his current girlfriend Daryl Hannah, he spent time with such beauties as Christina Haag, pictured above.

At 60, Jackie was still the toast of the town, as evidenced in this shot taken with Donald and Ivana Trump (and an unidentified man).

Despite the loss of two husbands, Jackie likes to have a man in her life. Here she is pictured with Maurice Tempelsman at a New York Public Library function.

A charming shot of young Jackie with her mother Janet at the Easthampton Fair on Long Island in 1935. Jackie was deeply affected by the loss of her mother to Alzheimer's disease in 1989.

CHAPTER THIRTEEN
National Monument at 34

In addition to facing these difficulties, which are the sad heritage of every widow, Jackie was beset by further problems which had no precedent. If—as she had said less than three years before—it was awful to lose your anonymity at the age of thirty-one, it was even worse to be transformed into a national monument at the age of thirty-four. Every action of Jackie's was reported, photographed, and analyzed. The incident of her dinner with Marlon Brando was only a foreshadowing. On St. Patrick's Day she left shamrocks on Jack's grave, and when word got around that the cemetery had planted them there, they were beseiged with requests for transplants. Solemn pilgrims from all over the country and the world, made their way to the grave at Arlington, and their thoughts and prayers were much appreciated by Jackie and the Kennedy family. But too many of them, meaning no harm, then made their next stop the sidewalk in front of the N Street house. The rudest stood for hours across the street, gawking and snapping pictures, and the most insensitive of them interrupted guests and official visitors on their way in or out of the door. Sightseeing buses were routed past her house, which had become another of the capitol's Points of Interest.

It wasn't only common people and tourists who sought Jackie out, praised her, sent her gifts, and tried to honor her in every way: the famous and powerful admired her just as much. A staggering variety of tributes were accorded her. She was made a life member of the National Geographical Society. A congresswoman proposed that Jackie become the next Ambassador to France. She was almost smothered in the flags which were sent to her in commemoration of the long weekend of mourning—Speaker McCormack along gave her six of those which had flown at half-staff over the Capitol in Jack's memory. Poet Archibald MacLeish was asked to write a dedication for the new Kennedy Center for the Performing Arts, but, another victim of the national crush on Jackie, he wrote a poem about her instead. "Jacqueline Kennedy, wife of the thirty-fifth President of the United States, who shared the ardor of his life and the moment of his death and made the darkest days the American people have known for a hundred years the deepest revelation of their inward strength," he wrote.

On what would have been Jack's forty-seventh birthday, she took Caroline and John-John to St.

Matthew's, but the throng of tourists on Rhode Island Avenue turned what should have been a solemn, private ceremony into an ordeal. The pulp fan magazines had discovered her, finding that Jackie's face on the cover was a more potent sales booster than that of Debbie Reynolds or even Liz Taylor. Compared to the cover lines today, those of the spring of 1964 seem remarkably tasteful. But they were enough to make Jackie keep her children away from newsstands. Pierre Salinger tried to intercede with the press, but his arguments weren't as persuasive as circulation figures.

This was the beginning of Jackie's much-discussed love-hate relationship with the press. On the one hand, their admiration for her was more than enough to please even the most immodest ego. On the other, their intrusive insensitivity was enough to disgust even those who were not particular friends or partisans of Jackie's. To Jackie herself, it has been a continuing and ever-growing source of anger and frustration. She may have asked herself just how much the American public demanded from her. Public life had taken much of Jack's time and attention away from her, and in the end it had taken his life. Now it appeared that the insatiable public wanted to dictate how she should act, and rob her of all privacy as well.

If Jackie had been born and bred a Kennedy herself, she might have taken it all in stride and perhaps even relished it. But she was raised as an aristocrat, not as a competitor. She was never meant to struggle—and it's doubtful that anyone could have struggled successfully against the wave of sentiment that was rapidly becoming known as the Kennedy Cult. She never wanted to be part of it, and she never knew quite how to handle it when it seemed to drown her in well-meaning but ill-considered public interest.

Politically, Jackie was a nonentity, but she was a nonentity with the biggest constituency of any American public figure since perhaps George Washington. In the weeks and months immediately following the assassination, before President Johnson was able to establish his own style and pace in the White House, Jackie was, if not the nation's leader, at least its focus of national allegiance. Johnson was a shadowy figure, wisely maintaining a low silhouette during his first months in office. Jackie, on the other hand, was an object of almost universal admiration. In an election, she might very well have beaten any professional politican the nation had to offer in the first months of 1964, including the incumbent president, Lyndon Johnson.

Johnson, a proud, vain, and sensitive man, who liked politics enough to keep his personal wounds concealed and his feelings under iron control, was probably more aware of this than Jackie ever was. Knowing that Jackie had no political ambitions at all, but nonetheless commanded enormous potential political clout, must have rankled in President Johnson's mind. Still he strove to be friendly with Jackie out of genuine affection and Southern chivalry—and perhaps out of good old Texas political savvy.

A Hyannis Port stringer for a news service

reported that Jackie was thinking of attending the 1964 Democratic National Convention, with the intention of stampeding the delegates into nominating Bobby Kennedy for the vice-presidential spot on the ticket. Anyone who knew Jackie even slightly ought to have perceived the absurdity of the tale, but normally astute editors permitted the story to go out on the wire. And when it was reported in the White House, it was taken with deadly seriousness, according to William Manchester.

Living under such intense and constant scrutiny was sheer hell for Jackie in her emotionally lacerated state. More and more she found it necessary to escape from Washington. In February, she spent a weekend at John Hay Whitney's Georgia plantation, with Mr. and Mrs. J. E. Sheffield, of South Carolina and New York, and with Lord and Lady Harlech and their daughter, Alice. As the British Ambassador to the U.S., Lord Harlech, then known as Sir David Ormsby-Gore, had been a good friend of Jack's. Later that year, Lady Harlech was to die tragically, and Jackie was to see Lord Harlech socially, often enough to give rise to rumors of marriage. But at this point, marriage was the furthest thing from Jackie's mind. What she wanted was privacy and some semblance of a normal life for herself and her children.

She took them to see the circus at the Coliseum in Washington, and John-John returned with a tiny turtle in a box. She visited friends in New York occasionally through the spring, and in late April took the children there for a week to attend the World's Fair. She planned to spend the summer in Hyannis Port. It was becoming evident to Jackie and to everyone around her that it wasn't possible to lead the kind of life she wanted in Washington.

Her troubles with her staff increased. The two Navy stewards, on loan from the White House, complained that their irregular hours were interfering with their studies for Navy examinations, and might interfere with their promotions. They had every other day off during the week, but never had two days in a row to spend with their families. Jackie was astonished at their complaints. "Well, what do they want? Do they want to go to Texas and work for the Johnsons from six in the morning till six at night?" she said to Mary Gallagher.

Over at the Executive Office Building, the devoted Evelyn Lincoln was performing her last duties for her late chief, sorting his papers and preparing the JFK Traveling Exhibit. She was one of the few people in the world with the ability, and the patience, to decipher Jack's notes and jottings. But the submerged resentment which most wives feel toward their husbands' secretaries was beginning to surface in Jackie—she became more and more critical of Evelyn's work, demanding to know just what it was that she *did* all day, anyway. A visit to the office brought it all to a head. There Jackie found that Evelyn had filled the spacious office with mementos of Jack, including a rocking chair, a PT-109 model, and enough photos of Jack and his family to cover the walls. As if it weren't enough to find Jack's old secretary laboring in this shrine to his memory, there was even a phonograph constantly playing Jack's favorite songs. For Jackie, it was all a bit much. "But these things are all mine!" she burst out, and told Evelyn what she was to do with them, instead of doling out mementos as she pleased.

At the end of May, Jackie went to New York where the JFK Traveling Exhibit was to open, in order to raise funds for the Kennedy Library. Then she planned to go to the cape for Memorial Day weekend, and asked Mary Gallagher to send one maid and two kitchen boys. The White House declined to let her have the Navy stewards, and Jackie had to hire her own help. After a fund-raising dinner in New York, Jackie went back to Hyannis Port for the summer, and Maud Shaw brought the children up from Washington.

Instead of returning to Washington at the end of the summer, Jackie moved to the Carlyle Hotel in New York, and then bought a $200,000 apartment at 1040 Fifth Avenue, overlooking Central Park. Her years in Washington were over, and her reign as America's Pop Princess was about to begin.

New Life in New York

Remaining for those months in Washington probably helped Jackie to work herself free of the shock and grief that had dominated her life since Patrick's death the year before, and Jack's assassination in November. It may have helped her to come to terms with the new realities of her life in Washington, and undoubtedly it was a sound decision so far as the children were concerned.

But having worked through her feelings and accepted the facts of her new life as Jack's widow, she found that staying on in Washington was impossible because she needed to set out on a life of her own now. Though she made much of her need for privacy and the obtrusiveness of the tourists, her decision to transplant herself and the children to New York was prompted just as much by a wish to start fresh.

They stayed briefly at the Carlyle Hotel, the Kennedys' favorite resting place in New York, until her fifteen-room apartment was ready. She enrolled Caroline in the city's most fashionable Catholic girls' school, the Convent of the Sacred Heart, and put John (no longer called John-John) into the equally fashionable St. David's school for boys.

Once again, with the help of Billy Baldwin, she decorated her fifteen-room co-op apartment with great originality and charm. The sunny living room was done in orange tones, its walls hung with drawings and paintings by the children and by Jackie herself. The windows were curtained to permit the best view of Central Park. Outside, on the terrace, crab-apple trees grew in square tubs painted turquoise. Her apartment had no dining room—guests for dinner sat at a table which was normally in a corner, covered by a floor-length suede cloth. Jackie's bedroom, its walls covered in raw silk in her favorite shade of off-white, was accented with shades of pink and bright green.

Jackie at first lived very quietly, and while New Yorkers are normally blasé about even the most notable celebrities in the world, they did turn their heads and gape when they saw the former First Lady and her children bicycling in the park. For the most part, however, they respected her need for privacy during her first year in the city. When at last she permitted herself to be photographed, during groundbreaking ceremonies for the Whitney Museum of Modern Art, the public was pleased that she looked like her old self again, in a black and white outfit with a fashionably short skirt.

To accommodate her horses and to give the children a place to enjoy country life, she rented an estate in Peapack, N.J., and joined an exclusive northern New Jersey hunt club. At 400 Park Avenue, she set up offices for Nancy and Pat to work in.

But quite obviously, she considered herself a private individual once again. Though she was ineligible to vote in the 1964 presidential election as a resident of Manhattan, she was still registered in Boston, and could easily have gone there to cast her vote—presumably for Lyndon Johnson. There were those who criticized her for not doing so. She did not attend Lyndon Johnson's inaugural, either, which drew further criticism, although not from the president himself.

The apartment was close to many of the people she loved best. Over at United Nations

Plaza, the Robert Kennedys had an apartment; her Aunt Maude lived in the same area, as did her stepbrother, and the Radziwills maintained an apartment close by.

She took a cruise on the Adriatic aboard the yacht of the Charles Wrightsmans—old friends —and was criticized for that. In Jackie's honor, President Johnson renamed the White House Rose Garden, which Jackie and Bunny Mellon had designed and which Jack had been so proud of, but Jackie did not attend the ceremonies. Though disappointed, the Johnsons understood, though there were others who did not.

Jackie once remarked, "If you bungle raising your children, I don't think whatever else you do well matters very much." After Jack's death, she began spending more and more time with her children, although she still left much of the day-to-day routine to a governess. She chose their schools with care, and while Jackie never involved herself in Parents' Committees, and seldom even allowed her name to be used on fund-raising letterheads for the schools, she did take an increasing interest in the children's homework.

Like Jackie herself, the children became celebrities, and fashion bell-wethers, before they were ready for long division. Their impeccable matching light-blue Harris tweed coats, with velvet collars, had become heartbreakingly familiar to television viewers of their father's funeral; John's little blunt-toed red shoes and Caroline's black velvet mourning hairband were familiar details, and now the details of their entire lives and their most informal wardrobes became matters of great public interest.

There was John's long English-style haircut, which mothers liked because it looked distinguished, because John wore it, and which kids surprisingly liked, too, because it reminded them of the Beatles. Crewcuts began to look like the stigma of middle-class nonchic to mothers with pretensions, and ordinary barbers across the country were suddenly asked to cut little boys' hair the way the barbers at the Carlyle did John's. Rowes of Bond Street, which has tailored the clothes of young members of the British Royal Family for a century, made many of John's garments, and Caroline's, as well.

Jackie took the children to museums, to Phebe's Whamburger on Madison Avenue, and to Rumplemayer's and Schraffts' for ice cream treats. They visited, quite frequently at first, Hyannis Port and Palm Beach to romp with their Kennedy cousins.

But she also began doing a little traveling herself; to Spain, to visit the Duke and Duchess of Alba and to wear a Spanish costume as she rode horseback in the procession at the Seville Fair; to Rome to visit the Spanish Ambassador to the Holy See and to have another private audience with the Pope; and to Cambodia to inspect the fabled ruins of Angkor Wat and be the guest of Prince Sihanouk. She was seen at the opera, the ballet, and the theater, with some of the most talented and distinguished men of our time— John Kenneth Galbraith, Leonard Bernstein, Alan Jay Lerner, Gian Carlo Menotti, George

Plimpton, Anthony Quinn, and, as Doris Lilly said, "I could go on and on."

Were they all actually beaux of Jackie's? Probably not. As a widow in a society where a woman is expected to be paraded on the arm of a man at least her social equal, Jackie discovered herself suddenly in the position of a single woman again. It would have been unseemly for her to be escorted by a Secret Service man to the brilliant galas and exclusive restaurants she fancied. And so Jackie developed the habit of asking gentlemen—often very properly married men —to escort her here and there. The men, of course, were generally thrilled at the prospect of being seen with the world's most admired woman, so chic and beautiful. Their wives, however, were sometimes less than pleased, particularly when it meant that they themselves had to stay home, or perhaps round up an escort of their own to the same event. One lady, rather irritated by Jackie, observed that "Jacqueline Kennedy borrows husbands the way other women borrow a cup of sugar!" She developed the habit of "inviting"—some people use the word "summoning"—the husbands of couples she knew to come to her apartment to have a little chat over a drink. She wouldn't ask the wives on these occasions and, again, the wives were disturbed. The men, however, were charmed by her wit and beauty, and that wispy voice that made you lean closer and closer to her so you could catch every well-chosen word.

"Men—single and married—were drawn to Jackie because they had an all-too-human weakness for who she was and what she had been through," a friend has been quoted as saying. "They were well aware that Jackie was a president's widow—and what a president! And don't think Jackie forgot for a second the historical role she'd played. But Jackie, like other women who exert such power, ended up feeling very patronizing to most men. She would only respect and marry one as powerful as she was and Onassis was one of the few who fit that description."

It is interesting to observe that both Jackie and Lee chose as their second husbands men who were much older and who had attained the kind of super-success in finance which Jack Bouvier had sought and failed to find. And both chose foreigners, as if rejecting the country which had treated them so ambiguously during their childhood.

"At least when you're with her, she's really with you and she makes you feel you matter to her," one of Jackie's male friends said recently. "Jackie doesn't look around the room trying to see who else is there. She zeros in on you with those wide-set eyes and listens to you with a shining, breathless intensity. She's no Mary McCarthy—she has islands of knowledge and puzzling dead spots—but she's talked to a lot of extraordinary people and she's remembered most of what they've told her."

Women sum this up tartly: "Jackie's an outrageous flirt!" "Jackie's an insincere flatterer!" Women, except perhaps for Lee, eventually get fed up with Jackie after long stretches of her company, but Jackie rarely spends much time with women anyway. She much prefers the company of men.

Plays Hide-And-Seek With Press

Jackie continued to go her own way, traveling, shopping, and playing hide-and-seek with the press. She never gave interviews, but did answer specific questions put to her through Nancy Tuckerman or Pamela Turnure. Sometimes she would allow a selected young photographer a shooting session, but she retained the right to approve individual photos. As for the working press, it had to take its chances catching her at the ballet or the theater. Like Garbo, Jackie's reluctance to seek publicity received a lot of publicity, and generated further interest in her.

Her sharp tongue, too, helped spread her fame. In 1966, a friend was talking about some mutual acquaintences with Jackie, and asked her if she had seen an interior decorator they both knew who was rather short. "Oh, yes," she said, "I did see him the other day. I almost stepped on him in the elevator." Imperious, accustomed to being obeyed without question, she was unbearably bossy with her friends at times, insisting they go where *she* wanted to, at her whim and convenience.

No one can tell just when she and Aristotle Onassis began to see each other regularly. Onassis, back again with Callas after the Lee Radziwill business, spent considerable time in

Europe and England as did Jackie. Onassis was well experienced in the arts of discretion, and could use them skillfully when he cared to. He knew well how to get publicity and attention, and, conversely, could cloak himself and his friends in utter secrecy when that suited him.

At any rate, something definitely was brewing between them as early as in 1968. This was the year that Bobby Kennedy began his own bid for the Democratic Presidential nomination, seeking to wrest it from the man who had succeeded his brother Jack. It was going to be an uphill fight, as Bobby was starting late, and supporters of anti-war spokesman Sen. Eugene McCarthy of Minnesota resented Bobby's joining the race. The Democratic establishment didn't much like him, either, of course—in Manchester's book, the extent of the friction between the two men was hinted at as early as 1963.

And just as Jack might have been glad, sometimes, that his wife's pregnancy kept her from participating much in the 1960 campaign, when her refined ways and her finishing-school education might have turned off earthy old pals, so Bobby was concerned, in 1968, about the effect Jackie might have on his own chances. The American people were ceasing to think of Jackie as a goddess, but they still felt she was some kind of widowed empress. If Jackie should ruin that helpful image with an unpopular marriage, it could dissipate some of the support for Bobby's bid, and Bobby, the underdog, needed all the help he could get. The fight meant a lot to him—in the years since Jack's death he had changed. Before, he had identified with Jack, believing that to elect his brother and keep him in power, just about any means were justified. After Bobby himself was elected senator from New York, with a largely black, Puerto Rican, and poor white constituency of his own, Bobby's political orientation changed. He grew weary of the unfulfilled promises of the federal government to the disadvantaged people of a rich country. On his own, for instance, he put together a high-powered group of businessmen and financiers to create a self-help program for Bedford-Stuyvesant, one of the worst ghetto areas in the nation. He supported United Farm Workers chief Cesar Chavez, long before the radical chic upper class of Manhattan stopped buying grapes. Bobby became his own man politically, and he began to care deeply, not about the power he could wield but the good it might do.

Probably no other motive would have been strong enough to overcome his wish to see Jackie happy again. As a devoutly religious man, and a bit of a moralist, he could scarcely have approved of Onassis—his antics with Onassis at the family dinner on the weekend of Jack's funeral were only half in jest. He probably wished he could have enforced Onassis' "pledge" to give all that money to the poor. Bobby was devoted to Jackie, and it probably grieved him to ask her to help with his campaign by postponing her marriage to Onassis until after the election. But Bobby had the temperament of a crusader, and, inwardly, he must have felt that ending the Vietnam war and mending the country's wounds at home were more important than Jackie's personal plans.

It is likely that Jackie would have listened to this sort of argument from no one but Bobby, and no one but Bobby could have made it stick.

In the spring of 1968, Jackie took a trip to Mexico, with Roswell Gilpatric, former Deputy Secretary of Defense and at that time a New York investment banker. Divorced three times, Gilpatric was a much older, distinguished, and attentive man, the sort Jackie has always been partial to. They traveled with a retinue to the Yucatan peninsula, where, says Gilpatric, "she wasn't content just to see the Mayan ruins by car in the daytime, as the average 20th-century tourist does. She also insisted on seeing them by moonlight on horseback, to get the feeling of the way it was the day before yesterday." On that trip, she threw herself into a pool near the ruins with all her clothes on, and cried for Gilpatric to do the same.

Rumors of a long-time romance between Jackie and Gilpatric were fanned once again — as they were to be brought to full inflammatory intensity after Jackie's marriage to Onassis when several personal letters she'd written to "dearest Ros" came to light.

When Jackie's friends are asked what they consider to have been her motives in marrying Onassis, the most usual answer is not, surprisingly, money, as it is "Bobby's death." It was a staggering loss to Jackie, who had come to depend on Bobby as a friend, confidant, and guide in a way that neither Jack nor her own father had been. His death left a total vacuum in her life, which made the masterful, wealthy, and powerful Onassis seem even more attractive than ever. To Onassis, Jackie was, most likely, the most precious specimen in his collection of celebrities. This list had, after all, included Sir Winston Churchill, Maria Callas, and Lee Radziwill. Like a lepidopterist collecting famous and beautiful people instead of butterflies, Onassis wanted the most glamorous species. And of her type, Jackie is unquestionably the prize. Onassis' defensiveness about his own origins, which were less humble than he perhaps feels that they were, probably led him to feel that some of Jackie's charisma might rub off on him, make him somehow more acceptable in the best circles. He didn't dream, and neither did Jackie, that precisely the opposite might occur.

CHAPTER FOURTEEN
Onassis Joins the Family

After Bobby's tragic and ironic death, Jackie and her sole surviving brother-in-law, Ted, cruised aboard the *Christina* in the Mediterranean. It was probably at this time that the final understandings between Jackie and Ari were reached. All three knew that the marriage would be controversial. Onassis was used to controversy, and Jackie felt herself above it all, but Ted, who had followed in the footsteps of two of the most intensely political men the country has ever produced, knew that this kind of controversy wasn't going to do him any good at all.

When Jackie returned to the U.S., she stopped in Boston to see the aging Cardinal Cushing. Cushing was well aware of what was going to take place—the word was out, and his phone was kept busy with calls from various members of the Kennedy family, friends of Jack's, and alumni of the New Frontier. The Cardinal later said, "They all wanted to stop all this from taking place—namely that Jack's widow, God rest him, would marry Aristotle Onassis."

Cushing was as devoted to Jackie as Bobby had been. He admired her grit and determination at the funeral, and her dedication to her fatherless children. But even without his great affection for her, the Cardinal honestly felt that this was a decision Jackie could alone make, and that the approval of outsiders was irrelevant. "I encouraged and helped her," he said later.

Onassis followed Jackie to New York, where they met often, dining at the Colony, eating Onassis' favorite spaghetti, or at Mykonos, a Greek restaurant. In September they went to Palm Beach, then to Hyannis Port, where Jackie introduced her husband-to-be to her former in-laws.

At that time, they planned to be married about Christmas, when Caroline and John were on vacation from school. Jackie knew, and had no doubt been told a thousand times by those attempting to dissuade her, that her marriage might hurt the democrats in the forthcoming presidential election. Hubert Humphrey was having trouble building campaign momentum, and Nixon was being successfully marketed all over the country. If Jackie married Onassis, she stood a good chance of contributing toward a Republican victory in November. Jackie, who likes to have enough time to plan things properly, at first thought the Christmas date would be fine.

Nobody is quite sure what happened to speed things up. A "completely knowledgeable source," probably one of Ted Kennedy's aides, leaked the news to the *Boston Herald-Traveler*. In a copyrighted story, the paper said that Jackie and Onassis "are making plans to be married within the next few weeks. At all events, it will take place before Christmas."

Momentarily, it drove the presidential campaign out of the public ken. Checking with Cardinal Cushing, the AP elicited not the expected "no comment" but that an official announcement "may be coming up tonight or tomorrow."

Richard Drayne, Ted Kennedy's spokesman, said, "We have no knowledge of Mrs. Kennedy's plans."

Nancy Tuckerman said, "All I know is that when this Lord Harlech thing was going on, Mrs. Kennedy said that if she ever did decide to get married the first thing she'd do would be tell the children and then she'd tell me to issue a statement. As far as I know, Mrs. Kennedy is not planning to get married."

Stephen Smith said, "I don't know anything about it. I can't confirm or deny it. If she were going to do it, Mrs. Kennedy's office would have a statement."

But in midafternoon, Janet Auchincloss revealed, through Nancy Tuckerman, "My daughter, Mrs. John F. Kennedy, is planning to marry Mr. Aristotle Onassis. The time and place have not been determined. I will have more information tomorrow."

As Jackie was to write to Ros Gilpatric later, "everything happened much more quickly than I'd planned." That very night she boarded an Olympic Airlines jet to Greece, accompanied by her children, her parents, her sisters-in-law—Jean Kennedy Smith and Pat Lawford—two governesses, and one Secret Service agent. The passengers originally scheduled to leave on that aircraft were "bumped" and forced to wait for another flight, an hour and a half later.

Meanwhile, Onassis told newsmen in Athens, "I can't say exactly when the wedding will be because I must first see and talk to her."

The plane carrying the wedding party landed at Andravida, in southern Greece, where Onassis had cleared all reporters and photographers from the field before the plane landed. They allowed one photo—Ari kissing Jackie modestly on the cheek—and then took off on another plane for the city of Acton, on the western coast of Greece. Not until then were the press admitted to the Andravida airport again, to learn what they could from the airline personnel who were, you recall, on Onassis' payroll. They were not particularly communicative.

Press Chase Speeded-up Wedding

All the press was able to learn at this point was that the wedding would be held on Sunday, October 20, on Onassis' very private island of Skorpios. Reporters dashed to the neighboring isle of Levkas, where they found to their immense chagrin that none of the inhabitants would take them to Skorpios. Onassis' island was ringed with patrol boats, from the Greek coast guard and from Onassis' personal navy, and military helicopters circled overhead. It was not an inviting prospect. Some reporters were lucky enough to acquire telescopes with which they scanned the island. The most they could see were painters and workmen refurbishing the island's tiny Greek Orthodox church, Caroline and John playing on the beach, and a couple of members of the wedding party swimming near the *Christina*. Reinforcements from the Greek army began arriving to bolster the secrecy. It pays to be on the right side of a ruling military junta.

Undaunted, a number of reporters acquired a powerful motor launch and ran the blockade of circling speedboats, reaching the dock where the *Christina* was moored. John Kennedy was riding in a mini-jeep, and the photographers reached for their cameras. The yacht's crewmen began shoving, and Achilleus Kapsambellis, head of Onassis' security force, waved a rock threateningly. A yacht crewman told the newsmen, "Unless you keep away we have orders to sink you!" It's not many weddings that are preceded with a possible naval battle.

The press corps refused to leave until Mrs. Kennedy came down the yacht's gangplank, and when she finally did—clad in white pants, a black turtleneck and, of course, Jackie-shades, she told them, "Telis and I are very happy." "Telis" is Onassis' jet-set nickname.

If the two principals in the wedding were happy, the Greeks themselves were in ecstasy. They were certain that with Jackie married to Onassis, Greece would regain much of the tourism which it had lost when the generals took over the government, ousting King Constantine. If the Acheans had managed to bring Helen back again from Troy, their joy might have been equal to that of the Greeks on their acquisition of Jackie.

The reception elsewhere was immediate, loud, and negative. "Lamentable, lamentable!" wailed the headlines in a Spanish newspaper. "He is foreign, he is old, he is indecently rich," scolded columnist Harriet Van Horne, "and he has the rough, dark looks of a Mafia villain on TV."

Onassis' liaison with Callas and his unsavory divorce were held against him, his shady business practices were once again aired, and the general reaction was first, "What could have possessed Jackie to do such a thing?" and, almost immediately, "Well, it must have been the money."

The consensus was that Jackie had somehow betrayed something. It was most often described as her duty to the memory of her husband, sometimes as her duty to her children, but these phrases were only masks for the truth—the American people felt that, somehow, Jackie owed something to them. It's a curious attitude, when you examine it coolly, because it would be hard to say exactly what America gave to Jackie to obligate her in this way.

She had grown up in considerable comfort, even during her mother's lean years as a divorcee, but though there were millions poorer than she in material things, there were some who were richer. Hers was not an "only in America" success story. When she was married to Jack Kennedy, he often spent time in public service, or seeking office within the American political system—while other husbands would have been able to spend time with their wives and families. And it was in the pursuit of his duties as president and as head of the Democratic party that he was killed at Jackie's side.

The nation had been her greatest, most powerful rival for Jack's attention and love, and in the end he had died pursuing that goal. In her steadfastness following his death, she had honored him, and through him, the nation. In return, the nation had given her boundless, unreasoning admiration, a heroine-worshipping fascination which soured whenever Jackie revealed a human frailty or made a public relations mistake. And which, ironically, Jackie had never sought or expected.

Jackie Mesmerized The World

Jackie had mesmerized the population of the world for the decade preceding the death of President Kennedy. She had become a glittering footnote to the events of our time. Beautiful, enigmatic, endlessly fascinating though she was, her influence had been limited—except in the fields of fashion, pop culture and the incomes of those who made a living by writing about her.

Aristotle Onassis, on the other hand, had profoundly influenced the lives of millions who had never known his name until he made Jacqueline Kennedy his bride. The immensely powerful men whose decisions shape our lives—they were the men who knew Onassis. This was a devious and slightly sinister factor that had to be taken into account. A man whose wealth alone was enough to make a king or break a nation and whose vast and intricate web of alliances, friends and men who owed him favors represented more potential raw power than heads of state cared to think about.

In considering Aristotle Socrates Onassis, the very first factor to recognize was money. Normally, a man's assets and income have little to do with the kind of human being he is. There are saints and scoundrels among the rich and the poor; human nature can't be rated by Dun and Bradstreet.

But as F. Scott Fitzgerald remarked, "The very rich are different from you and me." Ernest Hemingway growled the much-quoted reply, "Yeah, they have more money." He might have been talking about Onassis. With Onassis, money was what separated him from you and me and all but a handful of other men on this planet.

But you'd expect this of any man who found himself alone, friendless, and with about $60 to his name at the age of seventeen, and who went on to make his first million by the time he was twenty-five.

The additional millions he made afterward came a lot easier. Practice makes perfect.

At his death at an age estimated at between 69 and 75, there was just no way of calculating his wealth. He was certainly one of the richest men in the world, in a league with the House of Rothschild, the royal family of the Netherlands, and perhaps J. Paul Getty. Some analysts opined that Onassis was the richest. To most of us, comparisons at that level are meaningless.

But, as we have seen, money meant a great deal to Jackie. We have also seen that just as Jackie was drawn to the finest, most beautiful and rarest material objects, she also had an eye for quality in people. Cynics might say that in Jackie's scheme of things, quality equals money, but it isn't quite that simple. It is, of course, self-evident that Jackie prefers male companionship to female. And among men, she has a scale of values.

She prefers achievers. She is never attracted to second-raters. On this score, of course, her standards coincided precisely with those of the competitive Kennedys. It is important to Jackie that a man excel in his field, whatever it is. She has shown small patience with the idle, graceful rich boys who live on inherited wealth and let their talents lie fallow. She is drawn to men who can claim credit for accomplishments and initiative. Men like Jack Kennedy and Aristotle Onassis.

Which is not to say, of course, that money, independent of accomplishment, does not matter to her. Jackie is not one to starve beside an unsung genius in a garret. Her unsettled childhood, Jack Bouvier's failure as a father, and her education as a potential chatelaine for a well-to-do husband—all these influences made it impossible for Jackie to settle for a man of moderate means, or even to pay him much serious attention. She always recognized her need for a man who would take good care of her. Like Jack; like Onassis.

The little-girl need to be cherished in material ways had its parallel in Jackie's emotional constitution. The errant Jack Bouvier doomed Jackie to a lifelong quest for a loving, protective man she could depend upon. It's too simple—and too psychologically complex—to reduce it to the tired cliché, "She's just looking for a father figure." But in various ways it is striking to observe how many of the men close to her have been considerably older: Jack, Bobby, the elder Joe Kennedy, Gilpatrick and Onassis.

Money and accomplishment were not enough for Jackie, or it would have been simple for her to follow up on her own remark and "run off with Eddie Fisher." Or perhaps a Beatle.

No, Jackie's men had to be considerably older. There had to be a strong, indulgent presence to offer attention and support to the uncertain girl. Again, like both Jack and Onassis.

Finally, there's Jackie's sense of humor. That's an odd ingredient in a recipe for romance, but we mustn't lose sight of Jackie's impish side. Within the bounds of her intelligence and her breeding, she always delighted in the offbeat and the outrageous. If she had enjoyed a little more security in growing up, one suspects she would have taken great pleasure in creating a full-fledged scandal.

Marrying into the not-quite-there-yet Kennedy clan was in part, perhaps, Jackie's joke on her own upbringing. Probably she still enjoys a private giggle now and then, recalling that the ultra-eligible Jack was, after all, the grandson of a saloon-keeper. By comparison, her marriage to Onassis paralleled her marriage to Jack—on a grander scale.

PART FIVE

CHAPTER FIFTEEN
Emergence of Jackie O.

For two days, the Mediterranean sun smiled on Skorpios, the *Christina*, and the thwarted representatives of the world's press. If anything, Onassis' guards grew more adamant as time went on, and the strongest telephoto lenses could only catch a few grainy pictures of the wedding party, the island, and the yacht.

On Sunday, October 20, a huge pile of clouds moved in, heavy rains began falling, and the wind whipped up whitecaps on the placid Ionian Sea. The Greeks were again delighted—rain on a wedding day means prosperity, fertility, and good fortune.

Skilled, loyal Onassis sailors brought a thirty-two-year-old Greek Orthodox priest, the Rev. Polykarpos Athanassiou, chaplain of the University of Athens, to officiate at the ceremony.

Because the news media had threatened to

simply invade the island anyway if they were not allowed to cover the ceremonies, Onassis allowed them to form a pool for coverage. Perhaps he capitulated because he had begun to hear the feedback from the press around the world as editors, writers, and readers voiced their general horror at the thought of Jackie becoming Mrs. Onassis. Even so, the reporters were kept at bay on the flagged terrace before the church, and not permitted to go inside; the way was barred by a Secret Service agent, with a PT-109 tie clip.

The peasant women who had met the priest at the water's edge followed him up the hillside to the church, and remained outside in the rain, their faces shining with happiness. Greeks love weddings—it hardly matters who is getting married to whom.

Escorted by bodyguards, Onassis arrived in a double-breasted dark blue suit and a red tie. To reporters who knew the 5'8" Jackie, the sight of the diminutive, aging groom was almost ludicrous. He disappeared into the church to await his bride.

Meanwhile, more islanders had gathered along the walk from the dock to greet Jackie and her party as the *Christina's* launch brought them in from the yacht. They applauded as Jackie stepped onto the dock. She was smiling broadly, and the villagers applauded enthusiastically.

With Jackie were John and Caroline, Mr. and Mrs. Auchincloss, the Radziwills and their two children, and Pat Lawford and Jean Smith. They all walked up the path to the chapel, where the reporters were waiting. Jackie gave them a cheery "Hello!" and went inside.

Within were nearly all of Onassis' relatives—including his daughter, Christina, and his sister, Artemis—an assortment of business acquaintances, and the Managing Director of Olympic Airlines. Onassis himself appeared grim-faced and slightly troubled until his son, Alexander, slipped into his seat a moment just before the ceremony began. Then Onassis' face relaxed.

The Greek Orthodox marriage rite is complicated and full of mysticism, ancient tradition, and touching symbolism. Holding slim white candles, Jackie and Onassis stood before the priest in his golden robes at the altar, for the commencement of the ceremony. After a prayer, he put the rings on their right hands.

Onassis' sister was the "sponsor" of the wedding, and, according to custom, she exchanged the ring on Jackie's finger with that on Onassis'. The ceremony continued with prayers and ritual admonitions to the couple, and then two wreaths of white flowers, linked with a white satin ribbon, were placed on the heads of the couple. The Greek matron of honor, wife of the manager of Olympic Airlines, switched the two wreaths back and forth three times. A scripture reading followed, and the couple took a sip of wine from the same cup to symbolize their union. Then Father Polykarpos took Onassis' hand, Jackie took Ari's, and the three were led around the altar three times in what is called the Dance of Isaiah. After a final blessing, the guests threw rice, flowers, and sugared almonds at the newlyweds. The priest removed the wreaths from their heads, and the couple kissed. Caroline rushed up and kissed her mother, then Onassis; John kissed Jackie and shook hands with his new stepfather.

As the new Mrs. Onassis and her husband came out of the church, the soaked photographers and reporters crowded around them. "How do you feel?" someone asked Jackie. "We're very happy," she said breathlessly. "How do *you* feel?" somebody else asked Onassis, who frowned and said brusquely, "I feel very well, my boy."

Ari helped Jackie into a bright yellow golf cart, the children piled in behind them, and he drove down to the dock where the launch brought them to the reception aboard the *Christina*.

Champagne, of course, flowed like—well, like champagne at an Onassis party—and there was apparently limitless caviar in iced buckets. Roast suckling pig—a favorite dish of Onassis'—was the piece de resistance. A bouzouki band played nonstop, the toasts went 'round again and again, and the newly married couple danced together.

Every new marriage is beset by problems, as that of Jack Kennedy and Jacqueline Bouvier had been, and certainly that of Jackie and Onassis was no exception. Perhaps the most immediate problem was Jackie's children. And, for that matter, Ari's.

Caroline, who remembered her own father vividly, and who had been most upset after his death, was unhappiest of all. She did not like the prospect of a stepfather of any sort, and one who would take her mother away from her for long periods was the last thing she wanted. John, whose memories of his father were foggy, was more enthusiastic about his new life. Onassis showered both children with presents, which John delighted in, but which Caroline accepted with some wariness; being wary, perhaps, of Greeks bearing gifts.

Onassis' children, Christina and Alexander, were in their twenties, more independent, and more outspoken. Alexander, who had a girlfriend of his own, said, "I didn't need a stepmother, but my father needed a wife."

After the wedding, the press pulled out all stops—Jackie wasn't Mrs. Kennedy anymore, she was Mrs. Onassis, wife of that unpopular Greek shipowner, and no holds were barred. In France, where Jackie had scored such personal triumphs as First Lady, *Le Monde* moaned, "Jackie, whose staunch courage during John's funeral made such an impression, now chooses to shock by marrying a man who could be her father and whose career contradicts—rather strongly, to say the least—the liberal spirit that animated President Kennedy." It was typical.

Women's Wear Daily, the ultimate word in fashion and pop living, gave Onassis a nickname that will adhere to him for life: Daddy-O. (Jackie, no doubt retaliating, began her correspondence Jackie O.)

Maria Callas, in semiseclusion in Paris, said world-wearily, "First I lost my weight, then I lost my voice, now I've lost Onassis!" But perhaps there was a knowing smugness behind her feline smile. Late in November, less than a month after the wedding, Onassis stopped in Paris and took Callas to dinner. It was only the beginning of some utterly bizarre stories concerning Onassis and the women he had supposedly abandoned to marry Jackie.

Snoopy reporters from *Women's Wear Daily* discovered that he called on Maria at home shortly afterward, but she wouldn't unlock the door. The world then had to imagine the scene of Onassis, with Jackie's new wedding ring still bright upon his finger, standing outside Callas' house, yelling up at her closed window at some ungodly hour in the morning. The next day, lunching at the home of Baroness Van Zuylen, Onassis was read the riot act about the proper conduct of a new husband by his hostess. Onassis, it is reported, uttered a loud guffaw.

By January, gossips were saying that Callas had told Onassis off for the last time, blaming him for ruining her career at its peak. She received no settlement from her zillionnaire husband when their marriage split up; but then, at the time, she hardly needed one. Now, she said, she needed work in order to maintain her accustomed style of living. Insiders said that Onassis was still managing her finances, so presumably she needn't have worried. Still, she was quoted as saying, "I have erased him from my life, my heart, and my thoughts. He tried dangerously to ruin my career."

Callas' attempt to forget Onassis was more succesful than her efforts to get her career going again.

Judging by the kind of people involved, you could tell from the start that this was not to be any run-of-the-mill marriage. The two separated, geographically, only three days after the ceremony, with Ari going to Athens and Jackie to New York. Onassis had many business matters to attend to in Europe; Jackie busied herself with the JFK Memorial Mass in New York, and with flying to Virginia to see Ethel. After Onassis had flown briefly to New York (Jackie was not at the airport to meet him), the two flew, separately, to Greece for Christmas. In January, Jackie brought John and Caroline back to New York to resume school. She then zipped back to Athens for a bit of shopping while Ari was doing business in Rome, and then went on to Switzerland to see Lee.

One kind of wonders what they talked about, much less when.

Then in April, Jackie and Ari again cruised the Caribbean, perhaps to get reacquainted with each other.

The first year of their marriage was documented by reporter Fred Sparks, of the Bell-McClure Syndicate, who titled a series on the Onassises, "The $20 Million Honeymoon." The series, which ran in most major cities in the U.S. and in some other countries as well, boggled all but the most jaded imaginations. After all, everybody knew that Onassis was rich, but really!

The gems alone which he showered on Jackie as wedding gifts were estimated to be worth $1.1 million. During the following year, he presented her with additional trinkets which would have rung up to another $4 million if Tiffany's, Van Cleef .& Arpels, and other jewelry biggies had check-out counters.

When the Apollo II spacecraft made its historic journey to the moon, it coincided with Jackie's birthday. To commemorate the occasion, Onassis gave her a pair of gold earrings, replicas of the moon itself, set with diamonds as big as Ping-Pong balls. She also received one of the most famous gems in the world—the fabulous Krupp diamond, a forty-carat stone worth, a New York jeweler said, "a flat million."

All this added up to a lot more than the jewels which Onassis' first wife, Tina, had been able to acquire during their ten years of wedded bliss. In the divorce court, she declared her jewelry to be worth a mere $4 million in all.

Not all of Jackie's jewels were so important. She adored the "costume jewelry" Onassis showered on her—little bracelets and such which set him back a couple of thousand more or less and which the wealthy are fond of describing as "amusing." One of Jackie's favorite designers of such stuff is David Webb, whose bills (in 1969) to Jackie added up to about $60,000. Most of Webb's pieces started with an original idea submitted by Jackie which Webb then executed.

But there were other items in the "shower of gold" Onassis continued to rain upon Jackie. Onassis, who spent so much time away from his wife, made his presence felt by sending her a little something every now and then. He liked to know that when a servant brought in her breakfast tray with its accompanying bouquet of flowers Jackie would reach among the blooms to find, say, a little diamond-studded gold bracelet from Zolotas, Athens' best jeweler. At that point in her life, Jackie could have worn a different bracelet every day for several months without the bore of repetition.

But Jackie wears a good deal more than bracelets, and after only a year of marriage to Onassis, her expenditures were estimated to have been well over ten times as great as what she spent during all her years in the White House—Fred Sparks put it at well over a million and a quarter in U.S. dollars. In Jack's scheme of things, Jackie's compulsive spending was a political liability, but in Onassis' world, lack of spending ability in a wife would be an unthinkable embarrassment.

In the spring of 1969, Jackie had her first all-out shopping orgy. *Women's Wear Daily* observed that Daddy-O's new bride was the "retailer's best friend."

Jackie's Bottomless Closets

"Jackie Onassis continues to fill her bottomless closets. She is making Daddy-O's bills bigger than ever with her latest shopping spree," said WWD. "She is buying in carload lots!"

She bought a gingham full floor-length gown from Adolfo for $1250, and a red-and-blue creation to be worn over a leotard for $400. On one spring Saturday she ambled in the St. Laurent ready-to-wear boutique on Madison Avenue and "bought the place out," spending an estimated $3,000 in about an hour and a half.

She gradually shifted her fashion allegiance to the Italian designer, Valentino, who had designed her ecru lace wedding dress. Valentino's clothes are not exactly discount items; they start at around $2,500 and go up—way up. In her first years as Mrs. Onassis, Jackie spent about $30,000 with Valentino alone. But she balanced this with seven or eight outfits from Ciardi, whose average selling price was about $1,200 for a single dress at the time. Nicole Alphand, Jackie's friend when Jack was president and when Herve Alphand was French Ambassador to Washington, is *directrice* of the Cardin salon. Once Jackie bought a brown and white midi outfit there, ordering it in brown linen, asking for a slit up the back and the removal of the sleeves. With her unerring fashion instinct she turned it into a Jackie original.

But Jackie's real hang-up was shoes, including boots, slippers and sandals. She went to Veneziano's for loafers, Gucci's for comfortable walking shoes, and picked up a stock of elegant low-heel pumps from Casimir's in Rome, for starters. In her closets around the world, Jackie stocked enough shoes to wear a different pair every day for a year and a half without repeating herself.

Where those closets were was another index to Jackie's life as Jackie O. Her New York headquarters remained the apartment at 1040 Fifth Avenue where John and Caroline lived with the cook, maids and governesses most of the time, and where Jackie and Onassis stayed whenever they were in New York. Onassis, however, was reportedly depressed by those pedestrian digs and wanted to build a nice town house somewhere in the seventies—on mid-city property he owned. There was also a villa in Athens and one in Montevideo, an apartment on Avenue Foch in Paris and another in London as well as the entire island of Skorpios, which attracted a lot of attention from Jackie and Onassis directly after their wedding as work progressed on the magnificent palace under construction. Onassis also bought the former Barclay estate, next to the Auchincloss' Hammersmith Farm in Newport.

Then, there was the matter of the yacht. Quite understandably, Jackie was not pleased with keeping the *Christina* in the family after its long association with Maria Callas. Onassis, therefore, commissioned the building of a new yacht, to be the biggest and fastest in the world. The *Christina*, after all, started life as a frigate in the Canadian Navy, something that not even the installation of a mosaic-lined swimming pool and marble bidet could quite undo. The upkeep on the *Christina* was over $1,400,000 a year—a lot to spend on a yacht its owners didn't really like.

It is easy to be flip about people who possess such wealth, and to minimize the inconveniences and unpleasantness which their wealth and attendant fame may bring. But these are real problems, as much as the gnawing worry of making ends meet, and just as rich people can never really comprehend what it is like to be poor, so the nonrich will always have a difficult time sympathizing with the human pains of the super rich like Jackie and Onassis. There was hate mail. Most of it was intercepted before it reached the eyes of either Onassis or his wife, but some of it did get through. Some of it was even directed at John and Caroline.

Ari, who liked to do as he pleased, had for years surrounded himself with bodyguards, and strict security rivaling that of any head of state. Until her marriage, Jackie was watched over by the Secret Service, and the children would continue to receive this protection from the U.S. government until they were sixteen. Jackie never went anywhere without a bodyguard and her New York apartment was guarded round-the-clock at a cost of $1,200 a week.

In January, 1969, a plane with Jackie aboard had to be searched at Kennedy airport because police received a tip-off that a bomb was aboard. Such things happened again and again. Most such threats were the work of cranks, but there was no way to be sure except to check.

The *modus vivendi* of Jackie and Ari became the cause of great speculation. It soon was clear that each intended continuing to go his own way. When they were together they seemed to be affectionate enough, but then, there were weeks and months when they were separated. It was generally believed that Onassis continued to see Callas when he was in Paris. It was also taken for granted that Jackie's circle of New York friends and acquaintances had not changed because of the marriage. The two lived in different social sets.

"Jackie's a little bird that needs its freedom as well as its security," Onassis said once in a much-quoted interview, "and she gets them both from me." He was also quoted once as saying that they had agreed to spend only four months of the year in each other's company—a somewhat odd arrangement.

Such a midsummer-midwinter marriage was bound to elicit rumors of disaster almost from the start. There was the Christmas, for example, when Jackie and the children abruptly pulled out of a holiday season with Onassis to visit Lee Radziwill in London. Onassis promptly took off for Paris and you-know-who.

It all upset the eighty-year–old matriarch of the Kennedy clan sufficiently that Rose telephoned Jackie in London to ask whether Jackie might not return to Skorpios, instead of proceeding to New York, so that Rose could zip over there for a little sun. Jackie greeted her former mother-in-law with tears in her eyes, and people wondered whether it was only because they had not seen each other since Joseph Kennedy's funeral in November.

Apparently Rose's visit had some effect on the Onassis marriage. Jackie began signing her letters "Jackie K.O."—acknowledging the Kennedy phase of her life once more. Onassis began exhibiting a bit more discretion about his visits to Callas, and he and Jackie spent more time together. When Onassis went to St. Croix to conduct some negotiations about his realty holdings on the island, Jackie accompanied him. The two spent a long weekend at Jackie's apartment in New York after that, and later Jackie sent John and Caroline on a visit to their grandmother, Mrs. Auchincloss, while she joined Onassis in Greece.

Soon afterward, Onassis surprised the press by giving a candid interview in which he said that Callas was a remarkable woman to whom he had been greatly attached for a long time and whom he would continue to see. He emphasized, however, that Jackie was "the only woman in his life."

Then he said a peculiar thing—that their "personal arrangement" was working out better than he had expected. Apparently, their arrangement included unlimited personal freedom for them both, which must have pleased the wilfull Jackie very much indeed. Actually, the pair probably had little to say to each other, when you come right down to it. Remembering Tina Onassis' boredom with Onassis' buddies, and Jackie's exasperation with Jack's Last-Hurrah political pals, it was probably a very good thing that Jackie and Onassis laid down the ground rules for their marriage. It might have degenerated into total incompatibility.

CHAPTER SIXTEEN
First Lady of the Tabloids

Modern journalism has no counterpart for Jacqueline Kennedy Onassis. Without doubt she remains the single most publicized female of the twentieth century. She has left all competition standing lonely, forlorn and forgotten at the starting gate. Even that formidable headline collector, Elizabeth Taylor, has dropped back to the mid-section of the photo pages where she can occasionally be found gallavanting with millionaire Malcolm Forbes.

Jackie turned the already flourishing profession of gossip into a gold mine for tabloid newspapers around the world and into a field day for photographers like Ron Gallella who chose Jackie as his specialty with as much deliberation as a botanist selecting a rare species of vine as his life's work. If Jackie presumed that her marriage to Aristotle Onassis would provide her with the privacy she professed to desire for herself and her children, she sadly underrated her position as a world figure and the curiosity her tiniest action created.

As Mrs. Onassis there emerged a noticeable change in the press' attitude toward her. Where before she had been the widow of a martyred president, she was not fair game for anything that imaginative journalists could think of, and they played rough. Previously there had been concessions to the tragedy she had endured, and while gossip whirled around her, it was touched with sympathy and understanding. Stripped of the blood-stained clothes she wore back from Dallas and decked out in a million-dollar wardrobe detailed by Fred Cook, the lady was for burning. And the press fried her.

Jackie opened Pandora's box by behaving characteristically—doing exactly what she wanted—without considering the consequences, or what some would insist were her responsibilities.

Modern America had only one model for a presidential widow—the indomitable Eleanor Roosevelt. She had set her course in the White House by becoming an activist with a keen interest in liberal politics, women's rights, minorities and a variety of other causes considered radical in their day. By the time John Kennedy came to office, they had all become part of the American scene and her most violent enemies had long since forgotten and forgiven her. Mrs. Roosevelt had institutionalized political widowhood, establishing standards that were expected to be followed—if not in deed, at least in spirit.

It was fully believed that Jackie, following her widow's period of mourning, would take a genteel place in society as a mother and doer of good deeds—remarrying eventually, of course. No one could imagine such a beautiful, vibrant and well-loved woman turning her back on love and affection.

But the Jackie Kennedy who took television audiences through tours of *her* White House, breathlessly explaining how she had recreated the original decor of the Blue Room, was not quite the same as the real Jackie Kennedy, the autocratic mistress of a world that revolved largely around her own mercurial personality. With her marriage to Aristotle Onassis Americans began discovering that their lovely, soft-spoken, fragile Jackie was really as tough as steel and as given to human frailties as the next pretty young wife of a successful and attractive man.

The Jackie Doll

She would have to be tough to withstand all of the negative attention she was getting. There was the *Jackie Kennedy Doll*, which suddenly appeared in the market place, a life-size mannequin that "could float in the tub or cuddle up in bed" with its owner. The tabloids had a great time with that one. Typical of the kind of coverage Jackie endured was the following:

" 'Somebody gave me a Jackie Kennedy doll

for Christmas,' a TV comedian said. 'You wind it up and it knocks you down.'

"He was referring, of course, to the historic incident in which the former First Lady decked a news photographer with a judo flip. Since that memorable moment, Jacqueline Kennedy Onassis has been called simply Jackie KO.

"But there really is a Jackie doll. The Jet Set has been whispering about it for weeks. It's a perfect gift for the Man Who Has Everything—especially if he's a jaded bachelor with a slightly eccentric taste in toys.

"You don't wind it, however. You blow it up, like a balloon. Properly inflated, it is a life-size, life-like replica of Jackie. It is 5 feet 4 inches tall and measures 36–24–36. This is 1 inch shorter than the original—but 4 inches fuller around the bust.

"The doll has shoulder-length black hair, false eyelashes and a sultry expression that is instantly familiar to Jackie watchers. It sells for $9.95, which is a lot less than the $20 million a year it has cost Aristotle Onassis to maintain the original. A deluxe model is also available for $16.95. It comes complete with wig, bikini and other interesting accessories.

"The owner can purchase accessories such as transparent lingerie, black lace panties and bra, all tastefully designed for doll collectors who like to dress and undress their playthings. What else they do with the Jackie doll is anybody's guess—and just about everybody who has seen or heard about this naughty novelty is guessing.

"The Los Angeles firm that manufactures the

doll calls her Gretchen and insists that any resemblance to Jackie KO is strictly coincidental. But that strange coincidence has been enough to sell nearly 100,000 of the sexy toys.

"And most of the purchasers have been single men.

"The manufacturer originally made the dolls as portable dummies for traveling dress salesmen. Then word got around that some traveling salesmen preferred Jackie dolls to farmers' daughters. Soon the doll company was flooded with orders for the blowup beauty.

"It would take a Freud or Kinsey to explain what this American phenomenon means. But one thing is certain: There would be no market for scantily-clad Jackie dolls if Jacqueline Kennedy Onassis had not kicked over the pedestal on which she posed so long."

Rumors of Romance

The difference in ages between Ari and Jackie had to invite rumors of other romantic interests and they weren't long in coming. The ink had barely dried on the pre-nuptial financial agreement Jackie and Ari signed when she was reported in the company of a handsome young Greek architect. And besides Callas, Onassis was supposed to have acquired a companion young enough to be his daughter.

This invited a lengthy piece in *Uncensored*, which, like many printed in the exposé magazines, had more than a grain of truth to them.

They picked up their information from foreign newspapers, even the most responsible of which were not the least bit reticent about prying into Jackie's affairs or following her around for weeks on end to collect the material for a single story.

The Greeks have a word for it: Sympathetikos.

In English it's "sympathetic;" in Spanish it's *simpatico*.

It didn't exactly describe the relationship between Mr. and Mrs. Aristotle Socrates Onassis. But it certainly fit the friendship between Jackie O and a swarthily handsome Greek architect. And it may also be the best word for Ari's feelings for a curvy Greek singer—even though she told him, "Never on Sunday."

According to the Random House Dictionary, "sympathetic" has a variety of meanings including "acting or affected by, or pertaining to, a special natural sympathy or affinity; congenial; looking upon with favor."

If that doesn't grab you, how about this one? "Pertaining to vibrations, sounds, etc. produced by a body as the direct result of similar vibrations in a different body."

Jackie O and architect Alex Hadzimichailis seemed to be sharing some sort of sympathetikos vibrations. And the sounds emanating from the beautiful body of singer Marinella seem to have had Daddy O vibrating all over.

So it's not surprising that the jet set grapevine vibrated with rumors about the famous couple and their new interests. Some Jackie-watchers were predicting that America's former First Lady would divorce her Golden Greek and marry Alex. And as for Ari—well, everyone knew he always had a thing about bosomy singers.

One Christmas, while Jackie was holidaying in England with her children, Daddy O and Maria held a tender reunion in Paris. And guess who played Santa Claus?

In February, Ari and the prima donna attended a super party celebrating the premiere of her first movie, *Medea*. They also were seen together in several posh restaurants and nightclubs. Just like old times.

They got together again in May—Paris in the spring, and all that—while Jackie was in America on a mystery mission.

Supposedly, she returned to the U.S. on business concerning the John F. Kennedy Memorial Library. But the real reason for her unscheduled trip was an affair of the heart involving her pretty, 18-year-old stepdaughter, Christina Onassis.

Around the end of April, Christina phoned her father from Switzerland and told him she intended to break her engagement to Petros Goulandris, 23, one of those fabulous Greek shipping heirs. Onassis reportedly was shocked and saddened by Christina's decision, but before he could give her a full measure of fatherly advice she hung up and took off for New York.

Daddy O had been looking forward to still

another alliance of shipping families and fortunes, the kind he had once made himself on the occasion of his first marriage. Greek shipping families are notorious for sticking together like barnacles to hulls.

Jackie also had approved of the engagement. She liked Petros and considered him a perfect match for Chris. So she and Daddy O talked it over and decided she should jet to New York and try to persuade Chris to go through with the wedding.

The mission was unsuccessful. Failing to convince her stepdaughter that shipping heirs make the best mates, Jackie went on to Boston to visit the Kennedy clan. Then she returned to New York, intending to stay with her children, Caroline and John Jr., while they wound up the school year.

But Jackie got wound up before the term did. What tightened her spring was a flash from Paris that Ari and Maria were rekindling that old flame.

Fast as any fireman, Jackie sped to Paris to stamp out the sparks. What she told her playful spouse has not been recorded for posterity, but it must have sounded like a reading of the Riot Act. Soon after her arrival in France, she and Ari flew back to Greece together amid reports that he had agreed never to see Maria again.

Jackie and Ari supposedly planned to spend most of the summer on Skorpios, their own private island. But business called him to Athens frequently and, though his personal helicopter waited at Helinikon Airport to whisk him back to Jackie's side, he often remained in the capital overnight.

Left alone on the island, with only about 50 servants and her children for company, Jackie soon became bored. She decided to tour some of the other Greek isles, and she couldn't have found a better guide than Alex Hadzimichailis.

According to one report, they were introduced by the curator of the Archaeological Museum of Denakis, which Jackie was visiting on her own as Ari was too busy to accompany her. Though Jackie loves museums and other forms of culture, Ari's motto was: "If you've seen one ruin, you've seen them all."

Alex offered to show her the historic sights and off they went—to Crete, Corfu, Lefkada, Rhodes, Tinos and other sun-baked isles. They were also seen together in Athens, while Ari was there making money.

The French newspaper *France-Dimanche*, first Jackie-watching journal to spot the budding friendship, reported: "Jackie has been seen a great deal in the company of the Greek architect Alex Hadzimichailis.

"For instance, they were together on Rhodes on June 16 when they visited the Chapel of the Virgin which has an icon (religious painting) believed to have miraculous powers.

"Tradition has it that a visitor should make an offering of an item of jewelry and then make a request. Jackie's gift to the icon was a pair of earrings. Her companion gave a medallion."

301

What did they ask in return? Not even *France-Dimanche*, which followed them like their shadows, could answer that one.

The friendly couple also inspected the Spring of Fertility on the island of Lefkada and an ancient fort on Corfu, where they lunched at a seaside cafe. According to witnesses, Jackie ordered lobster and Alex cracked the shell and claws with his teeth "while she looked on like a lovesick school girl."

Alex insisted throughout that the only woman in his life was his wife.

"We are happily married," he said, "and any suggestions to the contrary are nonsense. I've met Mrs. Onassis several times and we get along fine. But it's ridiculous to suggest there's more to it than that."

Jackie Pressures Vatican

Some of the Jackie stories took years to come to light. The drama behind Jackie Kennedy's 1962 trip to Italy while she was First Lady was an example. A Milan newspaper waited until 1968 before it charged that Jackie used the power of her White House position to obtain a Vatican annulment of her sister's first marriage.

The story said that Jackie put pressure on the late Pope John XXIII and that he, in turn, influenced the *Sacred Rota*, the Vatican judiciary court, to grant the annulment.

Several major newspapers carried the article in 1968, but actually it was an old piece in the magazine field. *Uncensored* published the full details in February, 1963, which carried the controversial headline: WHEN JACKIE KENNEDY WENT TO ROME FOR AN ANNULMENT.

The *Uncensored* account of her trip stated:

"The former Caroline Lee Bouvier, after whom the president's famous daughter is named, wants the Vatican to annul her first marriage so she and her present husband, Prince Stanislas Radziwill, can be married in the Catholic Church.

"To keep her mission a secret, Jackie stayed away from the Vatican on her summer holiday. The annulment negotiations were carried out through couriers who shuttled back and forth between Rome and Ravello, between the palace of Pope John and the white-washed villa of America's First Lady.

"Mastermind of these maneuvers was multimillionaire Gianno Agnelli, whose family makes Fiat autos. Agnelli's yacht and several custombuilt Fiats ran a regular Rome-Ravello shuttle service during Jackie's stay. The yacht served as headquarters for several church dignitaries and civilian experts on Roman Catholic law as they conferred with Lee, Prince Stash and Mrs. Kennedy."

Jackie's Poor Relatives

When it comes to poor relatives the rich can't win. Jackie Kennedy was no exception when, in 1971, Edith Bouvier Beale, Jackie's aunt and her

daughter, known as "Little Edie," made headlines when the sanitation department of Suffolk
County told the two eccentrics to clean up the
estate and their house or face eviction.

Naturally, the headlines ran: JACKIE'S AUNT
FACES EVICTION—and the story and photographs that accompanied them were hardly un-
familiar. It was the account of two women who
lived in a once–palatial manor house and estate
who had allowed it to go to ruin because they
lacked both funds and the energy to cope with
its enormous demands.

They had been living for years as eccentric
hermits, surrounded by cats whose leavings had
not been cleaned for months. There were hundreds of opened cans of food around the house,
only partially eaten, decaying and giving off an
odor to which the women were apparently indifferent.

When Edith Beale's son, a prominent lawyer,
was told of the conditions and the threat of the
sanitation department to move out his mother
and sister—by force, if necessary—he was delighted. Beale hoped that the sanitation authorities might accomplish what he hadn't been able
to do in years of pleading—get them off the land
into a more economical and practical life–style.

Onassis appeared to understand the plight of
the old women more sympathetically than either
Edith's son or her niece, Jackie. They simply
didn't want to be moved. They expected to
remain just where they'd lived for so many years.
As eccentrics invariably do, they got their way.
Onassis gave them the money to meet the clean-

up demands of the authorities and to pay back water, gas and light bills.

Ari's Gravedigger Brother

Ari had his own problems with poor relations. Reporters discovered that his brother was working as a gravedigger for eight dollars a month. Reported one scandal sheet:

"A ghost from the past has come out of obscurity to haunt the Jet Set life of Aristotle and his fabulous wife, Jackie Kennedy. While they prowl the world in private planes, dwell on private islands, sail what is called the world's most luxurious yacht and maintain posh pads in New York and Paris, the 62-year-old brother of the billionaire ekes out a living in his native Greece as a gravedigger, earning about $8.00 a month. That is, in the months when Nikos is lucky enough to find work.

"Nikos' story reads stranger than fiction. He bridles when questioned about the authenticity of his claim to being Ari's brother. Nikos may be poorly dressed but his working clothes are clean and he possesses the confident air of a man who has made his own way."

"Of course I am the brother of Aristotle Onassis," he told reporters. "Our father, Socrates, came from Laodiki Adena. Our mother came from Kessaria and we were born in Smyrna where our parents were living at the time. Our mother was my father's second wife.

"Father was secretary in a French tobacco

factory. We were very poor. He and Mother didn't get along and they were divorced in 1911. I was three years old at the time. She took me with her while Ari stayed with Father. But Mother just couldn't go it alone. I was sent to an orphanage.

"I was adopted by a family named Melissas and took that name because in Greece my Turkish name, Onassis, was a drawback. At school the other kids called me 'Onassis, the Turk'—and that, my stepfather and I realized, would be a terrible handicap when I started looking for work.

"When my mother died in 1928 I began to search for my real father and my brother, Ari. Through the Red Cross I discovered that Ari was in Buenos Aires. I wrote him immediately but never received an answer. I tried twice again, but the results were no better."

When Ari, who was forming Olympic Airlines in the fifties opened an office in Saloniki, Nikos again attempted to communicate with him. "I was then fifty years old and had learned few skills. I had always been a laborer. I thought, however, I could earn my way as a porter. But I never got to meet Ari. I could only talk to secretaries. I think Ari was simply ashamed of the fact that his brother was a poor, illiterate working man—as though I did not still have dignity!

"I was shocked but that stopped any attempts on my part to get in touch with him. It didn't make sense. Obviously I was a part of his life that he wanted to forget—and I suppose he's entitled to his private feelings. But we both carry the blood of our parents. I have never done him harm—not even now when I am telling this publicly for the first time. You cannot hurt a billionaire—at least outwardly. But moneyed people sometimes know too well how to hurt the poor."

CHAPTER SEVENTEEN
Onassis Spins Into Spotlight

No one knew much about Onassis. But Jackie catapulted him into the limelight, and around New York, at least, those who got to know him grew extremely fond of the old boy. There was a twinkle in his eye that shot out of the wrinkled lids that were beginning to show signs of *myasthenia gravis,* one of the diseases that would eventually take the life of the extraordinarily energetic Greek millionaire.

Newspapermen found him approachable and easy to talk to—even if he studiously avoided saying anything quotable about either his private or business life. He possessed the peculiar talent of all successful mystery men—to remain just that: a mystery. He seemed to enjoy being in the limelight although that had not been exactly new to him—not when you consider his tumultuous years with Callas, the fights, the press conferences, the flights, and the reunions that punctuated an affair held in the full glare of photographers' flash bulbs.

The man's stamina was amazing—along with his drinking. Ari drank his American whiskey in straight shots, rarely bothering with a chaser. He could close up a watering spa like P.J. Clarke's, the second home of Broadway and jet set night owls, and insist on walking home at four in the morning in full control of himself. His limousine ambled along beside him in case Ari got tired. He seldom did. For a man his age—any age, for that matter—his endurance was amazing. He could refresh himself with a couple of hours sleep and often nights went by when he didn't bother to sleep. When asked about his energy, Ari's response was characteristically simple, "I don't need much sleep."

Ari used the Jackie years cleverly to enlarge his already extensive empire in America, but not always successfully. He ran afoul of local pressures when he tried to build a pipeline carrying Atlantic oil to areas along the New England coast. Ari's engineers assured everyone that it was perfectly safe, with no risk of spill, but it was no dice and the tycoon retreated.

He found no such obstacles, however, to his construction of a high-rise luxury apartment building right in midtown Manhattan, a building reflecting his fanatical devotion to elegant living. Selling apartments for as much as a quarter million dollars, Onassis offered around-the-clock service on a scale that would embarrass any of the city's fine hotels. Even the interiors of the building's closets had been hand-painted and the bathroom fixtures gold-plated. A concierge provided such services as ordering limousines for airport pick-ups and departures and a twenty-four-hour restaurant could produce everything from a hamburger to *crepes suzettes* on a few minutes' notice.

Luxury was intrinsic to the Onassis lifestyle and it showed in everything he did—whether it related to his own private life or his business. Yet New Yorkers and Parisians long knew Ari could be the most democratic of people. He gave the impression of doting on his ability to be just one of the crowd, whether knocking off American whiskey at P.J. Clarke's in New York or sipping champagne at Maxim's.

He had a favorite table at that celebrated Parisian cabaret and there were times in the last years of his life when Ari slipped into it alone. But he was never alone for long. People would crowd around him—drawn to what was undoubtedly an attractive, magnetic personality. There were British, American and social figures. Fashionable young women would keep coming up to him to give him a peck on the cheek and someone would say, "Ari, dear, we're going to be cruising around Skorpios next month. Will it be all right if we drop in?"

"Yes, yes," Ari always said, waving the girls away and going on with whatever story he was telling at the time. Ari was fascinated with his background, with his youth. His life engrossed him and he loved to tell about his struggles, his triumphs and his dreams. "He seldom talked about Jackie," a friend from those evenings at Maxim's remembered.

Often Onassis confided to his friends that he couldn't understand why people looked upon him as a mystery man and, too often, regarded him with suspicion. He believed he had an unfavorable image, he said, "because they think I'm a Greek with too much money."

"The worst thing that can happen to a man," Onassis once said, "is to become a celebrity. It is as though there was a law that you have to walk naked in public—no matter how well built you are, they make you look ridiculous."

He agreed with those who said he "always seemed to be at war with someone"—whether it was the United States government or world oil interests. "Taking up these challenges has been most dangerous and expensive, but I thank God," Onassis said, "that I have been able to afford it and that I have a strong stomach."

Said one newspaperman who decided to become an Onassis watcher instead of a Jackie snooper, "I'm sorry the old boy didn't make himself known before. He's a great character. A robber baron right out of another century. I hate to say it, but he was the kind of fellow that made this country great. Someone who knew how to get things done. You know, he'd make a helluva mayor."

If Ari made a host of new friends for himself in his meanderings around New York, it was hard to tell whether the same could be said for Jackie. People, especially those who knew her in the

Kennedy era, blew hot and cold. "She's changed so much," they kept telling one another. "You used to know where you stood with her. Now she's difficult to get to. Her moods change as fast as a child's. All that spoiling she's enjoyed all her life is beginning to show. And on a grown woman it isn't attractive."

Jackie Crashes

To millions of Americans, Jackie was much more than the nation's most beautiful First Lady and the world's most glamorous widow. She was revered, idolized, worshipped like a goddess. And she let her public down with an earth-shaking crash.

She seemed to care little for her country or the part she had played in its history that she seriously considered raising her children in Europe.

After her marriage to billionaire Aristotle Onassis, she planned to take Caroline and John out of their New York schools and have them educated abroad. This infuriated Edward Kennedy. He threatened a legal battle to keep the late president's children in this country, even though Jackie had the right to raise them as she chose.

The threat of unfavorable publicity and an irreconcilable split with the Kennedy family finally persuaded Jackie to continue raising her children as Americans—the way their father wanted.

Shortly after her spectacular Greek wedding, there were persistent reports that Jackie was pregnant. Then the jet set rocked with rumors that she had suffered a miscarriage and, in a moment of deep despondency, had tried to kill herself with an overdose of sleeping pills.

Usually well-informed sources said Jackie was saved by a seaman on the Onassis yacht who revived her and called a doctor. Onassis gave the seaman a reward of several thousand dollars, those sources claimed, but later fired him because he mentioned the suicide attempt to another member of the crew.

Whether or not Jackie actually tried suicide, her bizarre actions after she became the bride of Daddy-O made many old friends wonder out loud: Was Jackie cracking up? Or was her outrageous behavior merely a public expression of the way she always wanted to act but never dared to before?

The outstanding example, of course, was the curious case of the assaulted photographer.

Jackie and Ari were both curious about *I Am Curious (Yellow)*, the notorious Swedish movie. And so, on a golden Sunday afternoon one October, they went to the New York theater where the sexsational film was playing. They arrived at the theater separately, hoping to escape notice, but the manager spotted them and tipped off the press.

Three photographers, two from the *Daily News* and one from *Associated Press*, hurried to the 57th St. theater and took up positions in the lobby. They made no attempt to go inside. Jackie spotted them when she came out to the lobby, heading for the ladies' lounge.

She was wearing a leather miniskirt, sweater and head scarf. One observer noted: "She looked like a hooker."

Glancing nervously at the lensmen, Jackie started to duck back inside then changed her mind. She walked up to one of the photographers, grabbed him by the arm and said: "Wait here." With that, she breezed out of the theater.

News photographer Mel Finkelstein, a veteran Jackie-snapper, got in front of her on the sidewalk, trying for a picture. She knew who he was, having both posed for him and refused to pose scores of times. As she charged by, she grabbed his right arm, stuck out her left leg and flipped him over it, dumping Mel and his equipment all over the cold pavement.

"I've been flipped by the best," the 5-foot-10, 168-pound Finkelstein said later, "but this was the fastest, smoothest job I ever had to suffer."

While his wife was manhandling the lensman, Daddy-O remained inside the theater, enjoying the sex film to its finish. When he came out, he didn't say anything. He merely smiled.

The next day, Jackie denied flipping the photographer. She said he must have tripped over his own big feet. Her secretary, Nancy Tuckerman, insisted: "It's really silly to think Mrs. Onassis could flip a 168-pound man just like that."

Though the assault was witnessed by the two other cameramen and several passersby, Jackie stuck to her story. Some of the witnesses cheered her; others felt she had no right to attack a man who was only doing his job. But even her staunchest supporters couldn't understand why Jackie said she didn't do it—when she obviously did.

Newspapers all over the world carried a photo of the miniskirted Jackie striding past the fallen Finkelstein. The picture was worth a thousand denials and the incident made Jackie KO look ridiculous—a public posture she has carefully avoided in the past.

Jackie's judo expertise promptly became the subject of jokes hastily added to the repertoires of TV and nightclub comedians.

On the night after the assault, Bob Hope went before a national TV audience and opened fire with a machinegun-like burst of Jackie gags. Posing as her judo instructor, he said she had planned to take some jewels out of a gem-encrusted sword, presented to President Kennedy by the Shah of Iran, and sew them on her black belt.

The same night, on another channel, Carol Burnett did a devastating takeoff on Queen Elizabeth and then told her viewers to "tune in next week when our guests will include the talented Christine Keeler and a judo lesson by Jacqueline Onassis."

A few nights later, Jackie and Daddy-O visited a popular Manhattan saloon. They were ushered to a table in the rear, as far from the crowded bar as possible.

Instead, Jackie chose a table near the bar and next to the window, where she could be ogled by everyone who came in, went out or passed on the sidewalk. A crowd quickly gathered outside the window and at least two amateur photographers snapped the famous couple. On this occasion, Jackie apparently felt more public than private.

Around the same time, free-lance photographer Ron Galella caught Jackie and son John bicycle riding in Central Park. They were accompanied by a Secret Service agent. Galella rushed up, shooting as fast as he could.

Realizing she was on candid camera, Jackie smiled sweetly while ordering the Secret Service agent through clenched teeth: "Mr. Connelly, smash his camera."

Agent Connelly didn't do that, but he did have Galella arrested on a charge of harassment. In other countries, mainly Greece, Ireland and Spain, photographers who incurred Jackie's displeasure have been jailed, clubbed by cops and Onassis bodyguards and have had their equipment busted, along with their heads.

Jackie's image was further tarnished by revelations of her reckless spending habits. While on a shopping binge, Jackie could no more resist snapping up expensive baubles than an alcoholic can refuse a drink when a bottle is thrust under his nose.

Was Jackie "Hearing Voices?"

There were some who even went so far as to question Jackie's sanity. There were wild rumors at one time that she was "hearing voices" and had gone deeply into the occult. But as one sympathetic friend put it, "How would you feel if you turned a corner and saw a tabloid reading—JACKIE MAKES CONTACT WITH JACK KENNEDY'S SPIRIT. Wouldn't you get a little balmy? Or at least question your own mind?"

When the pressures were missing, Jackie could be charm itself. Like Ari, she took a fancy to P.J. Clarke's, only a few minutes' walk from her apartment. There were nights when she sat there at a table by a window and couldn't care less whether photographers snapped her munching a hamburger or chatting away with friends. She seldom dropped in at P.J.'s when Ari was there. There was the feeling that she wanted people to understand that their relationship, was in her mind at least, a free and easy marriage which gave each partner the independence he wanted.

Then there were the nights when Jackie's guard was up—when she sat sullen and uncommunicating—just spending time like any other lonely woman. Newsmen got in the habit of avoiding her when they found Jackie in that sort of mood. Despite herself, she continued to enjoy fair treatment in the hands of the legitimate press.

They respected her feelings about visiting Washington and the White House and it was common knowledge that she had accepted an invitation from Patricia Nixon to make a private visit before the unveiling of an official White

House portrait of President Kennedy. But it was kept secret until the meeting was over.

In a way what was happening to Jackie was a tragedy as great as the loss of her first husband. It was greater, for it would endure longer than the sorrow caused by the death of a partner. Eventually sorrow diminishes. But Jackie had become the victim of her own legend, the headlines she made, both true and false. She simply wasn't real—and it began to show. She was too young to be considered an eccentric, too old to be labelled a kook. So Jackie started belonging somewhere in between—a public character who evidently had tired of retreating behind a mask. The public began to know all her moods, good, bad, petulant, spoiled. Jackie had become a complicated person—hopelessly engulfed in the critical spotlight her very identity turned on.

PART SIX

CHAPTER EIGHTEEN
Jackie's Many Faces

As Mrs. Onassis, Jackie wore many faces—
each more difficult than the other. She was
called upon to be so many people simultaneously, wife, mother, widow, Lady Bountiful, fashion
plate, cultural ambassador and a good American
woman, although it would be hard to define
what the last entailed as there are probably as
many definitions of the role as there are American women.

There were times when Jackie succeeded remarkably well and some of the old affection for
her returned. News broadcasts showed her at
the ceremonies honoring John Kennedy's memory at Arlington, visiting the graves of her husband, her son and brother Bobby. Always at her
side were the children, Caroline and John, tiny
rocks she seemed to lean upon. And at the same
time the very expression of her face reflected
Jackie's determination that the children should

be aware of their heritage; that, like her, they were part of history and owed something to it.

Americans saw her too attending a performance of the Leonard Bernstein Modern Mass, written to commemorate the brief life of President Kennedy. There were the other obligations that came with being a president's widow—and Jackie met them quietly and with dignity. It was as though from time to time the spirit she showed during those first tortured months after the assassination had asserted itself for a moment—however fleeting, however difficult it may have been to endure.

There were times when being a prominent mother must have broken Jackie's heart, when no decision she made would be considered right. It happened when a pair of hoodlums knocked John off his bicycle in Central Park and made off with the wheel.

It was a nasty event in a child's life and most mothers would have felt free to handle it according to their own conscience. Jackie couldn't. Like everything involving the Kennedys the theft became news, and there was an uproar over the apparent neglect of the Secret Service detail in keeping young John within eye range. The New York police moved in and eventually collared the young thieves—a pair of boys believed to have been involved in a series of thefts from younger bicycle riders.

At first Jackie didn't want to prosecute, fearing the effect of testifying and the whole court scene on her son. Her fears were logical and probably shared by most mothers. One can hear a typical New York mother washing her hands of the whole thing, "Forget it. I don't want the kid any more mixed up in this than he is. We'll just keep him out of the park from now on."

The luxury of following her own intuition wasn't possible for Jackie and it was either go into court or risk public censure. She chose the route dictated by public opinion and thanks to the confidentiality of juvenile trials, apparently the matter was settled with no ill effect as far as young Kennedy was concerned.

Then there was the matter of photographer Ron Gallella.

Takes Photographer to Court

Gallella followed Jackie everywhere she went, on shopping tours, to the park with the children, to school. Evenings he was somewhere to be found when she stepped out for the theater or dinner parties.

It was as though Jackie had become an obsession with the photographer. It had to be that, for he couldn't possibly hope to recoup enough profit from all the time he spent trying to photograph her. It became a battle of wits between him, Jackie and the Secret Service men. He got on Jackie's nerves, and there were several incidents of lost temper that reached a point where they certainly couldn't be considered ladylike.

Finally, Jackie went to court—a step she loathed and took reluctantly, only after having been completely convinced that there was no other course open to her to spare her from the pressures produced by Gallella's constant Jackie-watching.

It was a half-baked victory for Jackie O. The judge felt freedom of the press was involved and that Jackie certainly rated as a public figure—someone who couldn't expect to draw the line at coverage of her shopping tours and other womanly activities. It was decided that Gallella would have to observe a strict rule of distance between him and his beloved subject. Jackie sighed. She'd really been given no relief at all. The man would still be there, part of her entourage, practically, and there was no way of describing the discomfiture he produced. As though she hadn't enough to contend with living constantly under the eye of the Secret Service whenever she was with her children.

In Europe Jackie was prey for the photographers of the scandal magazines and there was the usual Jackie-style uproar when one of them, using a long-range lens, managed to snap a shot of the former First Lady while she was sunbathing in the nude.

American papers turned down the opportunity to buy the rights to the blurred sneak shot, but it played all over Europe and wasn't exactly flattering to Jackie. What came out was a silhouette that looked dumpier than the streamlined silhouette Jackie offered the public when she appeared in her chic wardrobe.

The power Jackie had as the First Lady didn't exist any more. When she was in the White

House there was the clout of her husband's office to insure as gentle a presentation of Jackie as she desired. Like Caesar's wife she was above suspicion and could do no wrong.

Jackie couldn't help alienating the public no matter how she tried. She had long been accustomed to special privilege. She got in the habit of flying in government planes while the Kennedys occupied the White House and when she took a scheduled airliner she sat in a roped-off section reserved for her, her companions and Secret Service agents. Protection was important when Jackie ventured out in public. Wherever she went she was mobbed—and a woman can suffer a lot of damage to her clothes and make-up in an airport pile-up, not to mention welts and bruises.

Because Onassis owned Olympic Airlines, Jackie's flying privileges were more or less similar to those she enjoyed as First Lady—until the evening she followed a sudden impulse and booked herself to Athens at the last minute. To accommodate Jackie and give her the privacy of a roped–off section, a half–dozen passengers were bumped. The furor that ensued was typical of the sort of quarrel Jackie provoked. The displaced passengers were perfectly right. They wanted to know why Jackie couldn't travel in a single seat—just like everybody else.

Unfortunately for democratic principles, things don't work out that way when celebrities are involved—and Jackie was no ordinary celebrity. Moving them from place to place is a headache for the people involved. They draw crowds and the crowds endanger not only their own lives but those of the people who want to get close to them. The simplest way to move a big shot from one point to another is to isolate him to the greatest degree possible and pay the price later.

Washington authorities heard about the Jackie-Olympic-bumping incident and there were a few hints of reprisals aimed more at collecting newspaper space than ending the evil of V.I.P. treatment by Olympic or any other airlines. The men who did the protesting could never be sure when they might want V.I.P. treatment themselves.

As there had been little peace in the world of Jackie Kennedy there was none in the world of Jackie O. She was constantly on stage—always there to be criticized. She appreciated the various occasions when she was given praise.

Jackie possessed an uncanny capacity for smoking out the right causes to support and when she did work for charity or for a project she gave it the best she could—the kind of public appearance in person or on television that carried weight. Jackie might have been modest and spent some time licking envelopes to satisfy those who longed to see her as a do-gooder. By choosing to appear as the grand lady she understood her effectiveness and made it pay off.

Neither Jackie nor Ari ever avoided speculation about the incongruity of their marriage. Whether together or separated there were always the rumors that they were on the verge of splitting. Jackie maintained that she would stick with Ari "Until the bitter end." But as the months went by the conviction behind her promise seemed to dwindle. She couldn't help but feel chagrined when she read an editorial in the Italian magazine, *L'Espresso*, which said:

"Onassis is a grizzled satrap, with liver-colored skin, thick hair, fleshy nose, and wide horsey grin, who buys an island and then has it removed from all the maps to prevent the landing of castaways; and on the other hand Jackie is an ethereal-looking beauty of 39, renowned for her sophistication and her interest in the fine arts, and a former First Lady at that. Highly suitable?"

Inevitably, Jackie became the lady of many faces—faces that she could not always mask behind her cultivated cool. For her, no less than the little guy Jack Kennedy often talked about, "life wasn't fair."

CHAPTER NINETEEN
Ari Cancels Divorce

But both Jackie and Ari were victims of bitter tragedies. Death, terrible and unexpected, had stalked their lives, leaving scars that would never heal. In 1973 Alexander, Onassis' only son, was killed in the crash of a private plane.

At the time death took his son, Onassis was involved in his unsuccessful campaign to convince residents of a New Hampshire town that they should allow him to build a $600 million oil refinery there. The combination of events suddenly aged him.

In 1973 it was apparent that Onassis was in deteriorating health. He was suffering from myasthenia gravis. In the fall he spent a week in a New York hospital after he had been photographed with his eyelids taped up to keep them from drooping. This was the kind of incident that fired Ari's temper. As he hated photographers who were bent on catching him at flamboyant play he hated to have his infirmities noised about, especially with a photograph. Like most tycoons he feared the impact of any rumor of poor health on his empire. In his business the sniffles amounted to the kiss of death.

Any talk of a divorce with Jackie was quietly dropped and the forces that manage such things, the public relations men, went to work at presenting an image of a fully recovered Onassis taking off for Europe with his wife and going about his business.

The Onassis empire at the time was sorely in need of direction. Like many other conglomerates it was reeling under the impact of the world-wide recession, especially Olympic Airlines, which Ari had been running for the Greek government. It was in trouble and Onassis was negotiating to turn over its management to the government—a highly complicated maneuver in view of the mercurial political situation in Greece.

The last year of Onassis' life reflected his gallantry and zest for living. It was spent in and out of hospitals; many times he was registered under an assumed name. Those close to him knew it was a losing game, but Ari couldn't see it. He fought to live as ferociously as he battled his adversaries in business deals. And there were times when his recovery was so pronounced that you could almost believe what Ari insisted, that his health problems were all minor and that eventually he would be as good as new.

Jackie's profile was lower during this critical

period; her trans-Atlantic trips, quietly concealed by Olympic Airways, became fewer. She appeared to be spending most of her time at Onassis' side.

She was with her husband when he was stricken in Athens in February, 1975. He was taken by special plane to Paris where he underwent a gall bladder operation. The hospitalization produced a rash of speculation about Ari's actual condition. As if to give living proof of his own conviction that he was indestructible, Ari walked into the Paris hospital under his own steam and two days after being admitted, doctors said that he was up and around. The impression Ari's people seemed anxious to convey was that the whole business had been a silly mistake, Onassis wasn't sick at all, and he would be up and around in a matter of hours.

News photographs showed a worried Jackie at Ari's side in the dramatic flight from Athens and in Paris she could be seen imprisoned inside her car by a mob of the curious. It was a typical Jackie display—the courageous little woman constantly at her husband's side, bravely facing another tragedy in the long list of calamities that had haunted her.

What happened in the weeks between Ari's Paris hospitalization in early February and the tycoon's death in mid-March has had to be pieced together since an iron curtain of silence descended on the Onassis family. Jackie flew back to New York quietly and without fanfare, although she didn't go into hiding. She seemed as busy and cheery as a little bird as she took care of her children, participated in a drive to preserve Grand Central Station as a New York City landmark and kept up with her luncheon and dinner appointments as though she hadn't a care in the world.

In Paris, it was a different scene. Maria Callas came to the hospital to visit Ari, spending long hours at his bedside. Ari had become a shadow of his former self. The years of battling poor health began to show. He had suddenly become an old man.

Christina Onassis maintained an around-the-clock vigil at her father's bedside. Peter Goulandris, the young Greek merchant prince to whom Christina was engaged, came to the hospital. Ari had finally given in; he knew he was dying. He extracted a promise from the young couple that they would marry. He wanted to be sure that Christina's vast financial empire would be protected. These were solemn moments in the last hours of Onassis' life—layered with the traditions and habits of the Old World. The dying patriarch insured the perpetuation of his dynasty.

Although not unexpected, the news of Ari's death caught people by surprise and the first question everyone asked was, "Where's Jackie?" She was in New York and the Jackie people quickly went to work to create an impression of a grief-stricken widow returning to the death bed she had left only hours before. It wasn't true, of course. She had been in New York for a couple of weeks.

With the advantage of hindsight it appears that

Jackie risked the usual snide remarks in the press—and they materialized—to leave Onassis with his family in his last hours, with his daughter and sisters. Perhaps even with Maria Callas. Her role in his drama had long since been played, and there was no reason to hang in for the final curtain. Perhaps that was how Ari wanted it. Who will ever know? And does it really matter?

Caroline And John at Ari's Funeral

Jackie, Caroline and John were on their way again—to another funeral. The youngsters may well have wondered at the trick of fate that had cast them once again into the roles of chief mourners at an international display of grief.

They buried Aristotle Onassis in the quiet hillside on the island of Skorpios where he had married Jacqueline Kennedy six years earlier. Ari had told his sisters that he wanted his burial as simple as possible on this private island in the Ionian Sea, and he picked the spot, next to a small 18th Century chapel. On the other side a wing had been built to shelter the body of Alexander. An identical wing would be constructed to house Onassis' body.

The funeral cortege assembled at the fishing village of Nidri on the island of Lefkas, about two miles from Skorpios. Village women crowded around. Like the women from Athens, Paris, London, and New York who had come to mourn their Ari, the peasants were dressed in black, although they wore tattered shawls instead of furs, and sandals instead of Gucci shoes. Jackie wore a black leather trench coat.

The coffin was placed on a cabin cruiser, and the immediate family boarded a second launch. The rest of the mourners were carried across the bay by ferry. Waiting on the docks were Jackie's two children and her mother, Mrs. Hugh Auchincloss.

Near the dock, a weeping willow, freshening with green buds, drooped in the water. After the coffin was unloaded, the mourners walked slowly behind it up the hill as the chapel bell tolled slowly. In keeping with the desire for simplicity the procession was led by the village priest from Nidri. Jackie took John's arm. Her black leather coat featured a wrap-around belt and a back pleat, covering a black wool dress, black shoes with low heels and black stockings. Her head was bare and her chestnut hair fell to her shoulders. She wore large oval dark glasses. Caroline walked with her uncle, Senator Ted Kennedy.

Only a few of the sixty mourners were able to crowd into the tiny chapel for the services. As the priest prayed, Jackie seemed to lose her set expression for a few moments. Emotion quavered on her lips, but she quickly recovered.

Christina Onassis, whose inheritance made her one of the world's wealthiest women, appeared dazed throughout the ceremony and stared for several seconds at the grave. One of Ari's sisters had been led away from the grave, overwhelmed by grief.

The coffin was lowered into the concrete wall, and the mourners walked away, toward the *Christina*. A few months ago the girl who gave the yacht its name said, "Both my father and myself have learned how short life can be, and how suddenly death may strike." These were ominous words coming from a woman whose own life would end prematurely and abruptly.

With Onassis' death, the world lost one of its most extraordinary entrepreneurs. However, he left little legacy—no monuments, no great acts of philanthropy, no record of achievements other than a succession of business deals. All that remains is the memory of a vital, tough, self-made millionaire who clearly believed that living well was the best revenge and, more than most mortals, could do so.

The funeral behind her, another husband interred, Jackie flew off to Paris with her children and mother, accompanied by Ted Kennedy. Christina flew to the Riviera for what she promised her friends and family would be several weeks of rest. She said she needed them. The long hours at the hospital, the ceremonial trapping of the funeral—all had sapped the young woman's energies. Moreover, she fully realized the scope of the enormous responsibilities that would become hers in the months ahead as the administrator of her father's fortune.

The headlines reporting Onassis' death had barely dried before newsmen began speculating on the amount of Jackie's inheritance. The existence of a pre-nuptial agreement was taken for granted and the figure most Jackie watchers agreed upon was that the widow would receive an outright inheritance of two hundred million dollars and that each of the children could expect to receive about fifteen million from their stepfather.

The earth had barely been turned on Ari's grave when European correspondents for American newspapers leaped into print with predictions that there would be a long and bitter dispute over the Onassis estate, estimated at between $500 million and $1 billion.

Wrote Bernard Valery: "Reports from the island of Skorpios indicated hard feelings between the daughter and the widow. A legal source said that 'there will be endless grounds for lawsuits' after the Onassis will is read.

"He continued: 'each big tanker (Onassis owned about 50) was a company in itself with several shareholders, and they will fight. He (Onassis) was Greek-born, an Argentine citizen and a resident of several countries, including the United States and France. Their laws will have to be satisfied.

"The source added: 'Christina is a tough girl, and if she feels that Jackie gets too much, she'll fight it. And the Kennedys will not let the widow of the President be cheated.'"

Jackie and Christina weren't the only people whose feelings were affected by the disposition of Onassis' estate. The Greek government believed that Onassis may have left a sizable portion of his estate to a fund intended for the purchase of military equipment needed in the continued dispute with Turkey over Cyprus. A leading Greek newspaper began an offensive against the Onassis estate by criticizing the late industrialist for not donating a large part of his huge fortune to Greek charities.

A political columnist on an Athens daily said that Onassis was not sympathetic as far as the masses were concerned because he and other Greek millionaires did nothing for their country.

"They did not build schools, hospitals or asylums," he wrote, "nor did they donate any buildings which might help advance our country and perpetuate their name. The comment has been circulating a lot these days that they are bad Greeks. Some do not even have Greek nationality. Onassis carried an Argentine passport."

However, the column said: "Con men, perhaps, but other countries much greater than Greece cannot show such an abundance of them. Many Greeks have jobs thanks to them and earn good salaries. Greeks should take pride in the fact that a refugee boy named Onassis was considered one of the richest men in the world and married the first lady of America. It is something that matters to us as a race."

Onassis once said, "After you reach a certain point, money becomes unimportant. What matters is success. The sensible thing would be for me to stop now. But I can't. I have to keep aiming higher and higher—just for the thrill."

If Onassis knew how to make money, he also knew how to spend it. And so did Jackie. The high-living couple had spent an estiamted $15 million annually on such goodies as unborn baby lamb at between $35 and $550 a pound and fresh French bread flown in daily from Paris. The *Christina* was a floating Olympus with a fully equipped operating room, 42 extension telephones and a mosaic dance floor that, at the touch of a button, descended nine feet to provide the floor for a mammoth swimming pool. The fabulous parties aboard the *Christina* became the talk of society.

Jackie returned to New York and the young Kennedys resumed their juvenile life of attending school, playing and entertaining each other under the eyes of the Secret Service. For Jackie there were luncheons, teas, intimate parties at her home, nights at the international jaunts she doted on.

And with her second appearance on the world scene as a widow, speculation grew about her future. Luck and fate have interfered again and again in the unfinished story of Jacqueline Onassis and, even more important, her endlessly fascinating unpredictable personality has led her, again and again, to do the totally unexpected. Then, afterwards, one saw that she took the only course compatible with the person she is.

For in the end, Jackie is Jackie, just as each of us is his own self. It is impossible to change another person, through love, through force, or through the seductive influence of public opinion. Jackie dances to nobody's tune but her own. Her beauty, wit, elegance, and the life she has led have opened to her many more possible choices than the average woman. But what she has chosen has been, in a sense, decreed in advance.

It goes back, of course, to her childhood, her education and her upbringing. Her parents meant well, and within the limits of their own abilities, they did as well as most parents do. But Jackie was raised with a particular point of view—that a girl should grow up to be a pleasant companion for a man, a proud possession, a helpmate, an ornament to his life—a woman a man could be proud of. Her own abilities and talents were directed into channels which would make her a "good match" for a man who would treat her well.

She was expected to be entertaining, charming and very beautiful—to develop her taste so that she could choose the clothes, the home, the style of life that would enhance her own value and make it evident her husband was a solid, successful and worthwhile man.

If this meant that in the decade of her forties Jackie was to be known as "superconsumer" and "the retailer's best friend," that she has been identified with as the widow of a President and of the richest man in the world—well, according to her upbringing's scale of values, there are many worse values she might have suffered.

By another scale of values, however, it might be said that Jackie is a victim as much as a tarnished goddess. One wonders, for instance, if she might not be a happier and more fulfilled woman if she had defied her well-meaning mother and stepfather and gone ahead to accept the

Vogue Prix de Paris which she had won. Perhaps she might be living in her beloved Paris today, leading a very different life and perhaps enjoying it in more meaningful ways, with a different name, and a very different life story.

Jackie is one of the last of a traditional breed of women. She is one of the most perfect specimens of this breed, who see themselves, first of all, in terms of who their father and husband is, and tend to confuse money and possessions with love. Jackie had, and still has, the potential to earn, to do—on Jackie's terms. She is brilliant, talented, and imaginative. And it is interesting, as well as a little sad, to think what she might have been able to do as Jackie, and not as Mrs. Somebody.

But her history is as much a part of her as her abilities, and given the unique mix of qualities that go together to make Jackie, there is nobody else she could have been, no other life she could have lived. She is not a goddess or a philanthropist. She is Jackie. It is spellbinding to watch her in action, to see her run the amazing course of her life at the center of the world's stage. But if the rest of us are wise, the elegant spectacle of Jackie's life should do more than entertain us. It ought to teach us something.

Jackie didn't have to marry Aristotle Onassis to share his philosophy, "If women didn't exist, all the money in the world would have no meaning."

CHAPTER TWENTY
Jackie's Political Clout?

One of the questions the Jackie-watchers have ducked speculating about is the role Jackie might play in a Ted Kennedy president bid. Although Jackie has never been as close to Ted as she was to Bobby, she respects the youngest of the Kennedys and, like many others, agrees that of the three brothers, he has prepared himself more completely to assume the presidency.

How would she figure in his plans? As a campaigner or as a force behind the scenes?

Probably both. It is unlikely that an audience would turn away from Jackie Kennedy should she decide to hit the road and stump for her brother-in-law. They would admire her—feeling that Jackie was once more back in the Kennedy fold and, therefore, a part of America's political scene.

As for Ted, make no mistake, he would welcome Jackie's help. He knows how effective

Jackie had been in her young, unspoiled days as a senator's wife when by wearing the same red coat she could always be spotted by photographers and the press during JFK's primary campaign. And Ted knows too of the curious role Jackie played in the "dump LBJ movement" when in 1967 she embarked on a secret mission —one that was vital to the presidential plans of Robert Kennedy. The trip she made in the fall of that year to Cambodia and her stopover in Rome were deliberately calculated to embarrass President Johnson.

Jackie's press secretary informed the world that Jackie was going to Cambodia as "an ordinary tourist" to fulfil a childhood longing to see the ruins of Angor, where the Khmer civilization once flourished. No one pointed out that ordinary tourists were not welcome in Cambodia at the time. The tiny country's ruler, Prince Norodom Siahnouk, was as anti-American as he was pro-Peking.

Sihanouk's anti-Americanism didn't deter Jackie, however. She could have seen bigger and better ruins of ancient civilizations in Mexico or Peru. But no—her heart was set on Cambodia. Although she could have gone there at any time during the fifteen years preceding her trip she chose to make it at a time when relations between Cambodia and the United States were at their poorest.

Needless to say Jackie wasn't treated like an "ordinary tourist." To make sure that she was comfortable on the twelve hour flight from Rome to Cambodia, Alitalia Airlines converted the first-class lounge into a private bedroom for Jackie. It was the sort of accommodation Alitalia made for the Pope.

Prince Sihanouk greeted her like visiting royalty, installed her in Khemarin Palace, took her to feed the royal elephants and expressed the belief that the United States would not be at war in Vietnam if JFK were alive.

He said that Jackie's husband "lit a light that has never been relit and which we miss cruelly today."

The roly-poly prince either forgot or did not choose to remember the statement he approved for a broadcast by his official radio station after JFK was murdered. That statement thanked "divine protection" for causing the "complete destruction of Cambodia's enemies."

While Jackie was in Angkor, Sihanouk told a press conference: "America did not come to Asia to help yellow people; it came to exploit Asia as a neocolonialist power."

At another news conference he denounced "the criminal aggression against Vietnam that menaces our country."

Then he had Jackie's limousine driven past a display of an American plane that had been shot down over Cambodia. "Please excuse me," he said to newsmen accompanying them on the sightseeing excursion, "You Americans have killed many people."

He didn't mention that his country had become the sanctuary for Viet Cong terrorists but he virtually admitted it when he told American reporters, "I am grateful to President Johnson for stopping their hawks in their plans to make aggression against Cambodia."

Jackie's visit to Cambodia provided the prince with perfect propaganda. Though he had been denouncing America with tiresome regularity for years, few people outside his bamboo kingdom bothered to listen to his tirades. But as Jackie's host he shared the publicity spotlight with her and used the occasion to sound off louder and shriller than ever.

While he was escorting her around his colorful country, he carefully avoided the Cambodian camps where Viet Cong troops were based. Nor did he show her the Sihanouk Trail where food, clothing and weapons for the Communist guerrillas were transported without fear of attack from American planes.

After her sojourn with the puppet prince Jackie flew to visit the King and Queen of Thailand. It would have taken only a few extra hours for her to visit South Vietnam and say hello to the American troops—some of whom were sent there by her husband—but Jackie had no time for a gracious gesture which might have been a tremendous morale builder. She also turned down an invitation to visit the Philippines. Her polite snub hurt the prestige of pro-American president Mapagal and cast a shadow over the usually sunny relations between Manila and Washington.

In Rome, Jackie was surrounded by the usual crowd of reporters, photographers and well-wishers. She found time to visit an old friend,

Don Antonio Garriguesy Diaz Canabate, Spanish Ambassador to the Vatican, both on the way to Cambodia and on her return to the United States. The Spanish diplomat, a widower, was seized on as a possible contender in Jackie's marital sweepstakes which was running at fever pitch. There were also whispers about Jackie and her Cambodia escort, Lord Harlech, forty-nine, a former British diplomat and recent widower, and Michael Forrestal, forty, bachelor son of the late Defense Secretary James V. Forrestal.

American correspondents were thrown off the real story by trying to keep tabs on Jackie's romantic prospects. They got so preoccupied with her male companions that they barely noticed one unusual invitation Jackie accepted while she was in Rome.

It was a dinner invitation from Countess Rattazzi, known to the *Dolce Vita* set as Suni. She was the very, very rich, very, very social sister of Fiat heir Gianni Agnelli—Jackie's go-between in her annulment dealings with Pope John XXIII.

Although Jackie turned down dinner invitations from several other rich, very social Romans, plus some wealthy Americans she had known even before her White House days, she accepted Suni's so promptly that it seemed she'd been waiting for it.

What made the invitation unusual was that in the previous summer Countess Rattazzi flew to Vietnam in connection with her charitable work with the Red Cross. Soon after she returned to

Italy, an article on Vietnam appeared under her byline in the weekly *L'Espresso*, published by Gianni Agnelli's brother-in-law.

The anti-American article accused the United States of horrible war crimes. Naturally Italian society raised its eyebrows when a former First Lady showed up for dinner at the Rattazzi *palazzo*. After all, President Johnson inherited the Vietnam mess from JFK. Curiously, it was not even mentioned in the American press.

Its implications eventually became clear. By going out of her way to socialize with harsh critics of American policies in Vietnam as she did in Rome and Cambodia, Jackie was using her political clout and the prestige of her name to make it clear that she opposed President Johnson's handling of the war.

Soon after Jackie returned to the United States, Robert Kennedy came out and said in public what he had been saying in private for some time. He took issue with the Administration's policy in Vietnam and·added that his brother would have done things differently. However he failed to spell them out.

The groundwork Jackie lay bore fruit in the winter of 1968 when the New Hampshire primary presidential election produced forty-two percent of its votes as favoring the nomination of Eugene McCarthy, an anti-Vietnam War candidate. Obviously this reflected the country's deep rooted dissatisfaction with the Johnson Administration.

The surprising results in New Hampshire

shaped Robert Kennedy's decision to throw his hat into the ring. He could no longer be accused of being Johnson's spoiler. The day after he announced his candidacy Johnson made a speech sharply defending his actions in Asia— but they fell on deaf ears and a few weeks later Johnson announced his intention to resign as a presidential candidate.

Society Queen

Politically Jackie's in the position of an old hand who can say, "I did it before and I'll do it again." No one would reject her support—least of all, a clever political animal like brother-in-law Ted Kennedy. But her role in future Kennedy political campaigns remains in the future— something to be speculated about.

At sixty Jackie's endured so many slings and arrows that there is nothing more to hurt her in a public way. She has enjoyed her role as mother. Her children are devoted to her. They can all be proud of holding their heads high during moments of dreadful public exposure and hours of terrible tragedy. They have inherited the strength of the Kennedys and the courage of their mother.

Whatever she does with her life will make news—just as it always has. And Jackie's capacity for surprise is unlikely to diminish simply because she has passed the half century mark.

A long time ago Jackie said, "The American

public will forgive me anything—even if I ran off and married Eddie Fisher."

Jackie was wrong. Their love for Jackie turned to resentment and finally to outright disgust when she married Onassis. But the years have mellowed their outrage. Jackie has become part of the scene—a legend in her own lifetime. Sometimes amusing, more often, pathetic. No one can quite understand her public postures. There are her fleeting associations with "good causes" like the preservation of Grand Central Station as a landmark building. She knows her name will draw a crowd. She doles out her presence at charity affairs sparingly, obviously reluctant to diminish her "dollars and cents value" to projects she cares about.

Some intimates wondered at her insecurity; they shuddered at her extravagance. They complained of her coldness. They saw her as calculating and scheming. Then they balanced her shortcomings against her skill at being an almost perfect modern mother.

"You can't call her an egnima," said one Jackie watcher years ago. "We hear so much about her that we certainly are aware of everything she does, thinks or feels. No woman in history has ever been reported on so consistently and with such intimate detail.

"Jackie always wanted to make a name for herself. Well, that has certainly been accomplished. Jackie will never be put away on a shelf and forgotten as long as she lives. There will always be Jackie Kennedy stories somewhere.

Perhaps in her maturity they will become kinder. Perhaps Jackie will too."

These skeptics can put their minds at rest. The 1980s were an eventful decade for Jackie, one in which the world saw a gentler, kinder, Jackie, a confident, beautiful woman with a happy life ahead of her.

PART SEVEN

CHAPTER TWENTY-ONE
The Camelot Kids Come of Age

"The three of us have been alone for such a long time. We welcome a fourth person." John Kennedy Jr. toasted his new brother-in-law with these touching words at his sister's wedding. His remarks were something of a testimony to Jackie's devotion as a mother, spoken at an occasion that reminded the world that Jackie's children had grown up—and grown well.

Singlehandedly raising the children of an American hero was no easy task, but one that Jackie performed admirably. The record proves that Jackie has done an extraordinary job of bringing up two children in the glare of the spotlight. With precious few mishaps, Caroline and John have come of age gracefully; they have managed to emerge as individuals in their own right, quite capable of standing on their own merits and talents, and not just the Kennedy name.

The New York *Daily News* headlined a series about Caroline: "She's Rebel Caroline Oh! At 21," but this report was slightly exaggerated. The press has had a knack for taking events in the Kennedy children's lives—events not uncommon to most teenagers—and blowing them out of proportion. Growing up, Caroline was as fun-loving and social as her peers, but her family and friends have always known her to be serious, polite and well-mannered.

George Plimpton told *People* magazine: "When she was seven or eight, we'd lie on the floor and have the most amazing adult conversations." And Rose Kennedy's secretary, Barbara Gibson, remembered that Caroline was "very well-mannered, very quiet, cooperative, poised and calm, unlike many of the other [Kennedy] children. Caroline was the most trustworthy—I would lend her my car." These are hardly the characteristics of a "rebel."

Studious Caroline graduated from the Concord Academy and attended Radcliffe College, where she became politically active and participated in demonstrations against the Vietnam War. In the *Daily News* series, reporter Lester David wrote: "Caroline has developed a strong social conscience. She can build up a full head of steam over injustices. She pores over books on history, political science and international relations, reading them carefully. She is conversant with every responsible book written about her father although she skips the lurid accounts of his personal life."

The Caroline who graduated from Radcliffe was very much a Kennedy—and not just in looks. She does not share Jackie's fascination with clothes, and is more of a Kennedy than a Bouvier about money, tending to spend it carefully. She even turned down an opportunity to enjoy a debutante's ball, the kind of chance a young Jackie would never have dreamt of missing.

Caroline's career choices, however, reflect her mother's influence. After college, she hoped to become a photojournalist (reminiscent of Jackie's stint as an inquiring photographer), and worked as a copy girl for the New York *Daily News*. Then, sharing her mother's appreciation of painting and sculpture, she made a career change and went to work for the Metropolitan Museum of Art, eventually becoming a manager and coordinator.

Her involvement in the art world led to her meeting her husband, Ed Schlossberg. Caroline had dated writer Tom Carney for two-and-a-half years; they split in 1980, and she met Schlossberg at a dinner party shortly after.

An intellectual and artist 13 years her senior, Schlossberg is commonly called a "Renaissance Man" and "brilliant." The son of a textile manager, he is a Columbia University graduate with two Ph.Ds. He has worked as a $500-a-day consultant, runs a company that designs museum displays and interiors, and is the author of nine books. His art is offbeat and interesting: He has written poetry on Plexiglass aluminum and black cloth, and designed T-shirts for WilliWear with slogans that changed color depending on the wearer's body temperature.

Schlossberg may be avante garde, but he is certainly considered a good catch. Being a well-respected man with impressive associates, he easily won the acceptance of Jackie and the Kennedys. Bobby Kennedy's son Douglas told reporters, "Everyone thinks he's great. We see them a lot." The May-December factor was quickly dismissed as well, considering Jackie was considerably younger than Jack Kennedy.

Caroline dated Schlossberg for five years; in March 1986 they announced their engagement, and on July 19, 1986, they were married, with Jackie and the Kennedys' blessings.

It was a bright summer day that Caroline Kennedy became Caroline Schlossberg at the Church of Our Lady of Victory in Massachusetts as 400 guests looked on. Jackie, as usual, did an excellent job keeping the press at bay. Still, reporters managed to uncover some interesting tidbits: Caroline had registered at Bloomingdale's and Tiffany's; any children of Caroline and Schlossberg, who is Jewish, would be raised Catholic; the bride would not use the word "obey" in the 30-minute ceremony; and the four-tier wedding cake would be topped by two miniature Godzillas in wedding clothes.

Despite the air of celebrity surrounding it, the wedding proceeded as most weddings do. Caroline giggled during the ceremony with matron of honor Maria Shriver (herself newly married to Arnold Schwarzennager). Caroline walked down the aisle, radiantly beautiful in a white silk organza wedding gown appliqued with shamrocks designed by Caroline Herrera.

Jackie, stylish as ever, wore a pale green dress by the same designer, and was escorted teary-eyed from the church on the arm of Ted Kennedy.

The festive day ended with a fireworks celebration provided by George Plimpton, but perhaps the most beautiful moment was a lovely toast by Ted Kennedy: "I know my brother Jack is here tonight. I'm sure he'd say, 'Jackie, I love you, and Caroline, I'm very proud of you.'"

Caroline's married life has been led as quietly as her single life, despite the hopes of many that she would enter the political foray. A year before her marriage to Schlossberg, Caroline left the art world to attend the Columbia University School of Law. *New Republic* magazine even postulated that she might be the next Kennedy to reach the White House. These thoughts may have been premature: Caroline put her law career on hold after the birth of her daughter Rose in June 1988, adding another child to the Kennedy bloodline and making Jackie the chicest grandmother in America.

Whatever lies in store for Caroline, it looks as though she's well prepared to handle it. Close friend Alexandra Styron told *Vanity Fair* magazine, "Caroline seems to have come into her own in the last few years. I've never seen her happier than she is now. She looks beautiful. She's stick thin. Her skin is glowing. She and Ed are as much in love as any married people I've ever seen. They have a very quiet social life. Caroline is really an extremely unassuming, down-to-earth person." This positive report is rather remarkable, considering the tragedy and turmoil surrounding Caroline's childhood—and much of the credit goes to Jackie.

On a drizzly night in early 1989, New York State Police pulled a car over for speeding on the highway past JFK Airport. The driver had no insurance card or driver's license, and the officers made a routine arrest. But there was nothing routine about the accused: he was a law school graduate about to be made an assistant district attorney. And he was the son of the late John F. Kennedy.

John Kennedy, Jr. was eventually cleared of the charges (it turned out he *was* insured) and was allowed to take the job at the DA's office, but the incident, like most events in his life, made newspapers everywhere. The American public has been waiting for over a quarter of a century for John Kennedy Jr. to make a name for himself —either as a saint or a sinner—and even the smallest incidents in his life are thrown out to the masses like meat to a hungry wolf pack, in hopes that someday these pieces will fit neatly together and form a clear picture of the man. But unfortunately for the wolves—and fortunately for John Kennedy—there hasn't been all that much to chew on.

For the most part, John has succeeded in coming of age with little incident. His friends call him a "regular guy," an appelation which is mostly likely a disappointment to a country that has been patiently waiting for the appearance of the new John F. Kennedy II. But what John has tried to do is to live life as a human being, not as the shadowy spectre of an American legend. This, too, was Jackie's greatest wish, and she did everything she could to see that he led a normal life.

"I'm immensely impressed by John," Gita Mehta told *Vanity Fair*. "It was great gallantry on Jackie's part to send him to India for nine months during the twentieth anniversary of his father's assassination. I mean, he could have grown up terrified, with a state-of-siege mentality, but she had given him the courage to address a place as alien as India without any sense of fear. This is an example of how subtle and intelligent a parent she has been."

The result of Jackie's parenting is a strikingly handsome, extremely confident and endlessly interesting individual eager to make his mark on the world. This is quite an achievement, considering the incredible odds Jackie and John were up against.

John was only a toddler when he lost his father; shortly after he moved with his mother and sister to Manhattan. The next years of John's life were filled with splendor, upheaval and sadness. In 1966 he lost his Uncle Bobby, who had become a surrogate father to him, only to gain a stepfather not long after. John often accompanied his globe-trotting mother on her summer travels, which were often spent in the company of artists and writers—some of the most interesting and intelligent people in society. During the school year, John attended private school, where he was described as restless, disruptive and inattentive. He finally graduated from Phillips Academy in Andover, Massachusetts, after being left back for a year. At the time, he was seeing a psychiatrist.

John was not much of a social animal in those days. He did make appearances at New York's popular Xenon disco, although he spent less time there than his Kennedy cousins.

"John-John was special," club owner Howard Stein told *New York* magazine. "He was less a disco baby. He was shyer, ingenuous. He didn't leverage his name off the way kids of the famous do in my world. He had star quality. So every time he was there, he got his picture in the papers. It took a scandal for the other Kennedy kids to be photographed."

After high school, John attended Brown University, and it was there that he really seemed to grow. His college career uncovered two of his more notable hobbies. One is not so surprising: like his father did, he enjoys the company of women, and there were times on campus when he had a reputation for being a ladies' man. John's other pasttime is a bit of a surprise—he fell in love with acting, and seriously considered making it his career.

Not surprisingly, it was his prowess with women that drew the most attention at first. *People* magazine voted him the "Sexiest Man Alive" in 1988, (a distinction that friends say sorely embarassed John), and he has been linked romantically in the tabloids with Brooke Shields, Madonna, Daryl Hannah, Molly Ringwald and Princess Stephanie of Monaco. A friend of John's told *New York* Magazine, "The apple doesn't fall far from the tree. Girls come and go." When John was a college freshman, hopeful girls would sleep outside his dormitory.

Of course, some of these claims are exaggerated or distorted. Madonna, for example, supposedly initiated all contacts with John herself, arranging to be at functions where he would be, but the pop star's friends said nothing ever came of it, much to Madonna's dismay.

John has also sought the security of a steady girlfriend. He dated Brown student Sally Munro for awhile, but his current main squeeze is actress Christina Haag, a former housemate and sometimes co-star. Haag, the daughter of a retired businessman, is a Julliard graduate struggling to make it as an actress just like any other actress—though some say she's a bit luckier than most.

For a time, John considered becoming an actor himself. At Brown, he appeared in several stage productions, and in 1985 he set foot on a New York stage for the first time—the Irish Arts Center—to mixed reviews. John was even offered a part in a Robert Stigwood film—playing his father. Jackie was reportedly upset, and John turned down the role.

But John told the press that acting was just a hobby, after all, and he set his sights elsewhere. He was somewhat politically active in college; one summer he met government and student leaders in Zimbabwe, and even worked briefly in a mining camp (owned by Jackie's latest boyfriend, Maurice Tempelsman). John has worked for the University Conference for Democratic

Policy, which sponsored disarmament forums on Northeastern college campuses. And the summer after his junior year, Kennedy and his cousin Tim Shriver tutored underpriveledged children.

After graduating, John got his first taste of city government by accepting a $20,000-a-year job with New York City's Office of Business Development. John's boss, Larry Kieves, reported that he was a good worker. Another co-worker had fond memories of John changing from his bicycle clothes into his suit in the office, often leaving his shirttails hanging out.

John's next job was with the 42nd Street Development Corporation, where he conducted negotiations with developers and city agencies.

John's flair for practical jokes (a trait he shared with his father), found an outlet in the workplace. *New York* Magazine reported an incident in which John kidnapped a secretary's teddy bears, sent her a ransom note reading "We have the bears," and then executed them in a "mass mock hanging." In another incident, John sent a stripper to meet with a colleague who was interviewing candidates for a job.

John left the business world in 1986 to attend law school at New York University, and while his academic record wasn't the best, he graduated with an interest in criminal law and becoming a prosecutor. In 1988 he sought a position as Assistant DA in Brooklyn and got it, but there were a few matters to be cleared up first— namely, $2,300 in parking tickets.

This "scandal" was as typically low-key as

other incidents in his life which the press has been quick to latch on to—in reality, they're episodes typical of most young men: falling down drunk after his sister's wedding, being late with rent checks, constantly forgetting his keys and ringing his neighbors' buzzers, and, of course, his recent arrest for speeding. But behind this careless, youthful behavior is a well-rounded, active adult, one who is expected to make an excellent assistant district attorney.

Those with hopes for a political future for John have not given up: he was a hit introducing Ted Kennedy at the 1988 Democratic Convention, and he is active and capable working on such projects as the Fresh Air Fund, the Kennedy Library, and the City University of New York's plan to assist the disabled. But if John has his eye on political office, he hasn't said so publicly—yet.

Born of two remarkable parents, a victim of tragedy, an inheritor of wealth and fame, John Kennedy could easily have become spoiled, desperate, reckless or foolish. He is none of those things, and it is doubtful that without the love and support of his mother he could have come so far.

CHAPTER TWENTY-TWO
End of a Chapter

After Ari's death, Jackie managed to neatly and completely sever herself from the Onassis empire. It began with the settlement of the estate with Christina Onassis, which Jackie's lawyers handled fairly quietly and out of court. They realized they could never exact the full amount of money the widow was legally entitled to, nor did they ever dare hope to take control of Onassis' business empire. They left that to Christina while they argued for cash on the barrelhead. Jackie got what she wanted—twenty-six million dollars—plus the return of all her letters to Onassis and an agreement that Christina would never publicly discuss the settlement. Jackie made the same commitment.

Christina and Jackie seemed perfectly happy to be rid of one another, which came as no surprise to anyone. Their relationship had always been tenuous, but probably no more strained than the typical stepmother/ stepdaughter relationship, in which the rebellious stepdaughter resents the intrusive woman who has married her father—but on a much grander scale, of course.

Christina certainly played the role of rebel well. Although born with the proverbial silver spoon, her life had its share of troubles. Her parents were divorced when she was eight; her brother died tragically in 1973; her mother died just a year later, and Ari, to whom she was very devoted, died just a year after that.

Wealth is not always the best panacea for a troubled mind, and Christina lived life in the fast lane, battling obesity and entering a string of unsuccessful marriages. Christina defied Ari in 1971 by marrying millionaire builder Joseph Bolker; they were divorced only months later, apparently at Ari's insistence. Christina remarried three times after her father's death, but her luck wasn't much better. Her marriage to Greek shipping and banking heir Alexander Alreadis lasted 14 months; she was married to Soviet shipping agent Sergei Kanzov in 1978, and separated a year later.

In 1984, Christina began what looked to be her most promising union, with French businessman Thierry Roussel, but barely two years later her marriage to the man who wanted to "grow old at her side" ended. This time, however, Christina had something to show for it—her first and only child. On January 28, 1985, Athina Roussel was born—and Jackie became a stepgrandmother.

With the birth of Athina, the press noted that Christina seemed happy at last, but sadly, that happiness was to be short-lived. Christina died of a heart attack while vacationing in Argentina; she was barely 37 years old. Her death was termed "questionable" at first: The *New York Times* reported that "some pills found by her side were being analyzed." Reports of suicide were never substantiated, however, and most attributed the heart attack to years of fluctuating weight. Her body was taken to Skorpios to be buried near her father's grave; Jackie did not attend the funeral.

Christina's death left the question of who would inherit and control the Onassis empire. There was speculation that Jackie might step in, but Jackie, as usual, remained silent. Instead, the bulk of the Onassis fortune, estimated at about $250–$500 million, went to then-three-year-old Athina, making her the richest toddler on the planet. The world would have to wait some time to test the mettle of Aristotle Onassis' sole heir.

CHAPTER TWENTY-THREE
The Third Man

In the years after Onassis' death, one of Jackie's old friends began to emerge as an important figure in her life. In recent years, Maurice Tempelsman has taken a solid place at Jackie's side as her official "significant other."

At first glance, the unassuming diamond mogul is an odd voice for vibrant Jackie, but a closer look reveals that Tempelsman may be just what Jackie needs. Interestingly, Tempelsman combines the most desirable traits of Jackie's first two husbands: while he is not dashingly handsome, as Jack Kennedy was, he is highly intelligent and magnetic; like Ari, Tempelsman is a millionaire many times over. And Maurice has one edge over both of them: at 56, he's four years *younger* than Jackie.

Jackie's Belgian-born boyfriend came into the diamond business through his family. His father, Leon, started a small industrial diamond business after WWII. Maurice's dealings in the Belgian Congo led him into African politics; he has been involved in the President's Commission for the Observance of Human Rights, the International Peace Academy, and the Council on Foreign Relations.

It was this involvement in politics that brought Maurice into Jackie's life. After becoming an acquaintance of the Kennedys, Tempelsman aided the Kennedy administration in its dealings with Africa. His friendship with the famous family grew, and in 1968 he was one of 1,100 invited guests on Robert Kennedy's funeral train. When Lee Radziwill's divorced husband Prince Stanislaus Radziwill died, Tempelsman accompanied Jackie to the funeral in London.

While Tempelsman's relationship with Jackie grew, so did his fortune: in 1983, his family became partners with Lazare Kaplan, an extremely prestigious diamond firm. The deal was largely due to Tempeslman's savvy and shrewd business sense.

It may be this intelligence that draws Jackie to Tempelsman; in this, they are alike. And they seem to enjoy the same pursuits: dining out, entertaining friends with quiet dinners at home, and picnicking and sailing at Martha's Vineyard. To avoid the crowds, Maurice docks his 65-foot luxury yacht in the Vineyard, and he and Jackie travel to waterfront restaurants or the small surrounding islands.

Jackie's newest relationship is not without its hitches: while Tempelsman has been estranged from his wife, Rena, for years, they share an apartment in Manhattan, although it is reported to be so large that the two could co-exist there without ever bumping into one another.

So for those hoping to hear wedding bells for Jackie, it doesn't seem likely. But all in all, Tempelsman seems to be just what Jackie needs at this point in her life: a good friend and companion, someone whose company she enjoys. Of course he's no Jack Kennedy—but he makes Jackie happy, and that's all that counts.

CHAPTER TWENTY-FOUR
Jackie at Work and at Play

What do you get the woman who has everything? In Jackie's case, a career in publishing. After Ari's death, her role as a magnate's wife ended; she was still a young woman, and perhaps felt the need to do more with her life than shop and travel. Years before, Jackie had set foot in the world of publishing, and she decided to have a go at it again.

Jackie's first attempt to reenter the publishing world, with Viking Press, was not a success—in fact, it ended badly. What began as a good idea—to have well-connected Jackie negotiate book deals with prominent individuals—fizzled fast.

In the narrow, sensitive world of publishing, new faces are seldom welcomed with open arms. Although Jackie took only a part-time position that paid $200 a week, she met with superficial politeness at Viking and the few suggestions she made were received with icy indifference.

One Viking editor explained, "There was no way Jackie could ingratiate herself with the company. She was resented at the beginning and her presence became a nagging insult to the professionals in the company. Jackie felt this keenly, and it must have hurt her. Defensively, I suppose, she chose an arrogant way out of a situation when she quit Viking with the publication of Jeffrey Archer's novel, *Shall We Tell the President?* in which the action revolved around an assassination attempt on Ted Kennedy. Jackie knew about the book and had been consulted about its 'taste.' She voiced no objections until reviews appeared and the work was pronounced 'trash.' That's when Jackie decided to leave."

Jackie's resignation read: "Last spring when told of the book, I tried to separate my lives as a Viking employee and a Kennedy relative. But this fall, when it was suggested that I had something to do with acquiring the book and that I was not distressed by its publication, I felt I had to resign."

Whether this was evidence of Jackie's unbreakable ties to the Kennedy clan or simply a convenient way to escape a bad situation is left to interpretation. Whatever the case, it was a smart move: Jackie's second attempt at a publishing career, with Doubleday, has been a qualified success. Doubleday apparently has been wise enough to realize what an asset a famous name like Jackie's would be to their operation, and employees were able to set aside professional jealousies.

Jackie got off to a slow start, but Doubleday was patient, and it paid off: She scored with her first bestseller in 1986, an autobiography of ballerina Gelsey Kirkland. Later, she convinced her friend Carly Simon to pen a volume of autobiographical sketches. It was in 1988, however, that she landed her biggest fish: Michael Jackson's autobiography *Moonwalk*. The book, which featured a brief introduction by Jackie, became an instant bestseller. Ironically, Jackie was becoming successful at convincing celebrities to make their private lives public—something she would never agree to do herself.

Her colleagues at Doubleday are considerably warmer to her than they apparently were at Viking. One former associate told *People* magazine: "She is quiet and shy with a sense of humor that is endearing. The other editors take her seriously. She is the one they turn to for a second reading of a book proposal if it is related to anything cultural. Her remarks are always cogent and to the point."

In fact, Jackie seems to be valued as much for her natural talent as for her connections. Friend Gita Mehta told *Vanity Fair*, "She's really an extraordinary type of editor. I watched her do *A Second Paradise*, a book by my brother, Naveen Patnaik. Jackie sent Naveen pages of research material annotated by herself. It was obscure research. I know as a writer that to have that kind of attention by a commissioning editor is quite rare."

Nevertheless, publishing is still more of a hobby to Jackie than a full-fledged career. She only works three halfdays a week—hardly a strenuous work schedule, but one that gives her the opportunity to exercise her creative side and have time left over to enjoy herself.

"For the first time in her life, Jackie is really rich," wrote Edward Klein, an acquaintance of Jackie's, in a revealing article that appeared in the August 1989 issue of *Vanity Fair*. Klein was referring to Jackie's estimated $200 million fortune, which had increased from $25 million since Ari's death.

While most of us would consider ourselves "really rich" with $25 million, it's not difficult to understand why it would take considerably more to keep a woman like Jackie happy. It's not easy traveling and participating in outdoor recreation while maintaining a low profile; Jackie needs plenty of space in which to indulge her hobbies, and she's acquired plenty. Jackie owns over 400 acres on Martha's Vineyard, including the entire town of Gay Head; a hunt-country estate in northwest New Jersey (an area becoming as popular a retreat for the wealthy as the Vineyard—Malcolm Forbes owns a large estate in the area); and a fifteen-room co-op in Manhattan.

Jackie is in no way one of the "idle" rich, and spends much of her time enjoying sports and exercise particular to each one of her habitats.

Jackie makes Martha's Vineyard her home every August, where she manages to stay behind the scenes, for the most part. *People* magazine reported that locals have seen her several times at the trendy Oyster Bar. And the *New York Post* provided an amusing tidbit reported by *The Washingtonian* magazine, which charged that Jackie visits the Town Hall Cinema in Edgartown on the Vineyard, carrying a four-pack of Bartles & James Wine Coolers. Apparently, Jackie would drink the wine coolers during the film and leave the empty bottles on the seat, but the theater manager told the *Post* that the tale was untrue, claiming, "Her most scandalous behavior was to walk in with an ice cream cone."

Otherwise, Jackie's behavior seems to be low key. Tempelsman docks his yacht there, and he and Jackie go waterskiing and sailing, often taking a few friends along for picnics. Once a year, Klein reports, Jackie invites the Kennedys to a weekend clambake at her estate. About 100 people attend—Shrivers, Lawfords, Smiths and Kennedys. It's another example of how Jackie strives to look after her family. "Jackie makes the weekend a means for her and her children to restore their connections to all the relatives," Sargent Shriver said.

Sailing, swimming and waterskiing, however, aren't enough to fill the life of an active woman like Jackie. Her love of riding and hunting takes her to New Jersey on autumn weekends to ride hands with the Essex Hunt Club, where Jackie rides to compete as well as for enjoyment. She won the Lady Ardmore Challenge trophy in 1985 for vaulting fences up to 39 inches higher than her competitors. She also attends an annual steeplechase held in Peapack, N.J., but residents report that she keeps a low profile—considerably lower than her boisterous neighbor Malcolm Forbes, for example. Once a year Jackie enjoys hunting in Virginia, where she rides with friends at the Orange County Hunt Club.

A longtime friend of Jackie's told *Vanity Fair* about Jackie's passion for riding: "She's attracted by the excitement and the vividness provided by the outdoors—getting sopping wet. I've ridden with her in the most miserable conditions. She enjoys the wind and the rain."

Jackie isn't just a weekend or a summer athlete, but keeps active even in dour Manhattan. Her free time there is busy but predictable, reported *People* magazine in 1987: "Onassis keeps a tidy routine: comb-outs at Kenneth's, shopping on pricey Madison Avenue and midmorning jogs in Manhattan's Central Park." New York Road Runner President Fred Lebow described Jackie's running style as "dainty." Recently, Jackie had been running after dark to avoid notoriety, but the tragic "wilding" episode in Central Park in which a woman jogger was gang-raped prompted Jackie's friends to convince her to run in daylight again. Between six and seven at night, Jackie meditates and does yoga with an instructor in her apartment, and for that hour, Jackie is cut off from the world.

Jackie's nights are no less active than her days. While her attendance at social galas is limited,

Jackie and Maurice enjoy throwing intimate dinner parties in her co-op. These gatherings are reported to be "relaxed, cozy and understated." "She can talk on any subject," one guest said, "She makes you feel like you are the only person in the world." Jackie's charm has many facets, from winning the hearts of an entire country, to the gratitude of a few dinner guests.

Jackie's charisma has proven an asset in political as well as social matters. While she prefers to remain anonymous and invisible, she has been known to lend her support to causes close to home—with astonishing results. In 1987, a development firm proposed to build a skyscraper in Manhattan's Columbus Circle; the planned structure was quickly dubbed "The Shadow" because of the forbidding shadow—nearly a mile long—that the sun-blocking monstrosity would cast over Central Park and surrounding buildings. Jackie, a resident of the neighborhood that would be affected, became "the driving force behind the coalition marshaling to halt the project," wrote *New York* magazine. Journalist Bill Moyers was perhaps the most vocal opponent of the plan, but Jackie was able to give the movement something he couldn't: celebrity. Jackie was able to enlist the help of neighborhood residents Henry Kissinger and Walter Cronkite, and Celeste Holm, Betty Friedan, John Lindsay and architect I.M. Pei lent their names to the cause, largely due to Jackie's involvement. Jackie even held a press conference—a rare event for reclusive Jackie. Critics claimed that the project would do more good than harm to the city, and charged that opposing the plan had become the "in" thing to do among celebrities and socialites. Nevertheless, "The Shadow" was eventually stopped, and one wonders whether such a tremendous project could have been blocked without Jackie's influence.

CHAPTER TWENTY-FIVE
A Year of Reflection

1989 was a year of change for Jackie, and she weathered it with her usual grace and composure. In the span of a year Jackie turned sixty, shortly after losing her beloved mother to Alzheimer's disease.

Janet Lee Auchincloss died in Newport, Rhode Island, on Saturday, July 22, 1989. She was 81 years old. Oddly, she died on the same day that Rose Kennedy celebrated her 99th birthday with a large family party at Hyannis Port.

With Janet's death Jackie lost not only a mother, but a friend. Janet had always been there for Jackie, providing a stabilizing force after her divorce from Jackie's father, supporting Jackie during the difficult time after Jack Kennedy's assasination, and watching Jackie's children grow and thrive in a circus-like atmosphere.

Jackie is like her mother in many ways. It was Janet who bestowed Jackie with the sense of style and propriety that made Americans admire and adore their first lady, and Janet who instilled a sense of culture and appreciation of art and beauty in her daughter.

There are, in fact, many similarities between Janet's lifestyle and the manner in which Jackie has chosen to live her life. Mother and daughter shared a passion for horses. "My mother was a great horsewoman," Lee Radziwill told *Architectural Digest* in 1985, "and still rides occasionally." Like Jackie, Janet was never single for long—her marriage to Hugh D. Auchincloss lasted 30 years, and she married Bingham W. Morris not long after Auchincloss' death. And Janet's sense of style never faltered—seen at a family christening the December before her death, she looked quite lovely, and hardly like an 81-year-old great-grandmother.

Hammersmith, Janet Auchincloss' historic summer home in Newport, Rhode Island, was a testimony to the devotion and love Janet felt for her large and remarkable family. The house was filled with photographs of Jackie, Jack Kennedy, Lee Radziwill, and all of her grandchildren. Mrs. Auchincloss may not have been as visible or amusing as the Kennedy matriarch, but her influence on Jackie and the family was pervasive and positive.

If the last quarter of a century of Janet Lee Auchincloss' life can be viewed as a roadmap of what lies ahead for Jackie, the world can rest easy. If Jackie grows old only half as gracefully as her remarkable mother, she'll still be the most stylish woman appearing on America's magazine covers.

The death of Jackie's mother occured at a turning point in Jackie's life—her 60th birthday on July 28, 1989. The press was quick to latch onto the event, and took advantage of Jackie O's selling power to plaster her photo all over the media. It had been years since Jackie first captured the public's heart, but on her 60th birthday America was still as enthralled with its favorite celebrity as ever. "Looking as glamorous as ever, Jacqueline Kennedy Onassis is still turning heads and making headlines as one of New York's most famous residents," wrote the *New York Post*. "We should all look as good at 60!" There was truth to this remark: Many of the retrospectives written about Jackie to mark her birthday were accompanied by photos—many from years ago—and they served to illustrate how little Jackie has changed over the years. Perhaps this is one reason for America's fascination with her: Presidents may come and go, inflation may rise and fall, but Jackie will always be Jackie, radiant, confident, beautiful, a familiar face to a lost generation.

Jackie became perhaps even more glamorous, even daring, after her 60th birthday. In October 1989 the *New York Post* reported that Jackie had put blonde highlights in her hair. Her co-workers at Doubleday said that she had taken to showing up at work wearing mini-skirts! And why not? As the saying goes, if you've got it, flaunt it, and after all these years, Jackie's still got it.

CHAPTER TWENTY-SIX
Easter Weekend—1991

Easter weekend has not turned out to be a particularly happy time at the Kennedy compound in elegant Palm Beach. The 1984 Easter weekend ended in tragedy with the drug-overdose death of David Kennedy, the fourth child of Ethel and the late Robert Kennedy. Tragically, he died a few short days after his release from a drug rehabilitation center in Minnesota.

As unfortunate and tragic as the death of a young member of the Kennedy clan had been, its very nature commanded the sympathy as much as the curiosity of the American people. The death occurred in a hotel, away from the compound, and as a news story it quietly went away.

Not so the stormy events of 1991 when preliminary reports out of tony Palm Beach indicated that the police had paid a call to the Kennedy compound at 1:30 Easter Sunday afternoon. This represented the substance of the first item of news. It was, however, certainly not the last of a Kennedy story that would dominate headlines and broadcast news for a full year and months thereafter.

It was immediately taken for granted that the visit had something to do with Senator Edward Kennedy, and past actions being the barometer, it was assumed that some sexual hanky-panky and booze were involved. This suspicion was shot down fairly soon but a long period of time passed before the name of the subject of the inquiry was revealed. The Palm Beach police played their hand close to the vest while the media pored over the backgrounds of the various Kennedys who were at the compound on Easter or who had easy access to it.

The compound was purchased by Kennedy patriarch Joseph Kennedy in 1933 as a vacation home for his large family. During JFK's tenure as president, it was used as the winter White House. Called *La Gueria,* it is an old-fashioned Mediterranean-style mansion, a lesser work of the Palm Beach architect Addison Mizner. Supposedly, Joseph Kennedy bequeathed the oceanside property to a foundation. After his death various of the Kennedy families took turns occupying the place over the winter months.

When Jackie was First Lady she did not look forward to Palm Beach with great enthusiasm. The so-called mansion was the sort of place Bette Davis would survey, flip a cigarette and observe, "What a dump!" Even then it was too run-down to be considered acceptable by a woman of taste, and by the 90's it had deteriorated to a point at which Jackie, and her children, had gone out of the way to avoid spending time there.

They were absent during the 1990-91 season. Jean Kennedy Smith and her family were tenants of record for March, making Ted Kennedy a visitor during his sister's tenure. When eventually the word was flashed that Ted was not the subject of the police inquiry, the press turned up the name of a virtually unknown relative, William Kennedy Smith.

We are indebted to that fabled chronicler of American society, Dominick Dunne, for this account of Smith's lineage: "William Kennedy Smith, Willy Smith or Will Smith, as his lawyer renamed him for the trial, is the grandson of Joseph O. and Rose Kennedy, the nephew of President John F. Kennedy, the cousin of Assistant District Attorney John Fitzgerald Kennedy Jr. and Caroline Kennedy Schlossberg, cousin of Congressman Joseph P. Kennedy II, and the cousin of Maria Shriver and the cousin of some twenty-five others of varying degrees of celebrity and recognizability."

The public also learned that he was in his last year of medical school and was shopping around for a hospital where he might serve as an intern. Pictures of Will Smith began to surface revealing a gangly young man of average good looks who appeared to have trouble smiling. The reason for this became apparent when the Palm Beach police finally made public their interest in the Easter weekend festivities at the Kennedy compound.

It seems that in the course of Good Friday evening, there had been an uncommon amount of barhopping by the young Kennedys—those ensconced at the compound as well as those visiting elsewhere. It appears that after the rounds of the Palm Beach bars had finished, Patrick Kennedy, son of the senator, and Willy Smith returned to the compound and went to bed. Senator Kennedy, restless and evidently feeling lonely and sorry for himself, roused the young men and suggested that they hit the road for a final nightcap.

That proved a fatal decision. The three men ended up at a club called Au Bar, a popular late night hangout before the Kennedys' visit and a must see afterward. There is nothing flashy about Au Bar. It is simply an ordinary-looking establishment, certainly no sex den. Evidently, Willy separated himself from his cousin and uncle. When it became clear that he would find his own way home, apparently with transportation supplied by a young woman who had met the senator briefly, Ted and Patrick drove back to the compound.

That was where preliminary information about Good Friday evening ended until the Palm Beach police, after several days of shooting down various rumors, finally released the information that William Smith had been indicted for rape; his accuser being an unidentified resident of Palm

Beach. The rape had taken place at the Kennedy compound.

By the time the police inquiry was completed the compound had been emptied. All the Kennedys were at home and the telephone hummed with activity as members of the clan were called upon to supply support for young Willy. As one observer remarked, "They'll behave like bulldogs, tearing anyone to pieces who crosses them, and when it's over, they'll chew Willy to bits."

At least the first part of that prediction proved correct. Because so little was known about Willy Smith, relatives like Jackie and her children were reluctant to supply information. Hence press attention concentrated on the accuser. In a comparatively short space of time everything there was to know filled newspaper files, including her name. The Kennedys saw to that.

Plainly, the first step in the defense of Willy Smith was to discredit the alleged victim. That wasn't exactly difficult for the Kennedy operatives who scuttled around Palm Beach digging up as much information as they could. Putting a questionable face on their findings was not difficult. They were pros at character assassination.

The accuser, it appeared, had very few real friends. She was a single parent supported by her stepfather, a wealthy man and Kennedy hater. She had been in an accident and suffered back pains as a result. Hence, when she drank she "lost control.'' So the story went.

By the time reporters got around to probing Willy Smith more deeply, the so-called victim, if not discredited, would be fighting an uphill battle to convince any judge or jury that she had been seriously molested and forced into sex at the Kennedy compound. It was no secret that the woman's life-style was a major reason for the long delay between the complaint and the charge. The police feared what ultimately happened: The victim was suspect.

However, Willy Smith did not escape unscarred. There were reports that this was not the first rough sex incident he had been involved in. There were numerous relationships in his past that led to violence with young women. It was clear that Willy Smith suffered a personality change when he drank or, as was also accused, when he used drugs. Offering drugs to young women was one way he was supposed to have attracted them.

Numerous names surfaced of young women who had known the dark side of Willy Smith. They fell into the hands of the media. But when it came to making their experiences public, the women were more than reluctant. They seemed terrified of the consequences. It was no secret they feared the Kennedy clout. One young woman in England who appeared on the verge of going public suddenly changed her mind when wiser family heads prevailed and called off what was to have been a TV interview with the accuser's appearance and voice disguised.

"How many times can the Kennedy women straighten their backs and walk down the street?" asked a close friend of Pat Kennedy Lawford when the Palm Beach scandal broke. Evidently quite a few. For the Kennedys went about their business as usual, as if nothing untoward had happened to change the regular course of their lives.

Senator Kennedy showed up at the compound in Hyannis to be photographed with Rose Kennedy on Mother's Day. Willy and his brother, Steve, and his two sisters, Kym and Amanda, were photographed on the same Sunday going to Mass.

And what of Jacqueline Kennedy Onassis? Never had Jackie more reason to be grateful that over the years she had been gracefully distancing herself from the Kennedy clan. They could, of course, call upon her for internal support, but it was unlikely that she would go public with any comment, certainly not in the Willy Smith rape case.

So during the months of the sensational publicity, when the case was on everyone's lips, all over the press and TV, Jackie pursued her job with quiet dignity. And her children, who might sometimes disagree with her, knew better than to question Jackie's judgment in political matters. And Kennedy family matters inevitably became political.

A few weeks after Mother's Day had pictured so many Kennedys in appropriate postures, the clan gathered again in Philadelphia for the marriage of Max Kennedy, the ninth child of Robert and Ethel, to Victoria Anne Strauss. A photograph of the ushers reveals William Kennedy Smith at the end of a line of cousins in cutaway. His countenance is more solemn than usual. Listed in this group of ushers was John Kennedy Jr., but he was not seen among those photographed. According to gossip reporter Richard Johnson, John dropped out of his ushering assignment at the last moment because Jackie did not want him to be photographed with Willy Smith.

The snub annoyed the Kennedys but again reinforced the impression that Jackie sought to carve in stone. She forged her own destiny away from the clan. And so did her children.

CHAPTER TWENTY-SEVEN
The Trial

No trial in history commanded the audience television was able to produce for the proceedings that took place in a Florida courtroom when, in early December, 1991, Judge Mary Lupo sounded her gavel and the proceedings began in the rape trial of William Kennedy Smith—Will, as his attorney called him, Dr. Smith, as the television commentators sometimes referred to him.

Months of legal wrangling had preceded the court appearances of the principals and their attorneys. There had been motions to quash the indictment as well as rumors that the Kennedys would seek some sort of accommodation rather than allow the case to go to trial.

At stake were good names of two institutions, the state of Florida and the Kennedy family. A retreat by either party would diminish it in the eyes of society, so whatever accommodations they did reach were accomplished within the law and out in the open. So far as could be determined, the state of Florida certainly had gone out of its way to pay for an expensive prosecution. There were technical and other experts to match the best Kennedy money could buy.

The first victory for the Kennedys occurred on the very first day of the trial when Judge Lupo disallowed the testimony of three other women—a doctor, a medical student and a law student who claimed they had been sexually assaulted by Smith between 1983 and 1988. Obtaining the testimony of these three women and persuading them to come forward and testify publicly had been an incredibly difficult task for the prosecution and their inability to put such evidence on the record was a disheartening first blow.

In the months between Easter weekend and the last week before Christmas, much more was known of the accuser than Willy Smith; not much of it was favorable. She was Patricia Bowman, a young woman with a great many problems, not the least of which were her friends, Ann Mercer and Chuck Desidero. Chuck was the man who had accompanied Ann Mercer to the Kennedy compound when Patricia had called her after the alleged rape. He had removed an urn from the house to prove Patricia had been there. It was a mistake. As for Ann, she had made paid appearances on tabloid television, so when she appeared as a witness for the prosecution, she was handily demolished by defense attorney Roy Black.

Roy Black, at forty-six, had become a hugely successful criminal lawyer in Florida, and it was quickly apparent that the Kennedys had not been mistaken in entrusting him with the position of top gun in the group of lawyers, witnesses, experts and jury analysts assembled to defend Willy Smith. The prosecution was led by Moira Lasch, whose single dour expression and monotonous questioning of witnesses grated on the television audience. They lost no time in being critical legal experts. What her work did to the jury was reflected in their not guilty verdict, arrived at after three hours of deliberation. Not a single request for rereading of testimony nor clarification of any legal point had been made in spite of all the complexities the lawyers for both sides had created.

Of all the witnesses the most striking was Senator Edward Kennedy. Journalists, perhaps more than the average person, are aware of the phenomenon that one experiences in the presence of a person of power. He may be an ordinary Joe in every sense of the word, filled with frailties both personal and public, as Senator Kennedy certainly is. Yet when Kennedy walked into the courtroom to be questioned by Black and Lash, the gray-haired leader of the Kennedy clan folded his hands quietly in his lap and proceeded to outline his recollection of the fatal evening. He was a presence, barely pausing to hear the questions. He paid no attention to them whatsoever. He looked hale and hearty. A few weeks earlier he had made a speech admitting certain indiscretions in his life and apologizing for them. With that behind him, he was in total control. He might as well have been going to another wedding instead of a rape trial. The afternoon was his.

While Senator Kennedy could control certain hours of the trial in the courtroom, not every second belonged to the defense. Patricia Bowman proved a credible and sympathetic witness. And there were other minor victories for Moira Lasch.

Outside the courtroom, however, in the court of public opinion, the Kennedys held forth and ruled supreme. Theirs was a textbook performance of a prominent family closing ranks to defend one of their own. Will's mother, Jean, accompanied him to court every day and at the visitors' benches there were spaces set aside for others of the huge Kennedy clan, who, one by one, made their way to Palm Beach and Will's support.

No fancy cars were visible. No furs, No ostentation whatsoever. TV viewers met the Kennedys as simple folk who drove their own, often battered cars and even perhaps brown-bagged their lunches. On the way in and out of the courthouse Will stopped to talk to reporters, graciously answering reasonable questions and smiling away those that were inappropriate. And the family spoke freely of their faith in Will and their trust in God, the American Constitution and the justice they knew could be found in a Florida court.

One day the family was accompanied by a Jesuit priest, prompting a local to exclaim, "When will they wheel in Rose Kennedy?" But the hundred-year-old matriarch never appeared. There were few other public appearances of the Kennedy clan except on Sunday when they drove in their station wagon and rented cars to Mass.

The big question, of course, was would Jackie Onassis join the clan. She failed to appear although she did not object when John Kennedy, evidently feeling a responsibility to a peer of his generation, made a brief visit to Palm Beach. Caroline, however, was a no-show.

Jackie's feelings about the scandal had been a well-kept secret. It was as though she had confided them to no one. Only one thing was sure: she would not join the circus at Palm Beach. The family knew this and resented it.

Will Smith made his final appearance on television, at least in front of a Palm Beach courthouse, at the trial's conclusion. "They say that gratitude is the memory of the heart," Will began. "And I have enough memories in my heart to last a lifetime. I want to say thank you most of all to my mother. I don't think it's possible for a child ever to repay the debt they owe their parents. I can only hope to be as good a parent to my children as my mother has been to me."

Will's remark that gratitude is the memory of the heart was from Jean Batiste Massieu, a nineteenth-century teacher of deaf-mutes. The thanks and waving to the press being over, Will and his family beamed their way to their cars and headed off to the compound for a celebration. Typically American, if one believes the official information. Beer, pretzels, potato salad. Very common man.

CHAPTER TWENTY-EIGHT
Sunday in the Park

It was a mild, sunny Sunday in New York. Jackie, her daughter, Caroline Kennedy Schlossberg, her grandson, and her longtime companion, Maurice Tempelsman, were strolling through Central Park, just enjoying the outing.

Suddenly, a photographer approached them and the usually even-tempered Tempelsman exploded with rage. The photographer, shaken, backed away, but something was obviously wrong.

Jackie, looking even more frail and wan than usual, remained calm, but had to be supported by Tempelsman as they hurried away.

It was a very short walk in the park—and Jackie's last public appearance. She would be dead in four days.

After the William Kennedy Smith debacle, Jackie had grown more reclusive than ever. She was naturally aloof or perhaps inspired a sense of awe in almost everyone.

Sally Quinn said on television that she had attended large parties with Jackie, but noticed that even the most powerful men and women in the nation would never introduce themselves to her. Was it out of respect? Or were they simply retreating from a wall of privacy that Jackie had built up around herself over the years?

1991 closed out none too soon for the publicity-shy Jackie Onassis. She was able to breathe a sigh of relief that the horror of the Palm Beach Easter weekend was in the past, and that John Jr. had not been implicated. But 1992 would bring more problems for Jackie, both medical and personal.

Jackie continued to devote much of her time to her job as an editor at Doubleday and lent her considerable prestige to bolster various charitable causes. Her love of old buildings and an abiding interest in architecture never dimmed. She always fought to preserve the past for the benefit of the future. But she was worried about her son, John, and his off-and-on-again girlfriend, Daryl Hannah.

It was an open secret that Jackie disapproved of the relationship, and on one of the few occasions they had met, the two women had not gotten along well. Jackie wanted her son to get serious about his career in law and stop being the international playboy his father had been. He was more free spirited and yearned for the glamorous life Jackie had avoided in recent years.

She had put her foot down when young John told her he would rather be an actor than a lawyer. Perhaps it was the influence of Rose Kennedy, who had almost lost her husband to actress Gloria Swanson, that made Jackie leery of Tinseltown and its denizens.

Jogging in Central Park, spending time with her

grandchildren, and getting away from it all in Hyannis Port, Martha's Vineyard, and her New Jersey estate with Tempelsman, Jackie was the very model of the upper-class woman of leisure. But this idyllic life came to an end in December, 1993.

While visiting friends in Virginia she noticed a swelling in her groin. A local doctor diagnosed a swollen lymph node and prescribed antibiotics. No one thought her condition life threatening.

Although the swelling didn't completely vanish, Jackie felt well enough to cruise to the Caribbean at Christmastime. All was well until she developed a mysterious stomach pain and a cough that just wouldn't go away. She would have ignored it all stoically, but the swelling became worse and worse.

After she described her symptoms over the phone, her New York physician ordered her to return to the United States for a full medical work-up.

Outwardly tanned and healthy looking, Jackie checked into one of New York's premier medical institutions, New York Hospital-Cornell Medical Center, located on Sixty-eighth Street in Manhattan. Her physical examination revealed swollen lymph glands in her neck and armpit. But after a CAT scan, the news was worse: lymph nodes in her chest and deep in her abdomen were also affected. A biopsy was ordered.

Leaning more than ever on Maurice Tempelsman, Jackie waited quietly for the news. She hadn't told anyone else for fear of alarming them needlessly. The long hours passed slowly; the ring of the telephone was shattering, the diagnoses even more shattering.

Jackie had non-Hodgkin's lymphoma, a deadly cancer

of the lymph system. The cells within her were "primitive," the doctors told her, meaning that the disease was lethal. This was confirmed by experts at another hospital.

Sources close to Jackie said she took the news with the same dignity and grace she had displayed all her life, and she even refused another opinion. She asked what could be done for her and was told that the standard protocol was a series of four chemotherapy treatments.

It was early January, one of the snowiest on record, but there was a mood of optimism. Everyone believed there was a chance to stop the disease in its tracks and ensure Jackie an active life for years to come. She was only 64.

In fact, the first course of chemotherapy worked splendidly. The lymphoma had apparently gone into remission. Family and close friends were relieved, and Jackie felt as if she had a new lease on life. Vowing to spend even more time with her children and grandchildren, she was determined to live for the moment.

Her health, however, soon began to deteriorate. By the middle of March she complained of leg pains and exhibited a new symptom: confusion.

Doctors immediately ordered a sophisticated new test, an MRI, or magnetic resonance imaging. This incredibly complex machine found that although the lymphoma had vanished from her neck and abdomen, it had spread to the membranes covering her brain and spinal chord.

Neurologists confirmed that the cerebellum, a portion of her brain, had now been affected. This was a dangerous and puzzling complication. A CAT scan taken the previous November, after Jackie had tumbled from her horse, had not shown any sign of brain cancer. Now the lymphoma was located there. Jackie's doctors were frustrated: they had cured the disease, but were losing the patient because the disease had moved.

The only course of treatment was radiation therapy, with its attendant nausea and loss of appetite and hair. A health caseworker said that the treatment lasted about a month, until the middle of April. Strong jolts of radioactivity were sent into Jackie's brain and lower spinal chord.

Then on April fourteenth, Jackie was readmitted to the hospital because she had developed a perforated ulcer and was bleeding internally. Doctors said that it was associated with her previous chemotherapy, and they operated on her stomach that same day. They succeeded in stopping the bleeding, but the radiation was having little effect on the main cause of her problem, the lymphoma. The cancer continued to grow in her brain and spine unabated. The situation was extremely serious; the disease was out of control.

After consulting with the top people in the field, Jackie's physicians made a last-ditch effort to save her. A tube was implanted directly into the affected portion of her brain to deliver an anticancer drug to the site. The drug, highly useful in some cases, did not have any material effect on her lymphoma.

Friends were shocked at her appearance during this time and noted her loss of weight, slurred speech, and difficulty getting around. More disturbing was the terrible change in her personality. She seemed to be drawing into herself, husbanding her few remaining sparks of life. The doctors had given her three months to live.

That final Sunday in the park was the last chance she had to enjoy the beautiful weather. On Monday, it turned nasty.

Shaking with chills as miserable as the storm outside, Jackie became more and more confused. A distraught Maurice Tempelsman insisted that she be readmitted to New York Hospital. This time she was afflicted with acute pneumonia, the result of the chemotherapy and radiation treatments that had significantly weakened her system. She was treated with antibiotics on Monday and by Tuesday was getting better.

The final blow fell on Wednesday. During tests for her lymphoma, doctors were horrified to find that her disease had spread to her liver.

It was all over. They told her medicine had done everything it could for her. It was now up to God. One source close to the hospital said, "She had a very aggressive case...There was very little you could do for her except make her as comfortable as possible."

Jackie left the hospital that day, and because she had signed a living will stating her desire not to be hooked up to a life-support machine, she went home to die in the arms of her loved ones.

CHAPTER TWENTY-NINE
The Final Day

Thursday, May 19, 1994, was a dark and dreary day in New York City. A cold rain swept across the city, and nowhere was the weather more somber than in front of Jacqueline Kennedy Onassis's Fifth Avenue residence, fitting testimony of the tragedy that would take place later that day.

From early in the morning, the gathering at Jackie's bedside began. The first to arrive, shortly before ten a.m., was Lee Radziwill, Jackie's beloved sister. She was followed by Jackie's children, Caroline and John, and Caroline's husband, Edwin Schlossberg. And as if the occasion wasn't hard enough to bear, John had to dash from Central Park past photographers and reporters thronging three thick before the building. All of Jackie's loved ones looked stunned by the sudden and unexpected severity of her illness.

But the worst was yet to come for John and Caroline.

Not only were they about to lose the mother who had guided them through a difficult childhood and given them a strong sense of family; but they were once again at the center of the blinding limelight they have never been able to escape. Later in the day, when John was sneaking out for a moment, police had to help him through the crush and he was heard to ask "Where's my sister? Is someone watching out for my sister?" At the same time, Caroline was rushing to a nearby station wagon. Clearly upset, she almost stumbled over a cameraman who fell in her path, and the grief-stricken young mother said, "Good for you." All in all, the young Kennedys did their mother proud under the tragic circumstances, never once bowing to the public spectacle that grew out of their private mourning.

And what a spectacle it was! In death, as in life, Jackie couldn't escape the public's adoration. Even as the family joined together inside, outside on Fifth Avenue, reporters and curious onlookers had begun to gather. Despite the ever increasing rain and gloom, the tabloid journalists haunted the street, hoping for one last photo of Jackie or her family for the front page, one last byline inspired by the former First Lady.

As the day grew darker, a candlelight vigil began on the street. While more family members and friends braved the crowds to pay their last respects, people who had never seen Jackie anywhere but on television stopped to wish her well. Visitors from as far away as Japan and neighbors from as close as the building next door joined in remembering and mourning the former First Lady. Even the doorman of Jackie's building couldn't hide his grief. Everyone had a sense that they were taking part in a brief moment of history.

Before the end of the morning, a rumor that Monsignor George Bardes, Jackie's local parish priest, had administered last rites sent shock waves around the globe, and tributes poured in from kings and queens, celebrities and dignitaries, the well-known and the unknown.

By early afternoon, a veritable who's who of Kennedy family members filled Jackie's palatial 15-room home, and although many of them came full of hope, they all departed with the certainty that they had bid their final farewells to the woman millions have admired. Several of Jackie's neighbors on Martha's Vineyard, including singer Carly Simon, stopped by, only to leave visibly upset a short time later. Even John Jr.'s girlfriend, Daryl Hannah, made a brief appearance, despite Jackie's dislike for her. Ironically, Daryl Hannah was one of the last visitors to see Jackie alive.

Among Jackie's nieces and nephews present were William Kennedy Smith and Maria Shriver. After a 90-minute visit, U.S. Representative Joseph Kennedy II, a nephew, told reporters, "There is a lot of love in her room."

Almost all of JFK's surviving relatives stopped by for a final visit with the woman who, as Senator Edward Kennedy said, "was part of our family and part of our hearts for forty wonderful and unforgettable years and she will never really leave us."

Perhaps the most noticeably absent member of the Kennedy clan ws matriarch Rose Kennedy. But the 103-year-old mother of one president and two senators wasn't strong enough to make the journey from Hyannis Port to New York City.

Ted Kennedy and his new wife, Victoria, didn't arrive

until the early evening, but Pat Kennedy Lawford, Eunice and Sargent Shriver, and Ethel Kennedy—Bobby Kennedy's widow—spent different parts of the afternoon with their former sister-in-law. As Ethel Kennedy departed, she was heard to day that Jackie "needs everyone's prayers. She's struggling."

Despite Ethel Kennedy's gloomy, and ultimately true, comment, Ted Kennedy announced before nine p.m. that Jackie was "enormously grateful to all the people who've been kind enough to send notes and get-well wishes. She's resting comfortably and I look forward to seeing her tomorrow."

Then, at 10:15 p.m., the news came: Jackie had passed away peacefully with her beloved children at her bedside.

In the early morning hours of May 20, 1994, Carolyn Kennedy Schlossberg left her mother's bedside for a waiting car. John Kennedy Jr. rode away on his bike a short while later. Before them waited the grieving and ceremony of their mother's funeral; behind them lay cherished memories.

Besides her children and relatives, Jackie left behind longtime escort Maurice Tempelsman. For nearly two decades, the courtly financier had escorted Jackie to social and family affairs. Unfortunately, their chance for wedded happiness was thwarted by Tempelsman's wife, Lilly, who refused to divorce her husband. No one will ever know if Maurice Tempelsman would have been Jackie's last—and perhaps best—husband. But the love and support he gave her over the years helped Jackie through the best and worst of times.

Jacqueline Bouvier Kennedy Onassis will be buried in Arlington National Cemetary, next to her first husband, President John F. Kennedy, and their infant son, Patrick. Kathy Shenkle, a spokeswoman for the cemetery's historian's office, said, "There's room for her here. But I never thought of her actually coming here. I never thought she was going to die."

In closing the final chapter in the storybook life of the former First Lady, the essential question remains: how well did we know this very private woman who captured the heart of America and the world? Through the last years of her life, Jackie continued to shun the press. Whatever her reasons, she maintained a low profile while actively supporting the arts and contributing to society. Her greatest joy, however, came from the time she spent with her children and grandchildren, who remain her true legacy to the world.

Historian William Manchester, in researching *The Death of a President*, was fortunate to spend more than ten hours in private conversations with Jackie. The rare and sensational interview was recorded and it is kept under seal at the Kennedy Library in Boston. The tapes will remain there until the year 2067, when they are scheduled to be released to the public. Perhaps at that time, when the name Jackie O. conjures up the glamour and simplicity of a bygone era, future generations will, at last, come to understand the exceptional woman behind the myth.